The Michelin Tourist Services present **PLAN DE PARIS no 11** which is intended to help you to make a stay in the capital.

Information in this section is the latest available at the time of going to press ; improvements and alterations may account for certain discrepancies, we hope our readers will bear with us.

KEY TO THE GUIDE

Die Touristikabteilung der Michelin-Reifenwerke stellt Ihnen ihre Veröffentlichung **PLAN DE PARIS no 11** *vor, die eine praktische Hilfe für Ihren Parisaufenthalt sein soll.*

Die Ausgabe entspricht dem Stand zur Zeit der Drucklegung. Durch die Entwicklung der sich stetig wandelnden Hauptstadt können einige Angaben inzwischen veraltet sein. Wir bitten unsere Leser dafür um Verständnis.

ÜBERSICHT

Los Servicios de Turismo del Neumático Michelin le presentan su **PLAN DE PARIS no 11** *obra especialmente concebida para desenvolverse fácilmente en París.*

Esta edición corresponde a la situación actual, pero la evolución de la actividad de la capital puede hacer que determinadas informaciones caduquen. Esperamos que nuestros lectores lo comprendan.

LA CLAVE DE LA GUÍA

Tableau d'assemblage

Grands axes de circulation

Layout diagram

Main traffic artery

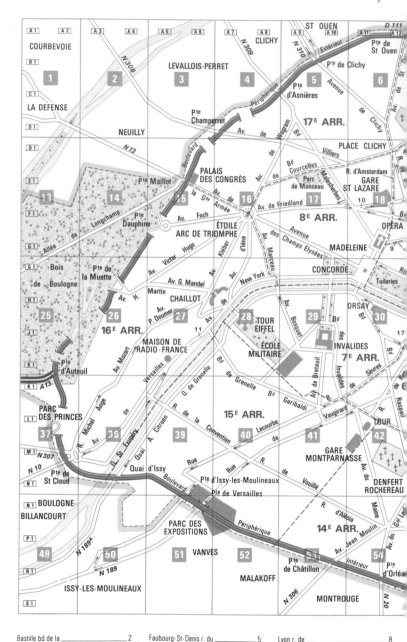

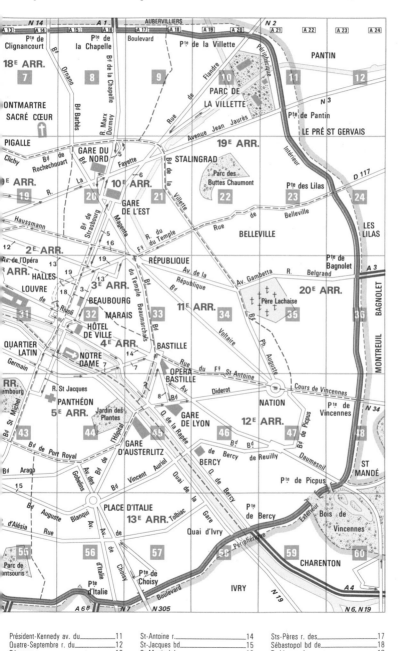

Les rues de Paris

Streets of Paris
Straßen von Paris
Calles de París

Index alphabétique des rues de Paris

Les deux premières colonnes renvoient à la page et au carroyage qui permettent de localiser la rue sur le plan *(découpage cartographique, p. 4 et 5)*. Dans certains cas, les lettres *N* (Nord) ou *S* (Sud) apportent une précision supplémentaire.

Les colonnes suivantes indiquent le nom de la rue, ainsi que le ou les arrondissements dont elle dépend.

L'Association Valentin Haüy, 5 rue Duroc, 75007 Paris, diffuse (prix 178 F) *la liste alphabétique des rues de Paris, transcrite en écriture braille.*

Index to the streets of Paris

The first two columns giving the page of plan and grid reference, enable you to locate a street on the map *(key map p. 4-5)*. In some cases the grid references may be followed by the letters *N* (North) or *S* (South) indicating the position of the street more closely.
The following columns give the street's name and its arrondissement, or two if it overlaps into a second.

Alphabetisches Straßenverzeichnis

Die beiden ersten Spalten enthalten die Angabe der Seite sowie die der Koordinaten des Planquadrates und erlauben Ihnen, die Straße auf dem Plan zu finden *(Seiteneinteilung s. S. 4-5)*. Manchmal wurde ein *N* (Norden) oder *S* (Süden) hinzugefügt, wodurch die Lage noch genauer bestimmt ist.
In den folgenden Spalten sind der Name der Straße und die Nummer des bzw. der entsprechenden Arrondissements angegeben.

Índice alfabético de las calles de París

Las dos primeras columnas le remiten a la página del plano y a las coordenadas de la cuadrícula que permiten localizar con exactitud la calle en el plano *(división cartográfica pág. 4-5)*. En algunos casos las letras *N* (Norte) o *S* (Sur) proporcionan una precisión complementaria.
Las columnas siguientes indican el nombre exacto de la calle, así como el o los distritos de que depende.

a

Plan n°	Repère	Nom	Arrondissement
31	J13	Abbaye r. de l'	6
43-44	L14-L-15	Abbé-Basset pl. de l'	5
53-54	P10-P11	Abbé-Carton r. de l'	14
43	L14-L13	Abbé-de-l'Epée r. de l'	5
56	R15	Abbé-G.-Henocque pl.	13
27	J6 N	Abbé-Gillet r. de l'	16
42	K11-L12	Abbé-Grégoire r. de l'	6
40	L7-N8	Abbé-Groult r. de l'	15
42	N11	Abbé-Jean-Lebeuf pl. de l'	14
32	H16-J16	Abbé-Migne r. de l'	4
7	C14	Abbé-Patureau r. de l'	18
28	K8	Abbé-Roger-Derry r. de l'	15
26-27	K4-K5	Abbé-Roussel av. de l'	16
4	C8	Abbé-Rousselot r. de l'	17
42	N11	Abbé-Soulange-Bodin r. de l'	14
19	D13	Abbesses pass. des	18
19	D13	Abbesses pl. des	18
7-19	D13	Abbesses r. des	18
20	E15	Abbeville r. d' n°s 1-17, 2-16	10
		n°s 19-fin, 18-fin	9
45	L18-K18	Abel r.	12
38	N3 N	Abel-Ferry r.	16
45-56	N15 S	Abel-Hovelacque r.	13
46	L19	Abel-Leblanc pass.	12
21	G18 N	Abel-Rabaud r.	11
18	D11	Abel-Truchet r.	17
31-20	G14-G15	Aboukir r. d'	2
7	C13 S	Abreuvoir r. de l'	18
16	E7	Acacias pass. des	17
16	E7	Acacias r. des	17
31	K13 N	Acadie pl. d'	6
35	H21	Achille r.	20
54	R11	Achille-Luchaire r.	14
7	C13-B13	Achille-Martinet r.	18
44	M15	Adanson sq.	5
23-35	G22	Adjudant-Réau r.	20
24	F23 S	Adjudant-Vincenot pl.	20
32	J15	Adolphe-Adam r.	4
40	M8	Adolphe-Chérioux pl.	15
54	P12 S	Adolphe-Focillon r.	14
31	H14 N	Adolphe-Jullien r.	1
18	D12	Adolphe-Max pl.	9
10	C20	Adolphe-Mille r.	19
53	R9-R10	Adolphe-Pinard bd	14
26	H4-G4	Adolphe-Yvon r.	16
22	F20 N	Adour villa de l'	19
26	J4 S	Adrien-Hébrard av.	16
19	F13	Adrien-Oudin pl.	9
35	J22 N	Adrienne cité	20
54	N12 S	Adrienne villa	14
28	J8-J9	Adrienne-Lecouvreur allée	7
42	N12 N	Adrienne-Simon villa	14
8	D16-C16	Affre r.	18
27	K5	Agar r.	16
19	E14	Agent-Bailly r. de l'	9
32-33	K16-K17	Agrippa-d'Aubigné r.	4
18	F11 S	d'Aguesseau r.	8
42	N11	Aide-Sociale sq. de l'	14
7	B14 S	Aimé-Lavy r.	18
16	D8 S	Aimé-Maillart pl.	17
56	R15-S15	Aimé-Morot r.	13
10	C19 N	Aisne r. de l'	19
21	F17 S	Aix r. d'	10
41	M10-N10	Alain r.	14
40	M8 S	Alain-Chartier r.	15
53	P9	Alain-Fournier sq.	14
28	K8	Alasseur r.	15
27-26	H5-H4	Albéric-Magnard r.	16
57	R18-P18	Albert r.	13
52	P7-P8	Albert-Bartholomé av.	15
52	P7	Albert-Bartholomé sq.	15
56	P16-N16	Albert-Bayer r.	13
21	E17	Albert-Camus r.	10
41	K9	Albert-de-Lapparent r.	7
28	H7 N	Albert-de-Mun av.	16
7	B14	Albert-Kahn pl.	18
56	R17	Albert-Londres pl.	13
48	M23 N	Albert-Malet r.	12
29	G9 S	Albert-1er cours	8
28	H7	Albert-1er-de-Monaco av.	16
22	E20	Albert-Robida villa	19
4	D7-C7	Albert-Samain r.	17
54	R11	Albert-Sorel r.	14
21-20	G17-F16	Albert-Thomas r.	10
48	L24-K24	Albert-Willemetz r.	20
43	N14 S	Albin-Cachot sq.	13
56	R15	Albin-Haller r.	13
27	J6 N	Alboni r. de l'	16
27	J6 N	Alboni sq.	16
55	P13 N	d'Alembert r.	14
42	L11	Alençon r. d'	15
55-53	P14-N10	Alésia r. d'	14
54	P11	Alésia villa d'	14
23	D22-E22	Alexander-Fleming r.	19
41	M10	Alexandre pass.	15
40-41	K8-K9	Alexandre-Cabanel r.	15
16	D7	Alexandre-Charpentier r.	17
34-35	K20-J21	Alexandre-Dumas r.	
		n°s 1-59, 2-72	11
		n°s 61 fin, 74-fin	20
7	B14 N	Alexandre-Lécuyer imp.	18
21	E17 N	Alexandre-Parodi r.	10
23	D21 S	Alexandre-Ribot villa	19
29	H10 N	Alexandre III pont	8-7
20	G15 N	Alexandrie r. d'	2
34	J20	Alexandrine pass.	11
28	J8 S	Alexis-Carrel r.	15
27	J5	Alfred-Bruneau r.	16
26	K3	Alfred-Capus sq.	16
44	L15	Alfred-Cornu r.	5
26	H4	Alfred-Dehodencq r.	16
26	H4	Alfred-Dehodencq sq.	16
17	E9	Alfred-de-Vigny r.	
		n°s 1-9, 2-16	8
		n°s 11-fin, 18-fin	17
53	P9 N	Alfred-Durand-Claye r.	14
57	S17 N	Alfred-Fouillée r.	13
4	C8 S	Alfred-Roll r.	17
19	D13 S	Alfred-Stevens pass.	9
19	D13 S	Alfred-Stevens r.	9
45	L17 N	Alger cour d'	12
30	G12 S	Alger r. d'	1
23	E22-D21	Algérie bd d'	19
21	F17	Alibert r.	10
53	P10 S	Alice sq.	14
46	K19 S	d'Aligre pl.	12
46	K19 S	d'Aligre r.	12

Plan n°	Repère	Nom	Arrondissement
32	J15-H16	Archives r. des nos 1-41, 2-56	4
		nos 43-fin, 58-fin	3
32	J15	Arcole pont d'	4
32	J15 S	Arcole r. d'	4
55	R13	Arcueil porte d'	14
55	R14-S14	Arcueil r. d'	14
10	C20	Ardennes r. des	19
44	L15	Arènes r. des	5
17	F10 N	Argenson r. d'	8
31	H13-G13	Argenteuil r. d'	1
15	G6 N	Argentine cité de l'	16
16	F7 N	Argentine r. d'	16
10	B19	Argonne pl. de l'	19
10	B20-B19	Argonne r. de l'	19
31	G14 S	Argout r. d'	2
37	M2 N	Arioste r. de l'	16
30	H11	Aristide-Briand r.	7
7-19	D13 N	Aristide-Bruand r.	18
41	M10	Aristide-Maillol r.	15
16	E7	Armaillé r. d'	17
6	B12 S	Armand villa	18
22	D19 S	Armand-Carrel pl.	19
22-21	D19-D18	Armand-Carrel r.	19
22	E20 N	Armand-Fallières villa	19
7	C13	Armand-Gauthier r.	18
41-42	L10-M11	Armand-Moisant r.	15
48	N23-M23	Armand-Rousseau av.	12
7	C13 S	Armée-d'Orient r. de l'	18
15	D6-D5	Armenonville r. d'	
		nos 1-11 bis, 2-10	17
		nos 13-fin, 12-fin	Neuilly
41	M10	Armorique r. de l'	15
6	A11 S	Arnault-Tzanck pl.	17
33	H17 S	Arquebusiers r. des	3
44	L15 N	Arras r. d'	5
42	L11 S	Arrivée r. de l'	15
33-45	K17	Arsenal r. de l'	4
16	F8	Arsène-Houssaye r.	8
41	M10	d'Arsonval r.	15
46	L20	d'Artagnan r.	12
6	B12	Arthur-Brière r.	17
21	F18	Arthur-Groussier r.	10
7	A13 S	Arthur-Ranc r.	18
22	E20	Arthur-Rozier r.	19
55	P13 S	Aristes r. des	14
17	F9	Artois r. d'	8
15	D6 S	Arts av. des	17
47	L21 N	Arts imp. des	12
42	N11 N	Arts pass. des	14
31	H13-J13	Arts pont des	1-6
6	C12 S	Arts villa des	18
33	H18 S	Asile pass. de l'	11
33	H18 S	Asile-Popincourt r. de l'	11
4	B8-C8	Asnières porte d'	17
42-43	K12-M13	Assas r. d'	6
42	N11	Asseline r.	14
27-26	K5-J4	Assomption r. de l'	16
18	F11	d'Astorg r.	8
42	L11	Astrolabe imp. de l'	15
18	E12	Athènes r. d'	9
21	F18 N	Atlas pass. de l'	19
21	F18-E18	Atlas r. de l'	19
18	F12	Auber r.	9
9	C17-D17	Aubervilliers imp. d'	19
9	A18	Aubervilliers porte d'	19
9	D17-A18	Aubervilliers r. d'	
		nos impairs 18e - nos pairs	19
16	D7-D8	Aublet villa	17
32	J16 N	Aubriot r.	4
35	J21 N	Aubry cité	20
32	H15 S	Aubry-le-Boucher r.	4
55	P13 S	Aude r. de l'	14
7-19	D13 N	Audran r.	18
35	K21	Auger r.	20
28-29	J8-J9	Augereau r.	7
21	G18	Auguste-Barbier	11
10	A20	Auguste-Baron pl.	19
28	K7-K8	Auguste-Bartholdi r.	15
56-55	P15-N14	Auguste-Blanqui bd	13
57	P17 N	Auguste-Blanqui villa	13
54	P11 S	Auguste-Cain r.	14
40	N7	Auguste-Chabrières cité	15
40	N7	Auguste-Chabrières r.	15
36	J23	Auguste-Chapuis r.	20
43	L13	Auguste-Comte r.	6
40	L8	Auguste-Dorchain r.	15
55	R14	Auguste-Lançon r.	13
34	J19 N	Auguste-Laurent r.	11
38	M4	Auguste-Maquet r.	16
34	H20	Auguste-Métivier pl.	20
42	M11 S	Auguste-Mie r.	14
56	R16 N	Auguste-Perret r.	13
53	P9	Auguste-Renoir sq.	14
16	F8-G7	Auguste-Vacquerie r.	16
39	L5	Auguste-Vitu r.	15
23	E21 S	Augustin-Thierry r.	19
19	E13	Aumale r. d'	9
56	P16 S	Aumont r.	13
16	D7	Aumont-Thiéville r.	17
34	H20 S	Aunay imp. d'	11
15	D6 S	d'Aurelle-de-Paladines bd	17
45-44	M17-M16	Austerlitz cité d'	5
45	L17	Austerlitz pont d'	12-5-13
45	M18-L17	Austerlitz port d'	13
45	M18-L17	Austerlitz quai d'	13
45	L18 N	Austerlitz r. d'	12
37	L2-L1	Auteuil bd d' nos 1-7 et 4	16
		autres nos	Boulogne
38	L4 N	Auteuil pl. d'	16
39-38	K5-M4	Auteuil pot d'	16
37	K2	Auteuil porte d'	16
38	L4-K3	Auteuil r. d'	16
32	K16 N	Ave Maria r. de l'	4
34	G19 S	Avenir cité de l'	11
23	F21 S	Avenir r. de l'	20
16-15	F7-F6	Avenue-du-Bois sq. de l'	16
15	F5	Avenue-Foch sq. de l'	16
4	C8	Aveyron sq. de l'	17
40	K8 S	Avre r. de l'	15
35-36	K21-J23	Avron r. d'	20
7	D14 N	Azaïs r.	18

Comment s'y retrouver dans la banlieue parisienne ?
Utilisez la **carte Michelin** *no 101 : claire, précise, à jour.*

Plan n°	Repère	Nom	Arrondissement
38	L4 *N*	Buis r. du	16
21	F18	Buisson-St-Louis pass.	10
21	F18	Buisson-St-Louis r. du	10
33-34	J18-J19	Bullourde pass.	11
56	P15 *S*	Buot r.	13
35	K21 *N*	Bureau imp. du	11

Plan n°	Repère	Nom	Arrondissement
35	J21 *S*	Bureau pass. du	11
21	F18-E18	Burnouf r.	19
7	D13-C13	Burq r.	18
56	P15	Butte-aux-Cailles r.	13
9	C17	Buzelin r.	18
47-35	K22-J21	Buzenval r. de	20

C

Plan n°	Repère	Nom	Arrondissement
55	P14-P13	Cabanis r.	14
55	R14 *S*	Cacheux r.	13
19	F14-E14	Cadet r.	9
40	N7	Cadix r. de	15
1	D14	Cadran imp. du	18
32-33	H16-H17	Caffarelli r.	3
56	R15-S15	Caffieri av.	13
11	D21 *N*	Cahors r. de	19
20	D16	Cail r.	10
33	J18 *S*	Caillard imp.	11
56	R16	Caillaux r.	13
48	L23-M24	Cailletet r.	12
9-21	D17 *N*	Caillé r.	18
20	G15 *N*	Caire galerie du	2
20	G15	Caire pass. du	2
20	G15	Caire pl. du	2
32	G15	Caire r. du	2
18	D12	Calais r. de	9
7	B13	Calmels imp.	18
7	B14-B13	Calmels r.	18
7	B13 *S*	Calmels prolongée r.	18
7	D14 *N*	Calvaire pl. du	18
7	D14	Calvaire r. du	18
18	F11	Cambacérès r.	8
23	E21	Cambo r. de	19
35	G21 *S*	Cambodge r. du	20
18-30	G12	Cambon r.	1
10	B19	Cambrai r. de	19
40	K8-L8	Cambronne pl.	15
40-41	L8-M9	Cambronne r.	15
53	P9	Camélias r. des	14
6	A12	Camille-Blaisot r.	17
34	J19-H19	Camille-Desmoulins r.	11
7	A13-A14	Camille-Flammarion r.	18
43	M13 *N*	Camille-Jullian pl.	6
6	D12	Camille-Tahan r.	18
27	H6 *S*	de Camoëns av.	16
43-42	M13-M12	Campagne-Première r.	14
44	N16	Campo-Formio r. de	13
53	P9	Camulogène r.	15
29	G9-G10	Canada pl. du	8
9	C17	Canada r. du	18
48	L23	Canart imp.	12
34	K19	Candie r. de	11
44	M15	de Candolle r.	5
31	K13 *N*	Canettes r. des	6
41	N10	du Cange r.	14
31-43	K13	Canivet r. du	6
47	M21 *S*	Cannebière r.	12
57	P18 *S*	Cantagrel r.	13
33	J18 *S*	Cantal cour du	11
35-36	G22-G23	Capitaine-Ferber r. du	20
6	C12 *N*	Capitaine-Lagache r. du	17
6	C12	Capitaine-Madon r. du	18
23-35	G22	Capitaine-Marchal r. du	20
39	L6	Capitaine-Ménard r. du	15
26-38	K4 *S*	Capitaine-Olchanski r. du	16

Plan n°	Repère	Nom	Arrondissement
28	J7 *S*	Capitaine-Scott r. du	15
36	G23 *S*	Capitaine-Tarron r. du	20
20	D15	Caplat r.	18
4	C7 *S*	Caporal-Peugeot r. du	17
47	N21 *N*	Capri r. de	12
6	D12 *N*	Capron r.	18
19-18	F13-F12	Capucines bd des	
		n°s impairs	2
		n°s pairs	9
18	G12 *N*	Capucines r. des	
		n°s impairs	1
		n°s pairs	2
40	M8	Carcel r.	15
6-5	B11-B10	Cardan r.	17
35-36	J22-J23	Cardeurs sq. des	20
31	J13 *S*	Cardinale r.	6
28	K8	Cardinal-Amette pl. du	15
7	D14 *N*	Cardinal-Dubois r. du	18
7	D14-C14	Cardinal-Guibert r. du	10
47	N22	Cardinal-Lavigerie pl.	12
44	K15 *S*	Cardinal-Lemoine cité du	5
44	K15-L15	Cardinal-Lemoine r. du	5
18	E12-D12	Cardinal-Mercier r.	9
5	D10	Cardinet pass.	17
16-6	D8-C11	Cardinet r.	17
22	E20	Carducci r.	19
38	M4-N4	Carlo-Sarrabezolles r.	15
44-43	K15-K14	Carmes r. des	5
16	F7-E7	Carnot av.	17
48	L23-M23	Carnot bd	12
18	D12-D11	Caroline r.	17
23	E22	Carolus-Duran r.	19
33	J17	Caron r.	4
6-7	C12-C13	Carpeaux r.	18
41-40	L9-L8	Carrier-Belleuse r.	15
34	J20	Carrière-Mainguet imp.	11
27	J6 *N*	Carrières imp. des	16
23	D21	Carrières-d'Amérique r.	19
31	H13	Carrousel pl. du	1
31	H13-J13	Carrousel pont du	1-7
36	G23-H23	Cartellier av.	20
40	M7	Casablanca r. de	15
22	G20-F20	Cascades r. des	20
31-43	K13	Casimir-Delavigne r.	6
30	H11-J11	Casimir-Périer r.	7
42	K12	Cassette r.	6
43	M13 *S*	Cassini r.	14
41-53	N10-P9	Castagnary r.	15
35	J21 *S*	Casteggio imp. de	20
18	F12-F11	de Castellane r.	8
33	K17-J17	Castex r.	4
30	G12 *S*	Castiglione r. de	1
42	M11	Catalogne pl. de	14
31	G14 *S*	Catinat r.	1
4	D7-C7	Catulle-Mendès r.	17

Plan n°	Repère	Nom	Arrondissement
7-19	D13 *N*	Cauchois r.	18
39	L5-M6	Cauchy r.	15
6-7	D12-C14	Caulaincourt r.	18
7	C13	Caulaincourt sq.	18
18	F12-E12	de Caumartin r.	9
28-40	K8	Cavalerie r. de la	15
6	D12 *N*	Cavallotti r.	18
8	C16-C15	Cavé r.	18
22	D19	Cavendish r.	19
7-19	D14 *N*	Cazotte r.	18
32	K16 *N*	Célestins port des	4
32	K16 *N*	Célestins quai des	4
42	N11 *N*	Cels imp.	14
42	N12-M11	Cels r.	14
34	G20	Cendriers r. des	20
44	M16-M15	Censier r.	5
41	L9 *N*	Cépré r.	15
33	K17	Cerisaie r. de la	4
17	G9 *N*	Cerisoles r. de	8
5	D9 *N*	Cernuschi r.	17
18	E11 *S*	César-Caire av.	8
41	L10-L9	César-Franck r.	15
34	K19-K20	Cesselin imp.	11
39	L5-M6	Cévennes r. des	15
31	G13	Chabanais r.	2
46	N19-N20	Chablis r. de	12
20	E15 *S*	Chabrol cité de	10
20	E16-E15	Chabrol r. de	10
48	L23-L24	du Chaffault r.	12
16-28	G8	Chaillot r. de la	16
16	G8	Chaillot sq. de	16
30	J12-K12	Chaise r. de la	7
5	B10-C10	Chalabre imp.	17
21	F18	Chalet r. du	10
26	J4	Chalets av. des	16
18	F7 *N*	Chalgrin r.	16
46	L19-K19	Chaligny r.	12
45	L18	Chalon cour de	12
46-45	L19-L18	Chalon r. de	12
46	M19	Chambertin r. de	12
53	N9-P9	Chambéry r. de	15
29	G9	Chambiges r.	8
26	K4	Chamfort r.	16
35	J22 *S*	Champagne cité	20
30	J11 *N*	Champagny r. de	7
28	K8	Champaubert av. de	15
55	N14 *S*	Champ-de-l'Alouette r. du	13
29	J9	Champ-de-Mars r. du	7
4	D7	Champerret porte de	17
28	J8 *S*	Champfleury r.	7
7-8	B14-B15	Championnet pass.	18
8-6	B15-B12	Championnet r.	18
6	B12	Championnet villa	18
7	B13 *N*	Champ-Marie pass. du	13
31-43	K14 *S*	Champollion r.	5
17	F9 *S*	Champs galerie des	8
30-16	G11-F8	Champs-Elysées av. des	8
29	H10 *N*	Champs-Elysées port des	8
17	G10-G9	Champs-Elysées rd-pt des	8
30	K11 *N*	de Chanaleilles r.	7
15	F5 *S*	Chancelier-Adenauer pl. du	16
40	M7	Chandon imp.	15
38	L3 *N*	Chanez r.	16
38	L3 *N*	Chanez villa	16
48	L23	Changarnier r.	12
31	J14	Change pont au	14

Plan n°	Repère	Nom	Arrondissement
32	K15-J15	Chanoinesse r.	4
26	G4	Chantemesse av.	16
33	K18	Chantier pass. du	12
44	K16-K15	Chantier r. des	5
19	E14	Chantilly r. de	9
32	J15 *S*	Chantres r. des	4
57	N18-P17	Chanvin pass.	13
34	K19-K20	Chanzy r.	11
15	E6-D6	Chapelle av. de la	17
21-20	D17-D15	Chapelle bd de la	
		nᵒˢ impairs	10
		nᵒˢ pairs	18
8	C16 *S*	Chapelle cité de la	18
8	B16 *S*	Chapelle imp. de la	18
20	D16	Chapelle pl. de la	18
8	A16	Chapelle porte de la	18
8	C16-A16	Chapelle r. de la	18
32	H16-H15	Chapon r.	3
19	D14	Chappe r.	18
19	E13-D13	Chaptal cité	9
19-18	E13-D12	Chaptal r.	9
38	M4 *N*	Chapu r.	16
55	R14	Charbonnel r.	13
20	D16-D15	Charbonnière r. de la	18
41	L9-L10	Charbonniers pass. des	15
57	N18-P17	Charcot r.	13
28	H7-J7	Chardin r.	16
38	L4-M3	Chardon-Lagache r.	16
10	B20-A19	Charente quai de la	19
59	P22	Charenton porte de	12
33-47	K18-N21	Charenton r. de	12
32	J16 *S*	Charlemagne pass.	4
32	J16 *S*	Charlemagne r.	4
6	B12 *N*	Charles-Albert pass.	18
45-34	K18-K19	Charles-Baudelaire r.	12
47	L22	Charles-Bénard villa	12
7	B14 *S*	Charles-Bernard pl.	18
57	R17	Charles-Bertheau r.	13
48	L19 *S*	Charles-Bossut r.	12
33-32	K17-J16	Charles-V r.	4
24	E23 *S*	Charles-Cros r.	20
34-33	J19-J18	Charles-Dallery pass.	11
47	N22	Charles-de-Foucauld av.	12
16	F7-F8	Charles-de-Gaulle av.	8-16-17
34	K19 *N*	Charles-Delescluze r.	11
27	J6	Charles-Dickens r.	16
27	J6 *N*	Charles-Dickens sq.	16
42	N12	Charles-Divry r.	14
19	D14	Charles-Dullin pl.	18
36	K23-J23	Charles-et-Robert r.	20
5-6	C10-C11	Charles-Fillion pl.	17
28	J7-K8	Charles-Floquet av.	7
56	R15-P15	Charles-Fourier r.	13
23	F21	Charles-Friedel r.	20
18	F12 *S*	Charles-Garnier pl.	9
5	D9 *N*	Charles-Gerhardt r.	17
29	G10	Charles-Girault av.	8
19	E14	Charles-Godon cité	9
9	A17	Charles-Hermite r.	18
15	G5 *N*	Charles-Lamoureux r.	16
41	L9 *S*	Charles-Laurent sq.	15
9	A17	Charles-Lauth r.	18
40	M7-M8	Charles-Lecocq r.	15
54	R11	Charles-le-Goffic r.	14
33	H17	Charles-Luizet r.	11
38	M3 *N*	Charles-Marie-Widor r.	16
39	L6 *N*	Charles-Michels pl.	15
23	E22	Charles-Monselet r.	19

15

18

Plan n°	Repère	Nom	Arrondissement
56	S16	Dr-Bourneville r. du	13
28	J8	Dr-Brouardel av. du	7
57	N17 S	Dr-Charles-Richet r.	13
6	C11 S	Dr-Félix-Lobligeois pl.	17
27-28	K6-K7	Dr-Finlay r. du	15
27	K6-J5	Dr-Germain-Sée r. du	16
24	E23	Dr-Gley av. du	20
47	M21	Dr-Goujon r. du	12
27	K5 N	Dr-Hayem pl. du	16
6	C11	Dr-Heulin r. du	17
40	L8-M8	Dr-Jacquemaire-Clemenceau r. du	15
28	G8	Dr-Jacques-Bertillon imp.	8
24	G23 N	Dr-Labbé r. du	20
9	C18	Dr-Lamaze r. du	19
17	E10-F9	Dr-Lancereaux r. du	8
56	R15	Dr-Landouzy r. du	13
54	S12 N	Dr-Lannelongue av. du	14
56	R16 N	Dr-Laurent r. du	13
56	R15	Dr-Lecène r. du	13
56	R16-R15	Dr-Leray r. du	13
56	R15-R16	Dr-Lucas-Championniere r.	13
56	P16 S	Dr-Magnan r. du	13
57	P17	Dr-Navarre r. du	13
23	G22 N	Dr-Paquelin r. du	20
6	B11	Dr-Paul-Brousse r. du	17
37	M2	Dr-Paul-Michaux pl. du	16
23	E21 S	Dr-Potain r. du	19
41	M10	Dr-Roux r. du	15
36	J23	Drs-Déjerine r. des	20
56	R16-R15	Dr-Tuffier r. du	13
57	N17 S	Dr-Victor-Hutinel r. du	13
57	R18 S	Dr-Yersin pl. du	13
38	N3 N	Dode-de-la-Brunerie av.	16
16	E7	Doisy pass.	17
44	L15 S	Dolomieu r.	5
32-31	K15-K14	Domat r.	5
40	N8	Dombasle imp	15
40	N8 N	Dombasle pass.	15
40	M8-N8	Dombasle r.	15
16	F7 S	Dome r. du	16
57	P18-P17	Domrémy r. de	13
38	K4 S	Donizetti r.	16
4	C8	Dordogne sq. de la	17
48	N23	Dorée porte (porte de Picpus)	12
11	C21 S	Dorées sente des	19
47	L21 N	Dorian av.	12
47	L21 N	Dorian r.	12
15	G6-F6	Dosnes r.	16
19-18	D13-D12	Douai r. de	9
54	P12 S	Douanier-Rousseau r. du	14
5	B9	Douaumont bd de	17
32	K15 N	Double pont au	4-5
8	C16-C15	Doudeauville r.	18
30	J12-K12	Dragon r. du	6
34	G19 S	Dranem r.	11
15	EG	Dreux r. de	16
7-19	D14 N	Drevet r.	18
46	K19 S	Driancourt pass.	12
19	F14	Drouot r.	9
34-46	K19	Druinot imp.	12
20	F16	Dubail pass.	10

Plan n°	Repère	Nom	Arrondissement
27	J5 N	Duban r.	16
18	E11-E12	Dublin pl. de	8
22	D19	Dubois pass.	19
35	H22	Dubourg cité	20
46	M20	Dubrunfaut r.	12
7	C14-B14	Duc r.	18
57	N17 S	Duchefdelaville imp.	13
57	N18-N17	Duchefdelaville r.	13
34	N19	Dudouy pass.	11
23	F21 S	Duée pass. de la	20
23	F21 S	Duée r. de la	20
27	G5 S	Dufrénoy r.	16
38	M3 S	Dufresne villa	16
46	M20	Dugommier r.	12
42	L12 N	Duguay-Trouin r.	6
7-8	B14-B15	Duhesme pass.	18
7	C13-B14	Duhesme r.	18
41	L10 S	Dulac r.	15
36	G23	Dulaure r.	20
18-5	D11-C10	Dulong r.	17
34-35	K20-K21	Dumas pass.	11
44	M16-N16	Duméril r.	13
16	G7-F8	Dumont-d'Urville r.	16
22	F19-E19	Dunes r. des	19
20-19	E16-D14	Dunkerque r. de	
		n°ˢ 1-47, 2-36 bis	10
		n°ˢ 49-fin. 38-fin	9
45-57	P18-N17	Dunois r.	13
45	N17	Dunois sq.	13
19	D13 S	Duperré r.	9
32-33	G16-G17	Dupetit-Thouars cité	3
33-32	G17-G16	Dupetit-Thouars r.	3
18	G12	Duphot r.	
		n°ˢ 1-21, 2-26	1
		n°ˢ 23-fin, 28-fin	8
42	K12	Dupin r.	6
15	E6 S	Duplan cité	16
28	K8	Dupleix pl.	15
28-40	K8	Dupleix r.	15
34	H19	Dupont cité	11
15	F6 N	Dupont villa	16
23-35	G22-G21	Dupont-de-l'Eure r.	20
28-29	H8-H9	Dupont-des-Loges r.	7
33	G17 S	Dupuis r.	3
8	C16	Dupuy imp.	18
57	R18	Dupuy-de-Lôme r.	13
31	K13	Dupuytren r.	6
29-41	J9-K10	Duquesne av.	7
47	M21	Durance r. de la	12
34	H19-H20	Duranti r.	11
7	D13-C13	Durantin r.	18
39-40	M6-M7	Duranton r.	15
18	F11 S	Duras r. de	8
7	B13 N	Durel cité	18
15	F6-E6	Duret r.	16
34	G20-H20	Duris passage	20
34	G20	Duris r.	20
34	G19	Durmar cité	11
41	K10-L10	Duroc r.	7
42-54	N12 S	Durouchoux r.	14
23	E22 S	Dury-Vasselon villa	20
32	G15	Dusoubs r.	2
53	P10	Duthy villa	14
41	M9	Dutot r.	15
29	G10	Dutuit av.	8
10-9	C19-C18	Duvergier r.	19
29	J9	Duvivier r.	7

e

f

Plan n°	Repère	Nom	Arrondissement
44	K16-L15	Fossés-St-Bernard r. des	5
43	L14	Fossés-St-Jacques r. des	5
44	M16	Fossés-St-Marcel r. des	5
32	K15	Fouarre r. du	5
56	R15-P15	Foubert pass.	13
28	H8 *N*	Foucault r.	16
24	F23	Fougères r. des	20
31-30	K13-K12	Four r. du	6
40	M8 *S*	Fourcade r.	15
16	E8-D8	Fourcroy r.	17
32	J16 *S*	Fourcy r. de	4
6	C11	Fourneyron r.	17
21	E18	Fours-à-Chaux pass. des	19
19	D14	Foyatier r.	18
5	B10-B11	Fragonard r.	17
32	H15-G15	Française r. n°s 1-5, 2-6	1
		n°s 7 fin, 8-fin	2
33	G17 *S*	Franche-Comté r. de	3
34	J19 *S*	Franchemont imp.	11
8	C16	Francis-Carco r.	18
7	A14	Francis-de-Croisset r.	18
56	S15	Francis-de-Miomandre r.	13
41	N10	Francis-de-Pressensé r.	14
6	A12 *S*	Francis-Garnier r.	17
21	E17	Francis-Jammes r.	10
22	F19-G19	Francis-Picabia r.	20
43	K13 *S*	Francis-Poulenc sq.	6
31	K14 *N*	Francisque-Gay r.	6
27	H6 *S*	Francisque-Sarcey r.	16
57	R18 *S*	Franc-Nohain r.	13
7	C14	Francœur r.	18
41	L9	François-Bonvin r.	15
40	M7	François-Coppée r.	15
34	J19	François-de-Neufchâteau r.	11
38	K4 *S*	François-Gérard r.	16
27-39	K5	François-Millet r.	16
32	J15-J16	François-Miron r.	4
40	M7	François-Mouthon r.	15
22	D20 *S*	François-Pinton r.	19
27	J5-H5	François-Ponsard r.	16
29	G9 *S*	François-1er pl.	8
29-16	G9-F8	François-1er r.	8
40	M8 *S*	François-Villon r.	15
28	H8	Franco-Russe av.	7
33-32	J17-H16	Francs-Bourgeois r. des	
		n°s impairs	4
		n°s pairs	3
27	H6 *S*	Franklin r.	16
29-17	G10-F10	Franklin-D.-Roosevelt av	8
41	N9	Fanquet r.	15
27-26	H5-H4	Franqueville r. de	16
20	E15	Franz-Liszt pl.	10
23	D21 *S*	Fraternité r. de la	19
17	F9	Frédéric-Bastiat r.	8
6	A12 *S*	Frédéric Brunet r.	17
22-23	F20-F21	Frédérick-Lemaître r.	20
29	J9 *S*	Frédéric-Le-Play av.	7
47	K22 *S*	Frédéric-Loliée r.	20
40	L7-M7	Frédéric-Magisson r.	15
39	M6	Frédéric-Mistral r.	15
23	E21-E22	Frédéric-Mourlon r.	19
32	K15	Frédéric-Sauton r.	5
7	A13 *S*	Frédéric-Schneider r.	18
41	N9 *N*	Frédéric-Vallois sq.	15
40	L8-K8	Frémicourt r.	15
27	J6 *N*	Frémiet av.	16
35	J22	Fréquel pass.	20
57	R17	Frères-d'Astier-de-la Vigerie r. des	13
24	F23-E23	Frères-Flavien r. des	20
40	L7-M7	Frères-Morane r. des	15
28	H8-G8	Frères-Périer r. des	16
50-51	P4-P5	Frères-Voisin allée des	15
50-51	P4-P5	Frères-Voisin bd des	15
28	H8-H7	Fresnel r.	16
28	G8 *S*	Freycinet r.	16
54	P12-R11	Friant r.	14
17-16	F9-F8	Friedland av. de	8
19	E13-D13	Frochot av.	9
19	E13-D13	Frochot r.	9
42	N12-M11	Froidevaux r.	14
33	H17	Froissart r.	3
33	J18 *N*	Froment r.	11
19	D13 *S*	Fromentin r.	9
45	M18 *S*	Fulton r.	13
31	J13 *S*	de Furstemberg r.	6
54	P11 *N*	Furtado-Heine r.	14
43	M13-M14	Fustel-de-Coulanges r.	5

g

Plan n°	Repère	Nom	Arrondissement
48	L23	Gabon r. du	12
30-17	G11-G10	Gabriel av.	8
17	D10	Gabriel-Fauré sq.	17
46	N20 *N*	Gabriel-Lamé r.	12
20	F15	Gabriel-Laumain r.	10
7	D14-D13	Gabrielle r.	18
42	L11 *S*	Gabrielle villa	15
22	F19	Gabrielle-d'Estrées allée	19
18	F11 *N*	Gabriel-Péri pl.	8
32	G16 *S*	Gabriel-Vicaire r.	3
41	M9 *S*	Gager-Gabillot r.	15
23	F22-E22	Gagliardini villa	20
19	G13 *N*	Gaillon pl.	2
19	G13 *N*	Gaillon r.	2
42	M11-M12	Gaîté imp. de la	14
42	M11	Gaîté r. de la	14
32-31	K15-K14	Galande r.	5
16	G7-F8	Galilée r. n°s 1-53 - 2-50	16
		n°s 55-fin - 52-fin	8
35	J22-H22	Galleron r.	20
28	G8 *S*	Galliera r. de	16
16	D7	Galvani r.	17
34-23	H20-E22	Gambetta av.	20
23	F22	Gambetta pass.	20
23	F22	Gambetta petite-imp.	20
35	G21 *S*	Gambetta pl.	20
33	G18 *S*	Gambey r.	11
56	R16-S16	Gandon r.	13
6	D12-C12	Ganneron r.	18
31-43	K13	Garancière r.	6
8	D15-C15	Gardes r. des	18
46-45	N19-M18	Gare port de la	13

24

Plan n°	Repère	Nom	Arrondissement
22	G19 N	Georges-Rouault allée	20
54	N11 S	Georges-Saché r.	14
16	F7 S	Georges-Ville r.	16
7	B13	Georgette-Agutte r.	18
23	F21	Georgina villa	20
19	D14 S	Gérando r.	9
56	P15 N	Gérard pass.	13
56	P15	Gérard r.	13
7	A13	Gérard-de-Nerval r.	18
26	G4	Gérard-Philipe r.	16
40	M8	Gerbert r.	15
34	J20 N	Gerbier r.	11
41	N10	Gergovie pass. de	14
41-54	N10-P11	Gergovie r. de	14
38	K3 S	Géricault r.	16
19	D13	Geremain-Pilon cité	18
19	D13	Germain-Pilon r.	18
4	C8 S	Gervex r.	17
32	J15	Gesvres quai de	4
45	M18 S	Giffard r.	13
7	A14	Ginette-Neveu r.	18
39-40	K6-L7	Ginoux r.	15
54	P11 S	Giordano-Bruno r.	14
7	C13 S	Girardon imp.	18
7	C13	Girardon r.	18
38	K3 S	Girodet r.	16
10	B20-A19	Gironde quai de la	19
31	J14 S	Gît-le-Cœur r.	6
43-55	M14-P14	Glacière r. de la	13
24	E23	Glaïeuls r. des	20
19-18	F13-F12	Gluck r.	9
55	R14	Glycines r. des	13
44-56	M15-N16	Gobelins av. des	
		nos 1-23 - 2-22	5
		nos 25-fin - 24-fin	13
44	N16-N15	Gobelins cité des	13
44	N15 N	Gobelins r. des	13
44	N15	Gobelins villa des	13
34	J19	Gobert r.	11
56	N16 S	Godefroy r.	13
34	J19	Godefroy-Cavaignac r.	11
35	H22 S	Godin villa	20
18	F12 S	Godot-de-Mauroy r.	9
28	G8 S	Gœthe r.	16
9-21	D17 N	Goix pass.	19
18	G12	Gomboust imp.	1
19-31	G13	Gomboust r.	1
21	G18 N	Goncourt r. des	11
34-46	K20	Gonnet r.	11
37	L2 N	Gordon-Bennett av.	16
47	M22	Gossec r.	12
35-47	K22 S	Got sq.	20
10-22	D20	Goubet r.	19
16	D8	Gounod r.	17
4	D8-C8	Gourgaud av.	17
56	R15 S	Gouthière r.	13
8-20	D15	Goutte-d'Or r. de la	18
16-15	D7-E6	Gouvion-St-Cyr bd	17
15-16	D6-D7	Gouvion-St-Cyr sq.	17
31	J13 S	Gozlin r.	6
21	F18	Grâce-de-Dieu cour de la	10
44	M15-L15	Gracieuse r.	5
16-15	D7-D6	Graisivaudan sq. du	17
40	L8	Gramme r.	15
19	G13-F13	de Gramont r.	2
42	N12	de Grancey r.	14
32	G15 S	Grand-Cerf pass. du	2
28	K8	Grande-Allée	15

Plan n°	Repère	Nom	Arrondissement
16-15	F7-E6	Grande-Armée av. de la	
		nos impairs	16
		nos pairs	17
16	E7 S	Grande-Armée villa de la	17
42	L12-M12	Grande-Chaumière r. de la	6
32	H15 N	Grande-Truanderie r. de la	1
28	K8	Grand Place	15
33	G17 S	Grand-Prieuré r. du	11
31	J14	Grands-Augustins quai des	6
31	J14 S	Grands-Augustins r. des	6
35-36	K21-K23	Grands-Champs r. des	20
32	K15	Grands-Degrés r. des	5
33	H17-J17	Grand-Veneur r. du	3
43	N14 N	Grangé sq.	13
21	F17-E18	Grange-aux-Belles r. de la	10
19	F14	Grange-Batelière r. de la	9
47	N21 N	Gravelle r. de	12
32	H16 N	Gravilliers pass. des	3
32	H16-G15	Gravilliers r. des	3
18	F12	Greffulhe r.	8
31	J13-K13	Grégoire-de-Tours r.	6
11	C21	Grenade r. de la	19
28-40	J7-K8	Grenelle bd de	15
27-39	K5-K6	Grenelle pont de	16-15
28-27	J7-K6	Grenelle port de	15
28-27	J7-K6	Grenelle quai de	15
30-29	K12-J9	Grenelle r. de nos 1-7 - 2-10	6
		nos 9-fin - 12-fin	7
40	K7 S	Grenelle villa de	15
32	G15 S	Greneta cour	2
32	G15 S	Greneta r. nos 1-15 - 2-10	3
		nos 17-fin - 12-fin	2
32	H15 N	Grenier-St-Lazare r.	3
32	J16 S	Grenier-sur-l'Eau r. du	4
35	H22 S	Grés pl. des	20
10	C19 N	Gresset r.	19
19	F13 S	Grétry r.	2
27	H6-G6	Greuze r.	16
30	J12	Gribeauval r. de	7
44	M16-M15	Gril r. du	5
22	D20 S	Grimaud imp.	19
41	K9 S	Grisel imp.	15
34	G19	Griset cité	11
35	J22	Gros imp.	20
27-39	K5	Gros r.	16
29	H9 N	Gros-Caillou port du	7
29	J9 N	Gros-Caillou r. du	7
7	B14-B13	Grosse-Bouteille imp.	18
23	G22-F22	Groupe-Manouchian r. du	20
9-8	C17-C16	Guadeloupe r. de la	18
18	E11 S	Guatemala pl. du	8
38	M3 S	Gudin r.	16
8	B16 N	Gué imp. du	18
24	F23	de Guébriant r.	20
19	D13	Guelma imp. de	18
33	J17 S	Guéménée imp.	4
31	J13	Guénégaud r.	6
34	K20	Guénot pass.	11
35-34	K21-K20	Guénot r.	11
32	G15	Guérin-Boisseau r.	2
16	E7-D7	Guersant r.	17
28	K8 N	du Guesclin pass.	15
28	K8 N	du Guesclin r.	15
27	H5	Guibert villa	16
27	J5-H5	Guichard r.	16
23	F21 S	Guignier pl. du	20
23	F21 S	Guignier r. du	20

h

■
I

Les rues de Paris sont numérotées par rapport à la Seine : la maison n° 1 est la plus proche du fleuve lorsque la rue s'en écarte, en amont lorsqu'elle lui est parallèle.

Numéros impairs à gauche, numéros pairs à droite.

j

Plan n°	Repère	Nom	Arrondissement
31	J13	Jacob r.	6
33	G18 S	Jacquard r.	11
6	C11 S	Jacquemont r.	17
6	C11 S	Jacquemont ville	17
30	H11-J11	Jacques-Bainville pl.	7
53	P9	Jacques-Baudry r.	15
17	D10	Jacques-Bingen r.	17
20	F16 S	Jacques-Bonsergent pl.	10
31	J13	Jacques-Callot r.	6
6	B12	Jacques-Cartier r.	18
33	K17 N	Jacques-Cœur r.	4
31	K13-J13	Jacques-Copeau pl.	6
6	C12 N	Jacques-Froment pl.	18
3-4	C6-C7	Jacques-Ibert r.	17
9-8	D17-D16	Jacques-Kablé r.	18
6	B12-B11	Jacques-Kellner r.	17
21	F17-F18	Jacques-Louvel-Tessier r.	10
40	M7 S	Jacques-Mawas r.	15
27	J5	Jacques-Offenbach r.	16
34	G20	Jacques-Prévert r.	20
19	F13	Jacques-Rouché pl.	9
28	J8	Jacques-Rueff pl.	7
33	K18 N	Jacques-Viguès cour	11
41	L10	Jacques-et-Thérèse-Trefouel r.	15
54-53	P11-P10	Jacquier r.	14
17	E9-D9	Jadin r.	17
53	P10	Jamot villa	14
22	F19-E19	Jandelle cité	19
23	E21	Janssen r.	19
35	G22-G21	Japon r. du	20
34	J19	Japy r.	11
31	K14-K13	Jardinet r. du	6
34	K20 N	Jardiniers imp. des	11
47	N21	Jardiniers r. des	12
32	K16-J16	Jardins-St-Paul r. des	4
33	J17	de Jarente r.	4
20	F16	Jarry r.	10
26	K4 N	Jasmin cour	16
26	K4 N	Jasmin r.	16
26	K4 N	Jasmin sq.	16
47	L21 N	Jaucourt r.	12
39-38	K8-M4	Javel port de	15
39-40	L5-M7	Javel r. de	15
57	P17-R17	Javelot r. du	13
34	G19 S	Jean-Aicard av.	11
58	P20-P19	Jean-Baptiste-Berlier r.	13
7	C13 S	Jean-Baptiste-Clément pl.	18
16	D7	Jean-Baptiste-Dumas r.	17
22	F20 N	Jean-Baptiste-Dumay r.	20
23	D22-D21	Jean-Baptiste-Semanaz r.	19
42	K12-L12	Jean-Bart r.	6
33	J17	Jean-Beausire imp.	4
33	J17 S	Jean-Beausire pass.	4
33	J17 S	Jean-Beausire r.	4
27	J6	Jean-Bologne r.	16
45	L18	Jean-Bouton r.	12
44	M15 N	Jean-Colvin r.	5
28	K8 N	Jean-Carriès r.	7
8	A15	Jean-Cocteau r.	18
57	P18-P17	Jean-Colly r.	13
8	B16	Jean-Cottin r.	18
41	L9	Jean-Daudin r.	15
44-43	K15-K14	Jean-de-Beauvais r.	5
43	N14-N13	Jean-Dolent r.	14
7	B13 N	Jean-Dollfus r.	18
32	K15-J15	Jean-du-Bellay r.	4
57	R17	Jean-Dunand r.	13
21	E18-E17	Jean-Falck sq.	10
42	L11 N	Jean-Ferrandi r.	6
40	M8 N	Jean-Formigé r.	15
42	L12-L11	Jean-François-Gerbillon r.	6
8	D16 N	Jean-François Lépine r.	18
16	F7-G8	Jean-Giraudoux r.	16
47	N22 N	Jean-Godard villa	12
29	G9	Jean-Goujon r.	8
7	A14-A13	Jean-Henri-Fabre r.	18
15	G5 N	Jean-Hugues r.	16
31	H14-G14	Jean-Jacques-Rousseau r.	1
9-11	D18-C21	Jean-Jaurès av.	19
31	J14-H14	Jean-Lantier r.	1
6	B12	Jean-Leclaire r.	17
38	K3-K4	Jean-Lorrain pl.	16
4	C8	Jean-Louis-Forain r.	17
34	K19 N	Jean-Macé r.	11
39-40	M6-M7	Jean-Maridor r.	15
56	P15	Jean-Marie-Jégo r.	13
22	E19 N	Jean-Ménans r.	19
17	G10-F10	Jean-Mermoz r.	8
21	F18	Jean-Moinon r.	10
15	G16	Jean-Monnet pl.	16
4	C7 S	Jean-Moréas r.	17
54	P12-R11	Jean-Moulin av.	14
57	P17	Jeanne-d'Arc pl.	13
57-44	P17-M16	Jeanne-d'Arc r.	13
40	M8 N	Jeanne-Hachette r.	15
29	H9-J9	Jean-Nicot pass.	7
29	H9	Jean-Nicot r.	7
4	C7-D7	Jean-Ostreicher r.	17
26	J4 S	Jean-Paul-Laurens sq.	16
28	H8	Jean-Paulhan allée	7
33	G17-G19	Jean-Pierre-Timbaud r.	11
21	F17	Jean-Poulmarch r.	10
23	E21	Jean-Quarré r.	19
28	J7	Jean-Rey r.	15
27	H5	Jean-Richepin r.	16
8	C16	Jean-Robert r.	18
21	F18	Jean-Rostand pl.	19
57	P17-N17	Jean-Sébastien-Bach r.	13
52	P8	Jean-Sicard r.	15
40	L8 N	Jean-Thébaud sq.	15
31	H14 S	Jean-Tison r.	1
7	A13 S	Jean-Varenne r.	18
36	H23	Jean-Veber r.	20
42	M11	Jean-Zay r.	14
21	G17-E17	Jemmapes quai de	10
45-44	N17-N16	Jenner r.	13
4	D7	Jérôme-Bellat sq.	17
8-20	D16 N	de Jessaint r.	18
33	G17 S	Jeu-de-Boules pass. du	11
19	G14 N	Jeûneurs r. des	2
32	H15	Joachim-du-Bellay pl.	1
53	P10	Joanès pass.	14
54-53	P11-P10	Joanès r.	14
40	N8	Jobbé-Duval r.	15

k

Echelle : 1 cm sur l'atlas représente 100 m sur le terrain.

Scale : 1 cm on the map represents 100 m on the ground (1 in. : 278 yards approx.)

Maßstab : 1 cm auf dem Atlas entspricht 100 m.

Escala : 1 cm sobre el atlas representa 100 m sobre el terreno.

Plan n°	Repère	Nom	Arrondissement
54	R12	Le Brix-et-Mesmin r.	14
44	M16-N15	Le Brun r.	13
23-35	G22	Le Bua r.	20
6	D12 N	Lechapelais r.	17
4	D8 N	Le Châtelier r.	17
33	H18 N	Léchevin r.	11
35	H22 S	Leclaire cité	20
43	N13	Leclerc r.	17
18	D12	Lécluse r.	17
6	C11	Lecomte r.	17
37	L2 S	Lecomte-du-Noüy r.	16
38	K4 S	Leconte-de-Lisle r.	16
38	K4 S	Leconte-de-Lisle villa	16
37	L2	Le Corbusier pl.	16
41-39	L10-N6	Lecourbe r.	15
40	M7 S	Lecourbe villa	15
54	P11 N	Lecuirot r.	14
7	C14	Lecuyer r.	18
55-56	P14-P15	Le Dantec r.	13
53	P10 S	Ledion r.	14
45-34	L17-J19	Ledru-Rollin av.	
		nos 1-87, 2-88	12
		nos 89-fin, 90-fin	11
52-53	N7-P9	Lefebvre bd	15
52	N7 S	Lefebvre r.	15
6	C12 N	Legendre pass.	17
17-6	D10-B12	Legendre r.	17
5	D10-D9	Léger imp.	17
54	R12-R11	Légion-Etrangère r. de la	14
43	L14 N	Le Goff r.	5
21-20	F17-F16	Legouvé r.	10
21	E18 S	Legrand r.	19
45	L18 N	Legraverend r.	12
7-6	B13-B12	Leibnitz r.	18
6-7	B12-B13	Leibnitz sq.	18
27	J5	Lekain r.	16
55	R14 N	Lemaignan r.	14
23	E22	Léman r. du	19
38	M3 S	Le Marois r.	16
6	C11 S	Lemercier cité	17
6	D12-C11	Lemercier r.	17
20	G15 N	Lemoine pass.	2
22	F19 S	Lémon r.	20
54	P12 S	Leneveux r.	14
18	E11-D12	Léningrad r. de	8
28	H7 S	Le Nôtre r.	16
20	E15 N	Lentonnet r.	9
28	G7	Léo-Delibes r.	16
8	D15 N	Léon pass.	18
8	C15	Léon r.	18
15	F6	Léonard-de-Vinci r.	16
34	J19 N	Léon-Blum pl.	11
57-56	S17-S16	Léon-Bollée av.	13
26	K4	Léon-Bonnat r.	16
28	J7	Léon-Bourgeois allée	7
28	G8 S	Léonce-Reynaud r.	16
19	G14 N	Léon-Cladel r.	2
17	E9-D9	Léon-Cogniet r.	17
17	D10	Léon-Cosnard r.	17
39	N6	Léon-Delagrange r.	15
40	M8 S	Léon-Delhomme r.	15
38	M3 S	Léon-Deubel pl.	16
52	P8	Léon-Dierx r.	15
18	D11 S	Léon-Droux r.	17
53	P10 N	Léone villa	14
24	F23	Léon-Frapié r.	20
34	J20-J19	Léon-Frot r.	11
36-48	J24-K24	Léon-Gaumont av.	20
10	C19 S	Léon-Giraud r.	19
40	N8	Léon-Guillot sq.	15
38	K4-L4	Léon-Heuzey av.	16
54	P11-N11	Léonidas r.	14
17-16	E9-D8	Léon-Jost r.	17
21	G17 N	Léon-Jouhaux r.	10
40	L8	Léon-Lhermitte r.	15
43	N14	Léon-Maurice-Nordmann r.	13
41	L10 N	Léon-Paul-Fargue pl.	6-7
40	M8 N	Léon-Séché r.	15
39	L5	Léontine r.	15
41	K9-L9	Léon-Vaudoyer r.	7
31	G14	Léopold-Bellan r.	2
26-27	K5-K4	Léopold-II av.	16
42	M12 N	Léopold-Robert r.	14
21	E18 N	Lepage cité	19
19	F13-E14	Le Peletier r.	9
19	D13	Lepic pass.	18
7	D13-C13	Lepic r.	18
57	P18	Leredde r.	13
32	K15-K16	Le Regrattier r.	4
40	N7-N8	Leriche r.	15
16-15	F7-F6	Leroux r.	16
23	F21 S	Leroy cité	20
26	J4 S	Leroy-Beaulieu sq.	16
47	L22 S	Leroy-Dupré r.	12
22	F19	Lesage cour	20
22	F19	Lesage r.	20
33	K17-J17	de Lesdiguières r.	4
34-35	J20-J21	Lespagnol r.	20
35	J22-H21	de Lesseps r.	20
16	F7-E7	Le Sueur r.	16
27	H6	Le Tasse r.	16
40	K7-L8	Letellier r.	15
40	K8 S	Letellier villa	15
7	B14	Letort imp.	18
7	B14	Letort r.	18
35	H22 N	Leuck-Mathieu r.	20
36-24	G23-F23	Le Vau r.	20
43	L13-M13	Le Verrier r.	6
22	F20	Levert r.	20
17	D10 S	Lévis imp. de	17
17	D10	Lévis pl. de	17
17	D10	Lévis r. de	17
33	K18 N	Lhomme pass.	11
43-44	L14-M15	Lhomond r.	5
40	N8	Lhuillier r.	15
42	N12-N11	Liancourt r.	14
34	J20 S	Liandier cité	11
55	R14 S	Liard r.	14
22	G20 N	Liban r. du	20
23	E21 N	Liberté r. de la	19
17	F9	Lido arcades du	8
18	E12-E11	Liège r. de nos 1-19, 2-18	9
		nos 21-fin, 20-fin	8
48	M23 N	Lieutenance sentier de la	12
23-35	G22	Lieutenant-Chauré r. du	20
7	A14-A13	Lieutenant-Colonel-Dax r.	18
37	M2	Lieutenant-Colonel-Deport r. du	16
53	P10 S	Lieutenant-Lapeyre r. du	14
53-54	N10-11	Lieutenant-Stéphane-Piobetta pl. du	14
53	N9-P9	Lieuvin r. du	15
35	J21 N	Ligner r.	20
23-24	E22-E23	Lilas porte des	20
23	E21	Lilas r. des	19
23	E21 N	Lilas villa des	19

m

Plan n°	Repère	Nom	Arrondissement
6	B12 *N*	Milord imp.	18
19	E14	Milton r.	9
55	R14	Mimosas sq. des	13
33	J17 *N*	Minimes r. des	3
41	L9 *N*	Miollis r.	15
39	L5	Mirabeau pont	16-15
39-38	L5-L4	Mirabeau r.	16
44	M15 *N*	de Mirbel r.	5
55	R13-R14	Mire allée de la	14
7	D13-C13	Mire r. de la	18
17	F10-E10	de Miromesnil r.	8
26-38	K4	Mission-Marchand r. de la	16
41	M10 *N*	Mizon r.	15
22	D19	Moderne av.	19
54	P11 *N*	Moderne villa	14
39	M5-M6	Modigliani r.	15
42	M11	Modigliani terrasse	15
18	F12-E12	Mogador r. de	9
6	C11-B11	Moines r. des	17
38	L3 *S*	Molière av.	16
32	H15	Molière pass.	3
31	G13 *S*	Molière r.	1
9	C17	Molin imp.	18
37	L2	Molitor porte	16
38	L4-L3	Molitor r.	16
38	L4	Molitor villa	16
17	E10	Mollien r.	8
5	C9 *S*	Monbel r. de	17
17	F9-E10	Monceau r. de	8
18	D11 *S*	Monceau sq.	17
16	D8	Monceau villa	17
6	C12	Moncey pass.	17
18	E12 *N*	Moncey r.	9
18	E12 *N*	Moncey sq.	9
32	H15 *N*	Mondétour r.	1
30	G11	Mondovi r. de	1
44	L15 *S*	Monge pl.	5
44	K15-M15	Monge r.	5
48	L24-L23	Mongenot r.	
		n°s 29-fin, 12-fin	12
		autres n°s	St-Mandé
21	E18 *S*	Monjol r.	19
31	H14 *S*	Monnaie r. de la	1
34	G20 *S*	Monplaisir imp.	20
17	D9	Monseigneur-Loutil pl.	17
21	E17	Monseigneur-Rodhain r.	10
29	K10	Monsieur r.	7
31-43	K13-K14	Monsieur-le-Prince r.	6
19	G13 *N*	Monsigny r.	2
35	J21	Monsoreau sq. de	20
44	K15-L15	Montagne-Ste-Geneviève r.	5
17-29	G9	Montaigne av.	8
30	J12	Montalembert r.	7
18	F11 *S*	Montalivet r.	8
40	N8	Montauban r.	15
39	K5 *S*	Mont-Blanc sq. du	16
54	P12	Montbrun pass.	14
54	P12	Montbrun r.	14
7	C13-B14	Montcalm r.	18
7	B13 *S*	Montcalm villa	18
7	B14 *N*	Mont-Cenis pass. du	18
7	C14-B14	Mont-Cenis r. du	18
18	D11	Mont-Dore r. du	17
32	K15	Montebello port de	5
32	K15	Montebello quai de	5
53	P9 *N*	Montebello r. de	15

Plan n°	Repère	Nom	Arrondissement
35	J21	Monte-Cristo r.	20
48	M23	Montempoivre porte de	12
47-48	M22-M23	Montempoivre r. de	12
47	M22	Montempoivre sentier de	12
23	E22 *S*	Montenegro pass. du	19
16	E8	Montenotte r. de	17
48	L23	Montéra r.	12
27	G5 *S*	de Montespan av.	16
31	H13 *N*	Montesquieu r.	1
48	N23	Montesquieu-Fezensac r.	12
15-27	G5	Montevidéo r. de	16
31	K13 *N*	de Montfaucon r.	6
46	L20	Montgallet pass.	12
46	L20 *S*	Montgallet r.	12
32	G16	Montgolfier r.	3
18	E12 *N*	Monthiers cité	9
20-19	E15-E14	de Montholon r.	9
35	G22	Montibœufs r. des	20
54	R12 *S*	Monticelli r.	14
34	J20 *N*	Mont-Louis imp. de	11
34	J20 *N*	Mont-Louis r. de	11
19	F14	Montmartre bd	
		n°s impairs 2e - n°s pairs	9
31	G14 *S*	Montmartre cité	2
19	F14 *S*	Montmartre galerie	2
7	A13-B13	Montmartre porte de	18
31-19	H14-F14	Montmartre r.	
		n°s 1-21, 2-36	1
		n°s 23-fin, 38-fin	2
38	K4-K3	de Montmorency av.	16
26	J3-K3	de Montmorency bd	16
32	H16-H15	de Montmorency r.	3
26-38	K3	de Montmorency villa	16
31	H14-G14	Montorgueil r.	
		n°s 1-35, 2-40	1
		n°s 37-fin, 42-fin	2
42-43	L11-M13	Montparnasse bd du	
		n°s impairs	6
		n°s 2-66	15
		n°s 68-fin	14
42	L12-M12	Montparnasse r. du	
		n°s 1-35, 2-40	6
		n°s 37-fin, 42-fin	14
31	G13 *S*	de Montpensier galerie	1
31	H13-G13	de Montpensier r.	1
36	J23-J24	Montreuil porte de	20
34-35	K19-K21	Montreuil r. de	11
54	R11	Montrouge porte de	14
55	R13	Montsouris allée de	14
55	R13	Montsouris sq. de	14
28	H8 *S*	de Montessuy r.	7
30	G12 *S*	Mont-Thabor r. du	1
42	L11	Mont-Tonnerre imp. du	15
19	F14	de Montyon r.	9
27	G5	Mony r.	16
21	G18 *N*	Morand r.	11
45	K18	Moreau r.	12
54	R11 *N*	Morère r.	14
22-34	G19	Moret r.	11
28	J8-K8	Morieux cité	15
40-53	N8-N9	Morillons r. des	15
33-45	K17	Morland bd	4
45	L17 *N*	Morland pont	12-4
35-47	K21	Morlet imp.	11
18	E12	Morlot r.	9
45	K17	Mornay r.	4
42	N11	de Moro-Giaffери pl.	14
36-23	G23-E22	Mortier bd	20

Plan n°	Repère	Nom	Arrondissement
34	H19 *S*	Morvan r. du	11
18	E12-D11	Moscou r. de	8
22	D19	Moselle pass. de la	19
9-21	D18 *N*	Moselle r. de la	19
7	B13 *N*	Moskowa cité de la	18
44	L15-M15	Mouffetard r.	5
33	H18 *S*	Moufle r.	11
45	L18	Moulin pass.	12
56	R16	Moulin-de-la-Pointe r. du	13
41-53	N10 *S*	Moulin-de-la-Vierge r. du	14
56	P15 *N*	Moulin-des-Prés pass.	13
56	P15-R16	Moulin-des-Prés r. du	13
56	P15 *S*	Moulinet pass. du	13
56	P16-P15	Moulinet r. du	13
22	G19-F19	Moulin-Joly r. du	11
31	G13	Moulins r. des	1
54	P11 *N*	Moulin-Vert imp. du	14
54	P12-N11	Moulin-Vert r. du	14
47	K22 *S*	Mounet-Sully r.	20
36	J23	Mouraud r.	20
46	L20	Mousset imp.	12

Plan n°	Repère	Nom	Arrondissement
47	L22 *S*	Mousset-Robert r.	12
32	J16 *N*	de Moussy r.	4
54	N12 *S*	Mouton-Duvernet r.	14
23-22	E21-E20	Mouzaïa r. de	19
46	L20 *S*	Moynet cité	12
27-26	J5-K4	Mozart av.	16
26	J4	Mozart sq.	16
26	J4-K4	Mozart villa	16
27-26	J5-J4	Muette chaussée de la	16
26	H4	Muette porte de la	16
19	G14	Mulhouse r. de	2
38	M3	Mulhouse villa	16
7	C14-D14	Muller r.	18
38	L3-M4	Murat bd	16
38	M3 *S*	Murat villa	16
34	H20-G20	Mûriers r. des	20
17	E9	Murillo r.	8
38	M4-M3	de Musset r.	16
44	K15 *S*	Mutualité sq. de la	5
8	C16-D15	Myrha r.	18
17	F10	Myron-Timothy-Herrick av.	8

n

Plan n°	Repère	Nom	Arrondissement
6	B11	Naboulet imp.	17
20	F16	Nancy r. de	10
34	H19-G19	Nanettes r. des	11
55	R13 *S*	Nansouty imp.	14
55	R13	Nansouty r.	14
10	C19-B19	Nantes r. de	19
41	N9	Nanteuil r.	15
18-17	E11-E10	Naples r. de	8
20	E15-E16	Napoléon III pl.	10
30	K12 *N*	Narbonne r. de	7
38	L4 *N*	Narcisse-Diaz r.	16
17	E10 *S*	Narvik pl. de	8
47	K21 *S*	Nation pl. de la n⁰ˢ impairs	11
		n⁰ˢ pairs	12
57	R18-R17	National pass.	13
58	P20	National pont	12-13
57	R17 *N*	Nationale imp.	13
57	P17	Nationale pl.	13
57	R17-N17	Natinale r.	13
28	H7	Nations-Unies av. des	16
7	C13	Nattier pl.	18
19	E13 *N*	Navarin r. de	9
44	L15	Navarre r. de	5
6	B12-B11	Navier r.	17
33	J17	Necker r.	4
29	J9 *N*	Négrier cité	7
28	J7-K7	Nélaton r.	15
33	G18 *S*	Nemours r. de	11
31	J13	de Nesle r.	6
31	J14	Neuf pont	1-6
15	E6	Neuilly av. de	16-17
8	B15	Neuve-de-la-Charbonnière r.	18
34	J20 *S*	Neuve-des-Boulets r.	11
33	G18-H18	Neuve-Popincourt r.	11
33	J17	Neuve-St-Pierre r.	4
16	E8	Néva r. de la	8
31	J13	Nevers imp. de	6
31	J13	Nevers r. de	6
16	F8 *S*	Newton r.	16
28	H8-J7	New-York av. de	16

Plan n°	Repère	Nom	Arrondissement
9-6	A17-B12	Ney bd	18
5-17	D9 *N*	Nicaragua pl. du	17
34	J20 *S*	Nice r. de	11
47	N21-M21	Nicolaï r.	12
36	J23 *N*	Nicolas imp.	20
41	L10-M10	Nicolas-Charlet r.	15
5	C9	Nicolas-Chuquet r.	17
32	J15-H15	Nicolas-Flamel r.	4
56	P16 *N*	Nicolas-Fortin r.	13
45-44	M17-M16	Nicolas-Houël r.	5
44	N15 *N*	Nicolas-Roret r.	13
54	R11	Nicolas-Taunay r.	14
6	C11 *S*	Nicolay sq.	17
7	C14	Nicolet r.	18
27	J6-H5	Nicolo r.	16
18	E8-D8	Niel av.	17
16	D8 *S*	Niel villa	17
42	N11	Niepce r.	14
57	R18 *N*	Nieuport villa	13
48	L23	Niger r. du	12
20-32	G15	Nil r. du	2
7	C14	Nobel r.	18
28	J7 *S*	Nocard r.	15
32	H15-H16	Noël cité	3
48	K23 *S*	Noël-Ballay r.	20
15	G5 *N*	Noisiel r. de	16
24	F23-E24	Noisy-le-sec r. de n⁰ˢ 1-47, 2-72	20
6	D11-C11	Nollet r.	17
6	C11	Nollet sq.	17
7	B13	Nollez cité	18
33	K18 *N*	Nom-de-Jésus cour du	11
32	J16 *S*	Nonnains-d'Hyères r. des	4
10-22	D19	Nord pass. du	19
8	B15 *S*	Nord r. du	18
33	H17 *N*	Normandie r. de	3
7	C14-C13	Norvins r.	18
32	J15	Notre-Dame pont	4
20	G15-F15	Notre-Dame-de-Bonne-Nouvelle r.	2

40

Plan nº	Repère	Nom	Arrondissement
39	N6	Pte-d'Issy r. de la	15
56	S16	Pte-d'Italie av. de la	13
57	S18-R17	Pte-d'Ivry av. de la	13
54	R12 S	Pte-d'Orléans av. de la	14
23	E22-D22	Pte-du-Pré-St-Gervais av. de la	19
32	H16 N	Portefoin r.	3
15	E6	Pte-Maillot pl. de la	16-17
37	L2	Pte-Molitor av. de la	16
37-38	L2-L3	Pte-Molitor pl. de la	16
6	B11-A11	Pte-Pouchet av. de la	17
8	C15 N	Portes-Blanches r. des	18
19	G13 N	Port-Mahon r. de	2
44-43	M15	Port-Royal bd de n°s 1-93	13
		n°s 95-fin 14ᵉ - n°s pairs	5
43	M14 S	Port-Royal cité de	13
43	M14 S	Port-Royal sq. de	13
16	F7 S	Portugais av. des	16
27	H5 S	Possoz pl.	16
44	M15 N	Postes pass. des	5
44	L15 S	Pot-de-Fer r. du	5
7	B13 N	Poteau pass. du	18
7	B14-B13	Poteau r. du	18
56	R15-S15	Poterne-des-Peupliers r.	13
31	G13 S	Potier pass.	1
9	B18-C18	Pottier cité	19
6	B11	Pouchet pass.	17
6	A11-B11	Pouchet porte	17
6	C11-B11	Pouchet r.	17
7	C13-D14	Poulbot r.	18
35	J21-K21	Poule imp.	20
8	C15 S	Poulet r.	18
32	K16	Poulletier r.	4
38	K4-K3	Poussin r.	16
56	P15 S	Pouy r. de	13
22	F19-E19	Pradier r.	19
20	G15-F15	Prado pass. du	10
33-45	K18 S	Prague r. de	12
35	H22	Prairies r. des	20
8	B16 N	Pré r. du	18
22	E19	Préault r.	19
30	J12	Pré-aux-Clercs r. du	7
32	H15	Prêcheurs r. des	1
23	D21-D22	Pré-St-Gervais porte du	19
23	E21 S	Pré-St-Gervais r. du	19
16	F8-F7	Presbourg r. de n°s 1-2	8
		n°s 3-fin,4-fin	16
22-21	F19-F18	Présentation r. de la	11
30	H11	Président-Ed.-Herriot pl.	7
28-27	J7-K5	Président-Kennedy av. du	16
29	K10	Président-Mithouard pl.	7
28	G8-H7	Président-Wilson av. du	
		n°s impairs, n°s 8-fin	16
		n°s 2-6	8

Plan nº	Repère	Nom	Arrondissement
28	K8 N	Presles imp. de	15
28	K8 N	Presles r. de	15
22	G19 N	Pressoir r. du	20
27	G6 S	Prêtres imp. des	16
31	H14 S	Prêtres-St-Germain-l'Auxerrois r. des	1
31	K14 N	Prêtres-St-Séverin r. des	5
53	P9 S	Prévost-Paradol r.	14
32	J16 S	Prévôt r. du	4
22-23	D20-D21	Prévoyance r. de la	19
44-56	N16	Primatice r.	13
33	J17-H18	Primevères imp. des	11
19	F13 S	Princes pass. des	2
31	K13 S	Princesse r.	6
5	C9 S	Printemps r. du	17
54	R12-P12	Prisse-d'Avennes r.	14
41	M9-N10	Procession r. de la	15
36	J24-J23	Prof.-André-Lemierre av. du	
		n°s impairs	20
		n°s pairs	Montreuil-Bagnolet
8-7	A15-A14	Professeur-Gosset r. du	18
54	R12-S12	Professeur-Hyacinthe-Vincent r. du	14
56	R16-R15	Prof.-Louis-Renault r. du	13
23	E21 N	Progrès villa du	19
17-16	E9-D8	de Prony r.	17
17	D10 S	Prosper-Goubaux pl.	
		n°s impairs	8
		n°s pairs	17
34	K20 N	Prost cité	11
48	M20 S	Proudhon r.	12
31	H14	Prouvaires r. des	1
19	F13 N	Provence av. de	9
19-18	F14-F12	Provence r. de	
		n°s 1-125, 2-118	9
		n°s 127-fin, 120-fin	8
35	J22 S	Providence imp. de la	20
56-55	R15-P14	Providence r. de la	13
26	J4-H4	Prudhon av.	16
34	H20	Pruniers r. des	20
19	D13	Puget r.	18
55	R13	Puits allée du	
44	L15 S	Puits-de-l'Ermite pl. du	5
44	L15-M15	Puits-de-l'Ermite r. du	5
5	C10 S	Pusy cité de	17
18	F11	Puteaux pass.	8
18	D11	Puteaux r.	17
4	D8 N	Puvis-de-Chavannes r.	17
35	H22-G22	Py r. de la	20
31-30	H13-H12	Pyramides pl. des	1
31	H13-G13	Pyramides r. des	1
47-22	K22-F20	Pyrénées r. des	20
35	J22-K22	Pyrénées villa des	20

q

Plan nº	Repère	Nom	Arrondissement
44	L15 S	de Quatrefages r.	5
32	H16	Quatre-Fils r. des	3
7	C13	Quatre-Frères-Casadesus pl. des	18
39	L6 N	Quatre-Frères-Peignot r.	15
19	G13-F13	Quatres-Septembre r. du	2
31	K13 N	Quatre-Vents r. des	6
31	J13 S	Québec pl. du	6

Plan nº	Repère	Nom	Arrondissement
33	J18 S	Quellard cour	11
16-17	G8-F9	Quentin-Bauchart r.	8
36	K23 N	Quercy sq. du	20
22	G19	Questre imp.	11
40	L8	Quinault r.	15
32	H15	Quincampoix r.	
		n°s 1-63, 2-64	4
		n°s 65-fin, 66-fin	3

r

Plan n°	Repère	Nom	Arrondissement
17	F10 *S*	Rabelais r.	8
38	K3	Racan sq.	16
18	D12	Rachel av.	18
38	L3 *S*	Racine imp.	16
31-43	K14-K13	Racine r.	6
31	G13 *S*	Radziwill r.	1
37	L2 *S*	Raffaëlli r.	16
26	K4	Raffet imp.	16
26	K4-K3	Raffet r.	16
46	L19	Raguinot pass.	12
47	M22 *N*	Rambervillers r. de	12
45-46	L18-L19	Rambouillet r. de	12
32-31	H16-H14	Rambuteau r.	
		n°s 1-73	4
		n°s 2-66	3
		n°s 75-fin, 68-fin	1
19	G13	Rameau r.	2
7-8	C14-C15	Ramey pass.	18
8-7	C15-C14	Ramey r.	18
22	F19	Rampal r.	19
33	G17	Rampon r.	11
22	F19	Ramponeau r.	20
35	H21	Ramus r.	20
35	J22	Rançon imp.	20
26	J4 *N*	Ranelagh av. du	16
27-26	K6-J4	Ranelagh r. du	16
26	J4	Ranelagh sq. du	16
47	M21	Raoul r.	12
42	M11 *N*	Raoul-Dautry pl.	15
35	G20	Raoul-Dufy r.	20
21	E17	Raoul-Follereau pl.	10
45	M18-L17	Rapée port de la	12
45	M18-L17	Rapée quai de la	12
26	H4-J4	Raphaël av.	16
28	H8-J8	Rapp av.	7
28	J8 *N*	Rapp sq.	7
30-42	J12-N12	Raspail bd	
		n°s 1-41, 2-46	7
		n°s 43-147, 48-136	6
		n°s 201-fin, 202-fin	14
36	J23	Rasselins r. des	20
43	L14-M14	Rataud r.	5
34	J19 *S*	Rauch pass.	11
7	D13 *N*	Ravignan r.	18
56	R16 *S*	Raymond pass.	13
42-53	M11-P9	Raymond-Losserand r.	14
4	C8	Raymond-Pitet r.	17
27-15	H6-F6	Raymond-Poincaré av.	16
27	J6-K5	Raynouard r.	16
27	J6 *N*	Raynouard sq.	16
32-19	G16-G14	Réaumur	
		n°s 1-49, 2-72	3
		n°s 51-fin, 74-fin	2
21-22	F18-F19	Rébeval r.	19
30	K12 *N*	Récamier r.	7
20	F16 *N*	Récollets pass. des	10
21-20	F17-F16	Récollets r. des	10
27-26	K5-J4	Recteur-Poincaré av. du	16
56	N15 *S*	Reculettes r. des	13
4-5	C8-C9	Redon r.	17
28	J7	Refuzniks allée des	7
42	K12 *S*	Regard r. du	6
42	K11 *S*	Régis r.	6

Plan n°	Repère	Nom	Arrondissement
36	J23 *S*	Réglises r. des	20
31-43	K13	Regnard r.	6
58-57	P19-R17	Regnault r.	13
20	F15-F16	Reilhac pass.	10
55	P14-R13	Reille av.	14
55	P14-P13	Reille imp.	14
4	C8	Reims bd de	17
57	P18	Reims r. de	13
30-29	G11-G10	Reine cours la	8
29	G9 *S*	Reine-Astrid pl. de la	8
44	M15-N15	Reine-Blanche r. de la	13
31	H14 *N*	Reine-de-Hongrie pass.	1
17	E9	Rembrandt r.	8
39-38	K5-K4	de Rémusat r.	16
10	D19	Rémi-Belleau villa	19
22-21	E19-E18	Rémy-de-Gourmont r.	19
55-54	P13-P12	Remy-Dumoncel r.	14
29-17	G9	Renaissance r. de la	8
23	E21 *N*	Renaissance villa de la	19
32	J15-H15	Renard r. du	4
16	E8-D8	Renaudes r. des	17
47	L22	Rendez-vous cité du	12
47	L22	Rendez-vous r. du	12
26	J4-K4	René-Bazin r.	16
7	A14-A13	René-Binet r.	18
20	G16 *N*	René-Boulanger r.	10
27	J6	René-Boylesve av.	16
31	H14	René-Cassin pl.	1
43-55	N13-R13	René-Coty av.	14
24	E23	René-Fonck av.	19
44	M16	René-Panhard r.	13
34	H20	René-Villermé r.	11
16	E8-D8	Rennequin r.	17
31-42	J13-L11	Rennes r. de	6
34	J20-H20	Repos r. du	20
33-34	G17-H20	République av. de la	11
21-33	G17	République pl. de la	
		n°s impairs	3
		n°s 2-10	11
		n°s 12-16	10
17	E9	Rép.-de-l'Equateur pl. de la	8
17	E9 *N*	Rép.-Dominicaine pl. de la	
		n°s impairs	8
		n°s pairs	17
57	P18 *S*	Résal r.	13
28	H8	Résistance pl. de la	7
18	G11 *N*	Retiro cité du	8
23	G21 *N*	Retrait pass. du	20
23-35	G21	Retrait r. du	20
46-47	M20-M21	Reuilly bd de	12
47	N22	Reuilly porte de	12
46-47	K20-M21	Reuilly r. de	12
35	J22	Réunion pl. de la	20
35	K22-J21	Réunion r. de la	20
38	L4 *S*	Réunion villa de la	16
36-48	K23	Reynaldo-Hahn r.	20
22	D19	Rhin r. du	19
11-23	D21 *S*	Rhin-et-Danube pl. de	19
4	C8	Rhône sq. du	17
26	K4	Ribera r.	16
35	J21 *N*	Riberolle villa	20
40	L8 *N*	Ribet imp.	15

S

Plan n°	Repère	Nom	Arrondissement
54	N12-N11	Sablière r. de la	14
27	G6-H6	Sablons r. des	16
15	E6-E5	Sablonville r. de	17
30	K12 N	Sabot r. du	6
7	C14 S	Sacré-Cœur cité du	18
23	E21 N	Sadi-Carnot villa	19
21	E18 N	Sadi-Lecointe r.	19
47-48	M22-M23	Sahel r. du	12
47	M22 N	Sahel villa du	12
15	F6-F5	Saïd villa	16
52	N7-N8	Saïda r. de la	15
16	F7 N	Saïgon r. de	16
54	N12 S	Saillard r.	14
54	R12	St-Alphonse imp.	14
41	N9	Saint-Amand r.	15
34-33	H19-H18	St-Ambroise pass.	11
33-34	H18-H19	St-Ambroise r.	11
31	K14 N	St-André-des-Arts pl.	6
31	J14-J13	St-André-des-Arts r.	6
6	B12 N	Saint-Ange pass.	17
6	B12 N	Saint-Ange villa	17
33	K18 N	St-Antoine pass.	11
33-32	J17-J16	St-Antoine r.	4
18	F11 N	St-Augustin pl.	8
19	G13 N	St-Augustin r.	2
31	J13 S	St-Benoît r.	6
34	K19	St-Bernard pass.	11
45-44	L17-K16	St-Bernard port	5
45-44	L17-K16	St-Bernard quai	5
34	K19	St-Bernard r.	11
35	H22 S	St-Blaise pl.	20
35-36	H22-J23	St-Blaise r.	20
32	J15 N	St-Bon r.	4
8	D16-D15	St-Bruno r.	18
39	L6 N	St-Charles imp.	15
40	K7 S	St-Charles pl.	15
39	L6-M6	St-Charles rd-pt	15
28-39	K7-M5	St-Charles r.	15
46	L20 N	St-Charles sq.	12
21	F18-E18	St-Chaumont cité	19
39	L5-L6	St-Christophe r.	15
33	H17 S	St-Claude imp.	3
33	H17 S	St-Claude r.	3
37	M2-N2	St-Cloud porte de	16
20	G16-G15	St-Denis bd n°s 1-9	3
		n°s 11-fin	2
		n°s pairs	10
20-32	G15	St-Denis galerie	2
32	G15 S	St-Denis imp.	2
31-20	J14-G15	St-Denis r. n°s 1-133, 2-104	1
		n°s 135-fin, 106-fin	2
28-27	G7-G6	St-Didier r.	16
30-28	J11-J8	St-Dominique r.	7
7	D14 N	St-Eleuthère r.	18
46	L20 N	St-Eloi cour	12
34	K19	St-Esprit cour du	11
44	L15 N	St-Etienne-du-Mont r.	5
31	H14 N	St-Eustache imp.	1
38	M4-N3	Saint-Exupéry quai	16
23	F22 S	St Fargeau pl.	20
23-24	F21-F23	St-Fargeau r.	20
16	E7	St-Ferdinand pl.	17
16-15	E7-E6	St-Ferdinand r.	17
32	H15 S	St-Fiacre imp.	4
19	G14-F14	St-Fiacre r.	2
18-30	G11	St-Florentin n°s pairs	1
		n°s impairs	8
7	G14 N	St-François imp.	18
19	E13	St-Georges pl.	9
19	F13-E13	St-Georges r.	9
44-30	K16-H11	St-Germain bd	
		n°s 1-73, 2-100	5
		n°s 75-175, 102-186	6
		n°s 177-fin, 188-fin	7
31	J13 S	St-Germain-des-Prés pl.	6
31	J14 N	St-Germain-l'Auxerrois	1
32	J15	St-Gervais pl.	4
33	J17 N	St-Gilles r.	3
55	P13	St-Gothard r. du	14
30	J12	St-Guillaume r.	7
44-43	N15-N14	St-Hippolyte r.	13
31-18	H14-G11	St-Honoré r.	
		n°s 1-271, 2-404	1
		n°s 273-fin, 406-fin	8
15-27	G8	St-Honoré-d'Eylau av.	16
34	H19 N	St-Hubert r.	11
30	G12 S	St-Hyacinthe r.	1
33	H18	St-Irénée sq.	11
43-55	N14-N13	St-Jacques bd	14
33	J18 S	St-Jacques cour	11
43	N13	St-Jacques pl.	14
31-43	K14-M14	St-Jacques r.	5
55	N13 S	St-Jacques villa	14
6	C11-C12	St-Jean r.	17
42	L11 N	St-Jean-Baptiste-de-la-Salle r.	6
8	D16-C16	St-Jérôme r.	18
31	H14	St-John-Perse allée	1
33	K18 N	St-Joseph cour	11
19	G14 N	St-Joseph r.	2
32	H15	St-Josse pl.	4
7	B13 N	St-Jules pass.	18
32-31	K15-K14	St-Julien-le-Pauvre r.	5
5	B10 N	Saint-Just r.	17
40	M7-N7	St-Lambert r.	15
20	E16 S	St-Laurent r.	10
19-18	E13-F12	St-Lazare r.	
		n°s 1-109, 2-106	9
		n°s 111-fin, 108-fin	8
33	K18-J18	St-Louis cour	11
32	K15 N	St-Louis pont	4
32	K16-K15	St-Louis-en-l'Ile r.	4
8	D15 N	St-Luc r.	18
47-48	L21-L23	St-Mandé av. de	12
48	L23	St-Mandé porte de	12
47	L22-L21	St-Mandé villa de	12
19	F14 S	St-Marc galerie	2
19	F14-F13	St-Marc r.	2
4	C8	de Saint-Marceaux r.	17
44	M16-M15	St-Marcel bd n°s impairs	13
		n°s pairs	5
20	G16	St-Martin bd n°s impairs	3
		n°s pairs	10
20	F16	St-Martin cité	10
32-20	J15-G16	St-Martin r. n°s 1-143, 2-152	4
		n°s 145-fin, 154-fin	3
8	D16-D15	St-Mathieu r.	18
34	H19 N	St-Maur pass.	11

Plan n°	Repère	Nom	Arrondissement
46	N19	**Tolbiac pont de**	12-13
58	P20-N19	**Tolbiac port de**	13
58-55	N19-P14	**Tolbiac r. de**	13
26	K3 *N*	**Tolstoï sq.**	16
55-54	N13-R12	**Tombe-Issoire r. de la**	14
20	D16	**Tombouctou r. de**	18
8	C16 *N*	**de Torcy pl.**	18
9-8	C17-C16	**de Torcy r.**	18
16	E7-D7	**Torricelli r.**	17
47	M22	**Toul r. de**	12
43	L14 *N*	**Toullier r.**	5
11	D21 *N*	**Toulouse r. de**	19
6	A12	**Toulouse-Lautrec r.**	17
27	H6-H5	**Tour r. de la**	16
27	H5 *N*	**Tour villa de la**	16
19	E13	**Tour-des-Dames r. de la**	9
42	N11	**Tour-de-Vanves pass.**	14
23	F22 *N*	**Tourelles pass. des**	20
23	F22 *N*	**Tourelles r. des**	20
7	C13 *S*	**Tourlaque r.**	18
44	L15-M15	**Tournefort r.**	5
32-44	K16	**Tournelle pont de la**	4-5
32-44	K16-K15	**Tournelle port de la**	5
32-44	K16-K15	**Tournelle quai de la**	5
33	J17	**Tournelles r. des**	
		nos 1-29 2-44	4
		nos 31-fin, 46-fin	3
47	M21 *S*	**Tourneux imp.**	12
47	M21 *S*	**Tourneux r.**	12
31-43	K13	**Tournon r. de**	6
40	L7 *N*	**Tournus r.**	15
22	F19	**Tourtille r. de**	20
29	J10-J9	**de Tourville av.**	7
56	P16 *S*	**Toussaint-Féron r.**	13
31	K13 *N*	**Toustain r.**	6
20	G15	**de Tracy r.**	2
8	B15	**Traëger cité**	18
16	F7	**Traktir r. de**	16
22	F20	**Transvaal r. du**	20
45	L17-K18	**Traversière r.**	12
17	E10 *S*	**Treilhard r.**	8
32	J16	**Trésor r. du**	4
7	C14-B14	**de Trétaigne r.**	18
19	F14-E14	**de Trévise cité**	9
19	F14-E14	**de Trévise r.**	9
32	G15 *S*	**Trinité pass. de la**	2
18	E12	**Trinité r. de la**	9
16	E7	**Tristan-Bernard pl.**	17
27-28	H6-H7	**Trocadéro et Onze-Novembre pl. du**	16
27	H6	**Trocadéro sq. du**	16
21-33	G18	**Trois-Bornes cité des**	11
21-33	G18	**Trois-Bornes r. des**	11
21-33	G18	**Trois-Couronnes r. des**	11
33	K18 *N*	**Trois-Frères cour des**	11
19	D14-D13	**Trois-Frères r. des**	18
32	K15	**Trois-Portes r. des**	5
33	J18 *N*	**Trois-Sœurs imp. des**	11
18	F12	**Tronchet r.** nos impairs, 2-26	8
		nos 28-fin	9
47	K21 *S*	**Trône av. du** nos impairs	11
		nos pairs	12
47	K21 *S*	**Trône pass. du**	11
18	F11	**Tronson-du-Coudray r.**	8
34	K19	**Trousseau r.**	11
16	E8 *S*	**Troyon r.**	17
56	R15 *N*	**Trubert-Bellier pass.**	13
19	D14-E14	**Trudaine av.**	9
19	E14	**Trudaine sq.**	9
6-5	D11-C10	**Truffaut r.**	17
33	H18	**Truillot imp.**	11
30	H12-H11	**Tuileries port des**	1
31-30	H13-H11	**Tuileries quai des**	1
7	B14 *N*	**Tulipes villa des**	18
35-47	K21	**Tunis r. de**	11
55	R13	**Tunisie av. de la**	14
22	E20-E19	**Tunnel r. du**	19
31-32	H14-G18	**Turbigo r. de**	
		nos 1-11, 2-14	1
		nos 13-31, 16-24	2
		nos 33-fin, 26-fin	3
33	J17-H17	**de Turenne r.**	
		nos 1-27, 2-22	
		nos 29-fin, 24-fin	3
19	E14-D14	**Turgot r.**	9
18	E12-D11	**Turin r. de**	8
35	K21	**Turquetil pass.**	11

u

Plan n°	Repère	Nom	Arrondissement
43	L14-M14	**Ulm r. d'**	5
57	P18 *N*	**Ulysse-Trélat r.**	13
29	J9	**Union pass. de l'**	7
16-28	G7	**Union sq. de l'**	16
30-28	J12-H8	**Université r. de l'**	7
26-38	K3	**d'Urfé sq.**	16
32	J15 *S*	**Ursins r. des**	4
43	L14 *S*	**Ursulines r. des**	5
16	G8 *N*	**Uruguay pl. de l'**	16
19	F14 *S*	**d'Uzès r.**	2

v

Plan n°	Repère	Nom	Arrondissement
29	J9	**Valadon r.**	7
43	M14-M13	**Val-de-Grâce r. du**	5
56-55	S15-S14	**Val-de-Marne r. du**	13
44	M15 *S*	**Valence r. de**	5
20	E15	**Valenciennes pl. de**	10
20	E16-E15	**Valenciennes r. de**	10
41	L10-L9	**Valentin-Haüy r.**	15
43	K14-L14	**Valette r.**	5
45	L17	**Valhubert pl.**	
		nos 1, 2 et 3	13
		nos 5-21 et 4	5
47	N21	**Vallée-de-Fécamp r.**	12
44	N16	**Vallet pass.**	13
30	J12	**Valmy imp. de**	7
21	G17-D17	**Valmy quai de**	10
17	E10 *N*	**de Valois av.**	8

Plan nº	Repère	Nom	Arrondissement
38	L4 *S*	Villa Réunion gde av.	16
53	N9 *S*	Villafranca r. de	15
28	K8	Village-Suisse	15
16	E7 *S*	Villaret-de-Joyeuse r.	17
16	E7 *S*	Villaret-de-Joyeuse sq.	17
29	K10 *N*	de Villars av.	7
16	E7	Villebois-Mareuil r.	17
31	G13	Villedo r.	1
33	J17-H17	Villehardouin r.	3
18	F11 *S*	Ville-l'Evêque r. de la	8
53	N10 *S*	Villemain av.	14
20	G15-F15	Ville-Neuve r. de la	2
30	J12-J11	Villersexel r. de	7
21	F18-D17	Villette bd de la	
		nos impairs	10
		nos pairs	19
10	A20	Villette porte de la	19
22	F20-E20	Villette r. de la	19
17-16	D10-D7	Villiers av. de	17
15	D6	Villiers porte de	17
23	G21 *N*	Villiers-de-l'Isle-Adam imp.	20
23-25	G21-G22	Villiers-de-l'Isle-Adam r.	20
45	M18 *N*	Villiot r.	12
57	N18	Vimoutiers r.de	13
21-20	F17-F16	Vinaigriers r. des	10
47-48	K22-L23	Vincennes cours de	
		nos impairs	20
		nos pairs	12
48	L23-L24	Vincennes porte de	12-20
45-44	M18-N16	Vincent-Auriol bd	13
7	B13	Vincent-Compoint r.	18
48	L23	Vincent-d'Indy av.	12
9	D18	Vincent-Scotto r.	19
18	G12 *N*	Vindé cité	1
27	H6 *S*	Vineuse r.	16
54	R12-R11	Vingt-Cinq-Août-1944 pl.	14

Plan nº	Repère	Nom	Arrondissement
30	G12 *S*	Vingt-neuf-Juillet r. du	1
18	D12 *S*	Vintimille r. de	9
40	L7	Violet pl.	15
40	K7-L7	Violet r.	15
40	L7	Violet villa	15
19	D14 *S*	Viollet-le-Duc r.	9
26	J4	Vion-Whitcomb av.	16
54	R12 *N*	Virginie villa	14
40	L8 *S*	Viroflay r. de	15
31	J13	Visconti r.	6
30	J11	Visitation pass. de la	7
56	R16	Vistule r. de la	13
27	H6-J5	Vital r.	16
35-36	J22-H23	Vitruve r.	20
36	H23	Vitruve sq.	20
57-58	R18-R19	Vitry porte de	13
16	D7	Vivarais sq. du	17
31	G13	Vivienne galerie	2
19-31	G13-F14	Vivienne r. nº 1	1
		nos pairs, nos 3-fin	2
35-36	K22-K23	Volga r. du	20
18	G12 *N*	Volney r.	2
41	L9-M9	Volontaires r. des	15
32	G16	Volta r.	3
33-35	G17-K21	Voltaire bd	11
34	K20 *N*	Voltaire cité	11
38	L3 *S*	Voltaire imp.	16
31-30	J13-H12	Voltaire quai	7
34	K20 *N*	Voltaire r.	11
55	R14	Volubilis r. des	13
33	J17	Vosges pl. des	
		nos 1-19, 2-22	4
		nos 21-fin, 24-fin	3
41	N9	Vouillé r. de	15
35	G21 *S*	Voulzie r. de la	20
48	L23 *N*	Voûte pass. de la	12
47-48	L22-L23	Voûte r. de la	12
55	N14 *S*	Vulpian r.	13

W

Plan nº	Repère	Nom	Arrondissement
16-5	F8-C9	Wagram av. de	
		nos impairs, nos 48-fin	17
		nos 2-46	8
5	C9 *S*	Wagram pl. de	17
16	E8 *S*	Wagram St-Honoré villa	8
15	E6 *N*	Waldeck-Rousseau r.	17
44	M16 *S*	Wallons r. des	13
16-17	F8-F9	Washington r.	8
41	M9-M10	Wassily-Kandinsky pl.	15
58	P19	Watt r.	13
44	N16 *N*	Watteau r.	13

Plan nº	Repère	Nom	Arrondissement
9	B18	Wattieaux pass.	19
47	N21	Wattignies imp.	12
46-47	M20-N22	Wattignies r. de	12
21	G17 *N*	Wauxhall cité du	10
15	F16 *N*	Weber r.	16
35	G21 *S*	Westermann r.	20
53	P9 *S*	Wilfrid-Laurier r.	14
38	L4	Wilhem r.	16
29	G10	Winston-Churchill av.	8
55	P14 *S*	Wurtz r.	13

X - Y

Plan nº	Repère	Nom	Arrondissement
57	P18-P17	Xaintrailles r.	13
31	K14 *N*	Xavier-Privas r.	5
57-56	N17-N16	Yóo Thomas r.	13
16-15	D7-D6	Yser bd de l'	17
40-41	M8-M9	Yvart r.	15
16	D7 *S*	Yves-du-Manoir av.	17

Plan nº	Repère	Nom	Arrondissement
21	G17-F17	Yves-Toudic r.	10
26	K4-J4	Yvette r. de l'	16
16	F7-F7	Yvon et Claire-Morandat pl.	17
16	E7 *S*	Yvon-Morandat pl.	17
19	D14-D13	Yvonne-Le-Tac r.	18
16	G7 *N*	Yvon-Villarceau	16

Des adresses utiles

Comment situer ces adresses :

— Dans Paris :

Page du plan	Carroyage		Adresse	Téléphone
32	J15	Mairie de Paris	pl. Hôtel-de-Ville, 4ᵉ	42 76 40 40

— En Banlieue :

Utilisez les plans de Banlieue MICHELIN nᵒ **18** *à* **24** *ou la carte MICHELIN nᵒ* **101**

nᵒ du plan ou de la carte	Carroyage ou pli		Adresse	Téléphone
20	B16	Parc d'Expositions de Paris-Nord	ZAC Paris-Nord II	48 63 30 30
101	pli 36	Hippodrome d'Évry (91)	Rte départementale 31	60 77 82 80

Useful addresses

Nützliche Adressen

Direcciones útiles

How to locate a street on the map — Lokalisierung dieser Adressen Cómo situar estas direcciones

— In Paris — En París :

Page of plan — Seite des Plans — n° de página del plano

↓
| 32 | J15 | **Mairie de Paris** | pl. Hôtel-de-Ville, 4ᵉ | 42 76 40 40 |

Grid reference — Koordinaten — cuadrícula
↑

— In the suburbs — In den Vororten — En las cercanías :

Use the MICHELIN plans nos 18 to 24 or the MICHELIN map 101
Auf den MICHELIN-Stadtplänen Nr. 18-24 oder der MICHELIN-Karte Nr. 101
Utilice los planos de cercanías MICHELIN n° 18 a 24 o el mapa MICHELIN n° 101

No of plan or map — Nr. des Plans oder der Karte — n° del plano o del mapa

↓
| 20 | D16 | **Parc d'Expositions de Paris-Nord** | ZAC Paris-Nord II | 48 63 30 30 |
| 101 | pli 36 | **Hippodrome d'Évry (91)** | Rte départementale 31 | 60 77 82 80 |
↑
Grid reference or map fold — Koordinaten oder Falte — cuadrícula o pliego

ADMINISTRATION
BEHÖRDEN, ADMINISTRACIÓN

17	F10	**Présidence de la République** (Palais de l'Élysée)	55 r. du Fg-St-Honoré, 8e	42 92 81 00
30	H11	**Assemblée Nationale**	126 r. de l'Université, 7e	42 97 60 00
31	H13	**Conseil Constitutionnel**	2 r. de Montpensier, 1er	42 96 10 13
28	H7	**Conseil Économique et Social**	1 av. d'Iéna, 16e	47 23 72 34
31	H13	**Conseil d'État**	pl. du Palais-Royal, 1er	42 61 52 29
43	K13	**Sénat**	15 r. de Vaugirard, 6e	42 34 20 00

Institutions de l'État, *Government Departments*
Staatliche Behörden, Instituciones del Estado

Gouvernement, *Government offices, Regierung, Gobierno*

30	J11	**Premier ministre** (Hôtel Matignon)	57 r. de Varenne, 7e	42 75 80 00

Ministères :

29	H10	**Affaires étrangères**	37 quai d'Orsay, 7e	47 53 53 53
29	H10	**Affaires européennes**	37 quai d'Orsay, 7e	45 55 95 40
29	K9	**Affaires sociales et emploi**	1 pl. de Fontenoy, 7e	40 56 60 00
30	J11	**Agriculture**	78 r. de Varenne, 7e	45 55 95 50
31	H13	**Budget**	93 r. de Rivoli, 1er	42 60 33 00
18	F11	**Collectivités locales**	2 pl. des Saussaies, 8e	42 66 28 30
30	H11	**Commerce, artisanat et services**	80 r. de Lille, 7e	45 56 24 24
28	H8	**Commerce extérieur**	41 quai Branly, 7e	45 50 71 11
29	K10	**Coopération**	20 r. Monsieur, 7e	47 83 10 10
31	H13	**Culture et communication**	3 r. de Valois, 1er	40 15 80 00
30	H11	**Défense**	14 r. St-Dominique, 7e	45 55 95 20
41	K10	**Départements et territoires** d'outre-mer	27 r. Oudinot, 7e	47 83 01 23
31	H13	**Économie, finances et privatisation** *(transfert prévu)*	93 r. de Rivoli, 1er	42 60 33 00
30	J11	**Éducation nationale**	110 r. de Grenelle, 7e	45 50 10 10
27	H6	**Environnement**	45 av. Georges-Mandel, 16e	46 47 31 32
30	J12	**Équipement, logement, aménagement** du territoire et transports	244 bd St-Germain, 7e	45 49 61 62
30	J11	**Fonction publique et plan**	69 r. de Varennes, 7e	42 75 80 00
30	J11	**Industrie, P. et T. et Tourisme**	101 r. de Grenelle, 7e	45 56 36 36
17	F10	**Intérieur**	pl. Beauvau, 8e	45 22 90 90
18	G12	**Justice**	13 pl. Vendôme, 1er	42 61 80 22
29	K9	**Postes & Télécommunications**	20 av. de Ségur, 7e	45 64 22 22
44	L15	**Recherche et enseignement supérieur**	1 r. Descartes, 5e	46 34 35 35
16	F8	**Réforme administrative**	53 av. d'Iéna, 16e	45 01 86 56
30	J11	**Relations avec le parlement**	72 r. de Varenne, 7e	42 75 80 00
29	K9	**Santé et famille**	8 av. de Ségur, 7e	40 56 60 00
17	F10	**Sécurité**	pl. Beauvau, 8e	45 22 90 90
27	J6	**Transports**	32, av. du Prés. Kennedy, 16e	46 47 31 32

Secrétariats d'Etat :

29	H10	**Affaires étrangères**	37 quai d'Orsay, 7e	45 55 95 40
29	K9	**Affaires sociales et emploi**	1 pl. de Fontenoy, 7e	40 56 60 00
30	J11	**Anciens combattants**	37 r. de Bellechasse, 7e	45 50 32 55
31	H13	**Culture et communication**	3 r. de Valois, 1er	40 15 80 00
30	H11	**Défense**	14 r. St-Dominique, 7e	45 55 95 20
30	J11	**Droits de l'homme**	58 r. de Varenne, 7e	42 75 80 00
30	J11	**Enseignement**	110 r. de Grenelle, 7e	45 50 10 10
41	M9	**Formation professionnelle**	61-65 r. Dutot, 15e	45 39 25 75
30	K11	**Francophonie**	32 r. de Babylone, 7e	42 75 80 00
40	N7	**Jeunesse et sports**	78 r. Olivier-de-Serres, 15e	48 28 40 00
29	K9	**Mer**	3 pl. de Fontenoy, 7e	42 73 55 05
30	H11	**Problèmes du Pacifique Sud**	35 r. St-Dominique, 7e	45 55 76 00
16	F8	**Rapatriés**	53 av. d'Iéna, 16e	45 01 86 56
29	K9	**Sécurité sociale**	8 av. de Ségur, 7e	40 56 60 00
30	J11	**Tourisme**	101 r. de Grenelle, 7e	45 56 36 36

Government Offices, Services and Public Bodies
Öffentliche Verwaltungen, Dienststellen, Ämter,
Administraciones, Servicios y Establecimientos públicos

51	R5	**Agence Nationale pour l'Emploi** (ANPE)	Issy-les-Moulineaux - 53 av. du Gén.-Leclerc	46 45 21 26
32	H16	**Archives de France**	60 r. Francs-Bourgeois, 3ᵉ	42 77 11 30
42	L12	**Aviation Civile** (Direction)	93 bd Montparnasse, 6ᵉ	45 44 38 39
31	H14	**Banque de France**	31 r. Croix-des-Petits-Champs, 1ᵉʳ	42 92 42 92
30	H12	**Caisse des Dépôts et Consignations**	56 r. de Lille, 7ᵉ	42 34 56 78
42	L11	**Caisse Nationale d'Epargne**	6 r. St. Romain, 6ᵉ	45 30 77 77
33	J17	**Caisse Nationale des Monuments Historiques et des Sites**	62 r. St-Antoine, 4ᵉ	42 74 22 22
28	G7	**Centre National de la Cinématographie**	12 r. de Lübeck, 16ᵉ	45 05 14 40
31	H14	**Centre National d'Etudes Spatiales**	2 pl. Maurice-Quentin, 1ᵉʳ	45 08 75 00
28	G8	**Chambres d'Agriculture**	9 av. George-V, 8ᵉ	47 23 55 40
44	K15	**Chambre de Commerce et d'Industrie**	22 r. Monge, 5ᵉ	46 34 49 53
16	G8	**Chambres de Métiers**	12 av. Marceau, 8ᵉ	47 23 61 55
28	J7	**Commissariat à l'Énergie Atomique** (CEA)	31-33 r. de la Fédération, 15ᵉ	40 56 10 00
15	F6	**Conseil Supérieur de la Pêche**	134 av. de Malakoff, 16ᵉ	45 01 20 20
31	J14	**Cour de Cassation**	5 quai de l'Horloge, 1ᵉʳ	43 29 12 55
30	G12	**Cour des Comptes**	13 r. Cambon, 1ᵉʳ	42 98 95 00
28	J7	**Délégation à l'Aménagement du Territoire et à l'Action régionale** (DATAR)	1 av. Charles-Floquet, 7ᵉ	47 83 61 20
45	L18	**Direction Générale des Impôts**	64 à 92 allée de Bercy, 12ᵉ	40 04 04 04
30	H12	**Documentation Française**	31 quai Voltaire, 7ᵉ	40 15 70 00
21	G17	**Douanes**	14 r. Yves-Toudic, 10ᵉ	42 40 50 00
17	E9	**Électricité de France** (EDF)	2 r. Louis-Murat, 8ᵉ	47 64 30 00
30	H11	**État-Major des Armées**	231 bd St-Germain, 7ᵉ	45 55 95 20
30	H11	— Terre	231 bd St-Germain, 7ᵉ	45 55 95 20
30	G11	— Marine	2 r. Royale, 8ᵉ	42 60 33 30
39	N6	— Air	26 bd Victor, 15ᵉ	45 52 43 21
5	C9	**Gaz de France** (GDF)	23 r. Ph.-Delorme, 17ᵉ	47 54 20 20
30	H11	**Génie Rural des Eaux et Forêt** (Conseil Général)	30 r. Las Cases, 7ᵉ	45 55 95 50
39	L6	**Imprimerie Nationale**	27 r. de la Convention, 15ᵉ	45 75 62 66
41	L9	**Institut National de la Consommation**	80 r. Lecourbe, 15ᵉ	45 67 35 58
53	R9	**Institut National Statistique Études Économiques** (INSEE)	18 bd Adolphe-Pinard, 14ᵉ	45 40 12 12
28	K7	**Journaux Officiels** (Direction)	26 r. Desaix, 15ᵉ	45 75 62 31
43	N14	**Maison d'Arrêt de la Santé**	42 r. de la Santé, 14ᵉ	43 37 12 50
22	C14	**Météorologie Nationale** (Direction)	Boulogne-Billancourt - 73-77 r. Sèvres	46 04 91 51
21	F17	**Métrologie**	46 r. Bichat, 10ᵉ	42 06 27 20
44	N15	**Mobilier National**	1 r. Berbier-du-Mets, 13ᵉ	43 37 12 60
31	J13	**Monnaies et Médailles**	11 quai de Conti, 6ᵉ	40 46 56 66
31	H13	**Musées de France** (Direction)	1 pl. du Carrousel, pav. Mollien, 1ᵉʳ	42 60 39 26
45	L18	**Observatoire Économique**	195 r. de Bercy 12ᵉ Tour Gamma A	43 45 73 74
16	E8	**Office National de la Chasse**	85 bis av. de Wagram, 17ᵉ	42 27 81 75
47	L21	**Office National des Forêts** (ONF)	2 av. de St-Mandé, 12ᵉ	43 46 11 68
41	M9	**Office National d'Immigration**	44 r. Bargue, 15ᵉ	47 83 80 20
29	H10	**Office National de la Navigation**	2 bd de La Tour-Maubourg, 7ᵉ	45 50 32 24
30	H11	**Ordre de la Légion d'Honneur**	1 r. de Solférino, 7ᵉ	45 55 95 16
29	J10	**Ordre National de la Libération**	51 bis bd La-Tour-Maubourg, 7ᵉ	47 05 35 15
30	H11	**Ordre National du Mérite**	1 r. de Solférino, 7ᵉ	45 55 95 16
28	J7	**Port Autonome de Paris**	2 quai de Grenelle, 15ᵉ	45 78 61 92
29	H9	**Société Nationale d'Exploitation Industrielle des Tabacs et Allumettes** (SEITA)	53 quai d'Orsay, 7ᵉ	45 56 61 50

Renseignements administratifs par téléphone 43 46 13 46

Administration parisienne
Paris Local Government
Städtische Verwaltungen, Administración parisina

Ville de Paris, **Town Halls, Bürgermeisterämter, Ciudad de París**

32	J15	**Mairie de Paris**		pl. Hôtel-de-Ville, 4e	42 76 40 40
31	H14	**Mairie du :**	**1er Arrondissement**	4 pl. du Louvre, 1er	42 60 38 01
31	G14	—	**2e** —	8 r. de la Banque, 2e	42 61 55 02
32	H16	—	**3e** —	2 r. Eugène-Spuller, 3e	42 74 20 03
32	J16	—	**4e** —	2 pl. Baudoyer, 4e	42 74 20 04
43	L14	—	**5e** —	21 pl. du Panthéon, 5e	43 29 21 75
31	K13	—	**6e** —	78 r. Bonaparte, 6e	43 29 12 78
30	J11	—	**7e** —	116 r. de Grenelle, 7e	45 51 07 07
18	E11	—	**8e** —	3 r. de Lisbonne, 8e	42 94 08 08
19	F14	—	**9e** —	6 r. Drouot, 9e	42 46 72 09
20	F16	—	**10e** —	72 r. du Fg St-Martin 10e	42 40 10 10
34	J19	—	**11e** —	pl. Léon Blum, 11e	43 79 20 23
46	M20	—	**12e** —	130 av. Daumesnil, 12e	43 46 06 03
56	N16	—	**13e** —	1 pl. d'Italie, 13e	47 07 13 13
42	N12	—	**14e** —	2 pl. Ferdinand-Brunot, 14e	45 45 67 14
40	M8	—	**15e** —	31 r. Péclet, 15e	48 28 40 12
27	H5	—	**16e** —	71 av. Henri-Martin, 16e	45 03 21 16
18	D11	—	**17e** —	18 r. des Batignolles, 17e	42 93 35 17
7	C14	—	**18e** —	1 pl. Jules-Joffrin, 18e	42 52 42 00
22	D19	—	**19e** —	5-7 pl. Armand-Carrel, 19e	42 41 19 19
35	G21	—	**20e** —	6 pl. Gambetta, 20e	43 58 20 20

Services de police (Sécurité publique 24 h/24 h)
Police services, Polizeidienststellen, Servicios de policía

31	J14	**Préfecture de Police**		9 bd du Palais, 4e	42 60 33 22
30	G12	**Commissariat du**	**1er Arrondissement**	49-51, pl. du Marché-St-Honoré 1er	42 61 09 19
31	G14	—	**2e** —	5 pl. des Petits-Pères 2e	42 60 96 87
32	H16	—	**3e** —	5 r. Perrée 3e	42 78 40 00
32	J16	—	**4e** —	pl. Baudoyer 4e	42 77 67 21
44	K15	—	**5e** —	4 r. de la Montagne Ste-Geneviève 5e	43 29 21 57
31	K13	—	**6e** —	78 r. Bonaparte 6e	43 29 76 10
29	H10	—	**7e** —	9 r. Fabert 7e	45 55 40 81
29	G10	—	**8e** —	av. du Gal-Eisenhower 8e	42 25 88 80
19	F13-F14	—	**9e** —	14 bis r. Chauchat 9e	42 46 30 26
21	E17	—	**10e** —	26 r. Louis-Blanc 10e	46 07 57 77
34	J19	—	**11e** —	107 bd Voltaire 11e	43 79 39 51
46	M20	—	**12e** —	3 r. Bignon 12e	46 28 26 85
44	N16	—	**13e** —	144 bd de l'Hôpital 13e	45 70 11 99
42	N11	—	**14e** —	114 av. du Maine 14e	43 20 14 80
40	M8	—	**15e** —	141 r. Lecourbe 15e	45 31 14 40
26	J4	—	**16e** —	62 av. Mozart 16e	45 27 03 78
18	D11	—	**17e** —	19 r. Truffaut 17e	42 93 05 50
7	B14-C14	—	**18e** —	74 r. du Mont-Cenis 18e	46 06 43 84
22	D19	—	**19e** —	2 r. André-Dubois 19e	46 07 57 79
35	G21	—	**20e** —	6 pl. Gambetta 20e	46 36 06 10

Au-delà de Paris et de sa banlieue, utilisez les cartes Michelin :

196 *à 1/100 000 — Environs de Paris*

237 *à 1/200 000 — Ile de France.*

Services, Sonstige Behörden und Ämter, Servicios administrativos

30	K11	**Préfecture d'Ile de France**	29, r. Barbet-de-Jouy, 7ᵉ	45 50 32 12
33	K17	**Préfecture de Paris** *(transfert prévu)*	17 bd Morland, 4ᵉ	42 77 15 50
32	J15	**Accueil de la Ville de Paris**	29 r. de Rivoli, 4ᵉ	42 76 43 43
43	N13	**Aéroports De Paris (ADP)**	291 bd Raspail, 14ᵉ	43 35 70 00
45	K17	**Archives de Paris**	30 quai Henri-IV, 4ᵉ	42 72 34 52
31	H14	**Bourse de Commerce**	2 r. de Viarmes, 1ᵉʳ	45 08 35 00
20	G16	**Bourse du Travail**	3 r. du Château-d'Eau, 10ᵉ	42 38 66 12
19	G14	**Bourse des Valeurs**	4 pl. de la Bourse, 2ᵉ	42 61 85 90
31	G14	**Caisse d'Épargne de Paris**	19 r. du Louvre, 1ᵉʳ	42 96 15 00
16	F8	**Chambre de Commerce et d'Industrie de Paris**	16 r. Chateaubriand, 8ᵉ	42 89 78 15
31	J14	**Cour d'Appel de Paris**	4 bd du Palais, 1ᵉʳ	43 29 12 55
32	H16	**Crédit Municipal de Paris**	55 r. des Francs-Bourgeois, 4ᵉ	42 71 25 43
52	N8	**Fourrière**	39 r. de Dantzig, 15ᵉ	45 31 14 80
29	J10	**Gouvernement Militaire**	Hôtel des Invalides, 7ᵉ	45 55 92 30
40	N8	**Objets Trouvés**	36 r. des Morillons, 15ᵉ	45 31 14 80
31	G14	**Paierie Générale du Trésor**	16 r. N.-D.-des Victoires, 2ᵉ	40 20 13 13
31	J14	**Palais de Justice**	4 bd du Palais, 1ᵉʳ	43 29 12 55
9	C17	**Pompes Funèbres Municipales**	104 r. d'Aubervilliers, 19ᵉ	42 00 33 15
42	M11	**Télécommunications**	8-10 bd de Vaugirard, 15ᵉ	45 40 33 33
32	J16	**Tribunal Administratif**	7 r. de Jouy, 4ᵉ	42 78 40 24
31	J14	**Tribunal de Commerce**	1 quai de la Corse, 4ᵉ	43 29 12 60
31	J14	**Tribunal de Grande Instance**	4 bd du Palais, 1ᵉʳ	43 29 12 55

Échelle : 1 cm sur le plan représente 100 m sur le terrain.

Scale : 1 cm on the map represents 100 m on the ground (1 in. : 278 yards approx.)

Maßstab : 1 cm auf dem Atlas entspricht 100 m.

Escala : 1 cm sobre el atlas reprensenta 100 m sobre el terreno.

AMBASSADES ET REPRÉSENTATIONS
FOREIGN REPRESENTATIVES,
BOTSCHAFTEN UND VERTRETUNGEN,
EMBAJADAS Y REPRESENTACIONES

Organismes Internationaux, *International organizations,*
Internationale Organisationen, Organizaciones internacionales

33	J18	Association Internationale de l'Hôtellerie	80, r. de la Roquette, 11ᵉ	47 00 84 57
30	J12	Bureau International du Travail (BIT)	205 bd St-Germain, 7ᵉ	45 48 92 02
		(Siège à Genève)		
16	F7	Centre de Conférences Internationales	19 av. Kléber, 16ᵉ	45 01 59 40
61	ABX	Centre International de l'Enfance	Bois de Boulogne -	
		(Château de Longchamp)	Carrefour de Longchamp	45 20 79 92
18	F11	Chambre de Com. France-Amérique Latine	97 bd Haussmann, 8ᵉ	42 66 38 32
16	G7	Chambre de Commerce Franco-Arabe	93 r. Lauriston, 16ᵉ	45 53 20 12
18	E12	— Franco-Asiatique	94 r. St-Lazare, 9ᵉ	45 26 67 01
29	G9	— Internationale	38 cours Albert-Iᵉʳ, 8ᵉ	45 62 34 56
15	G6	Communautés Européennes	61 r. des Belles-Feuilles, 16ᵉ	45 01 58 85
		(Siège à Bruxelles)		
29	H10	Conseil des Communes et Régions d'Europe	41 quai d'Orsay, 7ᵉ	45 51 40 01
16	G7	Conseil de l'Europe (Siège à Strasbourg)	55 av. Kléber, 16ᵉ	47 04 38 65
16	G7	Fédération Aéronautique Internationale	6 r. Galilée, 16ᵉ	47 20 91 85
30	G11	— Internationale de l'Automobile	8 pl. de la Concorde, 8ᵉ	42 65 99 51
28	G7	— Mondiale Anciens Combattants	16 r. Hamelin, 16ᵉ	47 04 33 00
17	D9	— Mondiale des Villes Jumelées	2 r. de Logelbach, 17ᵉ	47 66 75 10
31	K13	Librairie internationale (Interculture)	141 bd St-Germain, 6ᵉ	43 29 38 20
18	F11	Office International de la Vigne et du Vin	11 r. Roquépine, 8ᵉ	42 65 04 16
15	D5	Organisation de l'Aviation Civile	Neuilly -	
		Internationale	3 bis villa É.-Bergerat	46 37 96 96
26	H4	Organisation de Coopération et de	2 r. André-Pascal, 16ᵉ	45 24 82 00
		Développement Économiques (OCDE)		
41	L9	Organisation des Nations-Unies (ONU)	1 r. Miollis, 15ᵉ	45 68 48 72
		(Siège à New York)		
41	K9	Unesco	7 pl. de Fontenoy, 7ᵉ	45 68 10 00
28	H7	Union de l'Europe Occidentale (UEO)	43 av. du Prés. Wilson, 16ᵉ	47 23 54 32
17	D9	Union des Foires Internationales	35 bis r. Jouffroy, 17ᵉ	47 66 17 17
28	J7	Union Internationale des Chemins de Fer	14-16 r. Jean-Rey, 15ᵉ	42 73 01 20

Représentations étrangères,
Foreign Representatives, Ausländische Vertretungen,
Representaciones extranjeras

Afghanistan - Cap. Kaboul

26	J4	Ambassade	32 av. Raphaël, 16ᵉ	45 27 66 09

Afrique du Sud - Cap. Pretoria

29	H9	Ambassade	59 quai d'Orsay, 7ᵉ	45 55 92 37
18	G12	Office du Tourisme Sud-Africain	9 bd de la Madeleine, 1ᵉʳ	42 61 82 30
18	G12	South African Airways	12 r. de la Paix, 2ᵉ	42 61 57 87

Albanie - Cap. Tirana

27	G6	Ambassade	131 r. de la Pompe, 16ᵉ	45 53 51 32

Algérie - Cap. Alger

17	E10	Ambassade	50 r. de Lisbonne, 8ᵉ	42 25 70 70
16	F7	Consulat	11 r. d'Argentine, 16ᵉ	45 00 99 50
19	G13	Air Algérie	28 av. de l'Opéra, 2ᵉ	42 96 12 09
40	M7	Centre Culturel	171 r. de la Croix-Nivert, 15ᵉ	45 54 95 31

Allemagne (République Démocratique-RDA) - Cap. Berlin

15	F6	Ambassade	24 r. Marbeau, 16ᵉ	45 00 00 10
31	K13	Centre culturel	117 bd St-Germain, 6ᵉ	46 34 25 99
14	D3	Représentation commerciale	Neuilly - 179 av. Ch.-de-Gaulle	47 47 45 17

Allemagne (République Fédérale-RFA) - Cap. Bonn

29	G10	**Ambassade**	13 av. Franklin-Roosevelt, 8ᵉ	42 99 78 00
28	G8	— (Section consulaire)	34 av. d'Iéna, 16ᵉ	42 99 78 00
39	L5	**Chambre Officielle Franco-Allemande de Commerce et d'Industrie**	18 r. Balard, 15ᵉ	45 75 62 56
19	E14	**Chemin de Fer Fédéral Allemand**	24 r. Condorcet, 9ᵉ	48 78 50 26
19	F13	**DER-Voyages, Deutsches Reisebüro**	28-30 r. Louis-le-Grand, 2ᵉ	47 42 07 09
17	F10	**Der Spiegel**	17 av. Matignon, 8ᵉ	42 56 12 11
27	H5	**Deutsches Historisches Institut**	9 r. Maspéro, 16ᵉ	45 20 25 55
17	F10	**Die Welt**	31 r. du Colisée, 8ᵉ	43 59 09 74
17	F10	**Frankfurter Allgemeine Zeitung**	11 r. de Mirosmesnil, 8ᵉ	42 65 49 87
28	G7	**Goethe-Institut**	17 av. d'Iéna, 16ᵉ	47 23 61 21
18	G11	**KD German Rhine-Line** (navigation)	9 r. du Fg-St-Honoré, 8ᵉ	47 42 52 27
44	M15	**Librairie Calligrammes**	8 r. de la Collégiale, 5ᵉ	43 36 85 07
32	H15	— **Marissal Bücher**	42 r. Rambuteau, 3ᵉ	42 74 37 47
31	J14	— **Martin Flinker**	68 quai des Orfèvres, 1ᵉʳ	43 54 48 60
43	M13	— **le Roi des Aulnes**	159 bis bd du Montparnasse, 6ᵉ	43 26 86 92
18	G11	**Lufthansa** (Cie aérienne)	21-23 r. Royale, 8ᵉ	42 65 19 19
55	R14	**Office Franco-Allemand pour la Jeunesse**	51 r. de l'Amiral-Mouchez, 13ᵉ	45 81 11 66
18	G12	**Office du Tourisme**	9 bd de la Madeleine, 1ᵉʳ	40 20 01 88
17	F10	**Stern**	17 av. Matignon, 8ᵉ	42 56 13 78

Angola - Cap. Luanda

16	F7	**Ambassade**	19 av. Foch, 16ᵉ	45 01 58 20
16	F7	**Consulat**	40 r. Chalgrin, 16ᵉ	45 01 96 94

Arabie Saoudite - Cap. Riyad

17	E9	**Ambassade**	5 av. Hoche, 8ᵉ	47 66 02 06
14	E3	**Consulat**	Neuilly - 29 rue des Graviers	47 47 62 63
16	F8	**Saudia** (Cie aérienne)	55 av. Georges V, 8ᵉ	47 23 72 22

Argentine - Cap. Buenos Aires

16	G7	**Ambassade**	6 r. Cimarosa, 16ᵉ	45 53 14 69
16	G7	**Consulat Général**	imp. Kléber 16ᵉ	45 53 22 25
17	F9	**Aerolineas Argentinas**	77 av. Champs-Élysées, 8ᵉ	43 59 02 96
28	G8	**Centre Culturel Argentin**	27 av. Pierre-Iᵉʳ-de-Serbie, 16ᵉ	47 20 30 60

Australie - Cap. Canberra

28	J7	**Ambassade**	4, r. Jean-Rey, 15ᵉ	40 59 33 00
28	J7	**Office du Tourisme**	4 r. Jean-Rey 15ᵉ	45 79 80 44
18	F12	**Qantas** (Cie aérienne)	7 r. Scribe, 9ᵉ	42 66 53 05

Autriche - Cap. Vienne

29	H10	**Ambassade**	6 r. Fabert, 7ᵉ	45 55 95 66
28	H8	— (Section Consulaire)	12 r. Ed-Valentin, 7ᵉ	47 05 27 17
18	F12	**Austrian Airlines**	47 av. de l'Opéra, 2ᵉ	47 42 55 05
18	F11	**Délégation commerciale**	22 r. de l'Arcade, 8ᵉ	42 65 67 35
41	K10	**Institut Autrichien**	30 bd des Invalides, 7ᵉ	47 05 27 10
18	F12	**Office National du Tourisme**	47 av. de l'Opéra, 2ᵉ	47 42 78 57

Bahrein - Cap. Manama

27	G6	**Ambassade**	15 av. Raymond-Poincaré, 16ᵉ	45 53 01 19
27	G6	**Consulat**	—	45 53 43 79

Bangladesh - Cap. Dacca

27	H6	**Ambassade**	5 square Pétrarque, 16ᵉ	45 53 41 20

Belgique - Cap. Bruxelles

16	F8	**Ambassade**	9 r. de Tilsitt, 17ᵉ	43 80 61 00
16	F7	**Service des visas**	1 av. Mac-Mahon, 17ᵉ	42 27 45 40
32	H15	**Centre Wallonie-Bruxelles**	127-129 r. St-Martin, 4ᵉ	42 71 26 16
17	F9	**Chambre de Commerce Belgo-Luxemb.**	174 bd Haussmann, 8ᵉ	45 62 44 87
18	F12	**Chemins de Fer Belges**	21 bd des Capucines, 2ᵉ	47 42 40 41
18	F12	**Office de Tourisme**	21 bd des Capucines, 2ᵉ	47 42 41 18
18	G12	**Sabena** (Cie aérienne)	19 r. de la Paix, 2ᵉ	47 42 47 47
18	D12	**« Le Soir »** de Bruxelles	90 r. d'Amsterdam, 9ᵉ	42 82 90 10

Bénin - Cap. Porto Novo

16	F7	**Ambassade**	87 av. Victor-Hugo, 16e	45 00 98 82
42	L11	**Consulat**	89 r. du Cherche-Midi, 6e	42 22 31 91

Birmanie - Cap. Rangoun

17	E9	**Ambassade**	60 r. de Courcelles, 8e	42 25 56 95

Bolivie - Cap. La Paz

27	J6	**Ambassade**	12 av. du Prés.-Kennedy, 16e	42 24 93 44
27	J6	**Consulat**	—	45 25 47 14
31	K13	**Institut Bolivien du Tourisme**	8 r. Mabillon, 6e	42 70 48 53
31	K13	**Lloyd Aereo Boliviano**	—	43 29 40 40

Brésil - Cap. Brasilia

29	G9	**Ambassade**	34 cours Albert-Ier, 8e	42 25 92 50
16	F8	**Consulat Général**	122 av. Champs-Élysées, 8e	43 59 89 30
17	G9	**Varig** (Cie aérienne)	27 av. Champs-Élysées, 8e	47 23 55 44

Bulgarie - Cap. Sofia

28	H8	**Ambassade**	1 av. Rapp, 7e	45 51 85 90
18	F12	**Balkan** (Cie aérienne)	4 r. Scribe, 9e	47 42 66 66
31	G13	**Office National du Tourisme**	45 av. de l'Opéra, 2e	42 61 69 68

Burkina Faso (anc. Haute-Volta) - Cap. Ouagadougou

17	F9	**Ambassade**	159 bd Haussmann, 8e	43 59 21 85

Burundi - Cap. Bujumbura

27	H5	**Ambassade**	3 r. Octave-Feuillet, 16e	45 20 60 61

Cameroun - Cap. Yaoundé

38	K3	**Ambassade**	73 r. d'Auteuil, 16e	47 43 98 33
18	F12	**Cameroon Airlines**	12 bd des Capucines, 9e	47 42 78 17
18	E12	**Cameroon Shipping Lines**	38 r. de Liège, 8e	42 93 50 70

Canada - Cap. Ottawa

29	G9	**Ambassade**	35 av. Montaigne, 8e	47 23 01 01
18	F12	**Air Canada**	24 bd des Capucines, 9e	47 42 21 21
18	G12	**Canadian Airlines International**	15 r. de la Paix, 2e	42 61 72 34
17	F10	**Canadian Broadcasting Corporation** (CBC)	17 av. Matignon, 8e	43 59 11 85
18	F12	**Canadien National** (chemins de fer)	1 r. Scribe, 9e	47 42 76 50
29	H10	**Centre Culturel**	5 rue de Constantine, 7e	45 51 35 73
29	G10	**Chambre de Commerce France-Canada**	9 av. Franklin Roosevelt, 8e	43 59 32 38
15	F6	**Délégation Générale du Québec**	66 r. Pergolèse, 16e	45 02 14 10
17	F9	**Délégation de l'Ontario**	109 r. du Fg.-St-Honoré, 8e	45 63 16 34
29	G9	**Division du Tourisme de l'Ambassade**	35 av. Montaigne, 8e	47 23 01 01
17	D9	**Off.-Franco-Québécois pour la Jeunesse**	5 r. de Logelbach, 17e	47 66 04 76

Centrafrique - Cap. Bangui

26	J3	**Ambassade**	29 bd de Montmorency, 16e	42 24 42 56

Chili - Cap. Santiago

29	J9	**Ambassade**	2 av. de La Motte-Picquet, 7e	45 51 46 68
29	J10	**Consulat**	64 bd de La-Tour-Maubourg, 7e	47 05 46 61
29	G10	**Service commercial**	9-11 av. F. D.-Roosevelt, 8e	42 89 32 38

Chine - Cap. Pékin

28	G8	**Ambassade**	11 av. George-V, 8e	47 23 34 45
50	R4	**Service consulaire**	Issy-les-Moulineaux - 9 av. Victor-Cresson	47 36 77 90
15	F6	**Compagnie aérienne de Chine** (CAAC)	47 r. Pergolèse, 16e	45 00 19 94
31	G13	**Office du Tourisme**	51 r. Ste-Anne, 2e	42 96 95 48
28	G7	**Service commercial**	21 r. Amiral d'Estaing, 16e	47 20 86 82
50	R4	**Service culturel**	Issy-les-Moulineaux - 9 av. Victor-Cresson	47 36 77 04

Chypre - Cap. Nicosie

16	G7	**Ambassade**	23 av. Galilée, 16e	47 20 86 28
16	F8	**Cyprus Airways**	37 r. Jean-Giraudoux, 16e	45 01 93 38
18	G12	**Office du Tourisme**	15 r. de la Paix, 2e	42 61 42 49

Colombie - Cap. Bogota

18	F11	**Ambassade**	22 r. de l'Élysée, 8e	42 65 46 08
16	G8	**Consulat**	11 bis r. Christophe-Colomb, 8e	47 23 36 05
18	G12	**Avianca** (Cie aérienne)	9 bd de la Madeleine, 1er	42 60 35 22
18	F11	**Office National du Tourisme**	22 r. de l'Élysée, 8e	42 66 58 84

Comores - Cap. Moroni

16	E8	**Ambassade**	15 r. de la Néva, 8e	47 63 81 78

Congo - Cap. Brazzaville

16	F7	**Ambassade**	37 bis r. Paul-Valéry, 16e	45 00 60 57

Corée - Cap. Séoul

30	J11	**Ambassade**	125 r. de Grenelle, 7e	47 53 01 01
18	F11	**Centre Coréen du Commerce Extérieur**	25-27 r. d'Astorg, 8e	47 42 00 17
28	H7	**Centre culturel**	2 av. d'Iéna, 16e	47 20 83 86
18	G12	**Korean Air** (Cie aérienne)	9 bd de la Madeleine, 1er	42 61 58 46
42	M11	**Office National du Tourisme**	Tour Montparnasse, 15e	45 38 71 23

Costa Rica - Cap. San José

27	H5	**Ambassade**	74 av. Paul-Doumer, 16e	45 04 50 93
27	H5	**Consulat**	—	45 04 32 16
27	H5	**Office National du Tourisme**	—	45 04 50 93

Côte-d'Ivoire -Cap. Yamoussoukro

15	F6	**Ambassade**	102 av. Raymond-Poincaré, 16e	45 01 53 10
12	G7	**Service des visas**	8, r. Dumont-d'Urville, 16e	47 20 35 09
41	K9-K10	**Centre de Commerce Intern. d'Abidjan**	21 av. de Saxe, 7e	45 67 35 38
26	H4	**Délégation du Tourisme**	24 bd Suchet, 16e	42 88 62 92

Cuba - Cap. La Havane

28	K8	**Ambassade**	16 r. de Presles, 15e	45 67 55 35
28	K8	**Consulat**	14 r. de Presles, 15e	45 67 55 35
19	G13	**Office du Tourisme**	24 r. du 4-Septembre, 2e	47 42 54 15
19	G13	**Cubana de Aviación**	—	47 42 91 21

Danemark - Cap. Copenhague

16	F8	**Ambassade**	77 av. Marceau, 16e	47 23 54 20
16	F8	**DSB Voyages**	142 av. Champs-Élysées, 8e	43 59 20 06
16	F8	**Office National du Tourisme**	142 av. Champs-Élysées, 8e	45 62 17 02
18	F12	**Scandinavian Airlines System (SAS)**	30 bd des Capucines, 9e	47 42 06 14

Djibouti - Cap. Djibouti

15	G5	**Ambassade**	26 r. Émile-Ménier, 16e	47 27 49 22

Dominicaine (République) - Cap. Saint-Domingue

16	F7	**Ambassade**	2 r. Georges-Ville, 16e	45 00 77 71

Égypte - Cap. Le Caire

16	G8	**Ambassade**	56 av. d'Iéna, 16e	47 20 97 70
15	F6	**Consulat**	58 av. Foch, 16e	45 00 69 23
17	F9	**Bureau du Tourisme**	90 av. Champs-Élysées, 8e	45 62 94 42
43	L13	**Centre Culturel**	111 bd St-Michel, 5e	46 33 75 67
18	F12	**Egyptair**	1 bis r. Auber, 9e	42 66 55 59

Émirats Arabes Unis (EAU) - Cap. Abou Dabi

27	G5	**Ambassade**	3, r. de Lota, 16e	45 53 94 04

Équateur - Cap. Quito

17	E10	**Ambassade**	34 av. de Messine, 8e	45 61 10 21
17	E10	**Consulat**	34 av. de Messine, 8e	45 61 10 04

Espagne - Cap. Madrid

28	G8	**Ambassade**	13, av. Georges-V, 8e	47 23 61 83
5	D9	**Consulat Général**	165 bd Malesherbes, 17e	47 66 03 32
19	G13	**Chambre de Commerce d'Espagne**	32 av. de l'Opéra, 2e	47 42 45 74
29	G9	**Iberia** (Cie aérienne)	31 av. Montaigne, 8e	47 23 01 23
31	J13	**Librairie Espagnole**	72 r. de Seine, 6e	43 54 56 26
28	G8	**Office culturel**	11 av. Marceau, 16e	47 20 83 45
16	G8	**Office National du Tourisme**	43 ter av. Pierre-1er-de-Serbie, 8e	47 20 90 54
28	G8	**Réseau des Chemins de fer** (RENFE)	1-3 av. Marceau, 16e	47 23 52 01
31	H14	**Maison d'Andorre** (Principauté d'Andorre)	111 r. St-Honoré 1er	45 08 50 28

Etats-Unis d'Amérique (USA) - Cap. Washington

30	G11	**Ambassade**	2 av. Gabriel, 8ᵉ	42 96 12 02
30	G11	**Consulat**	2, r. St-Florentin, 1ᵉʳ	42 96 12 02
22	A9	**American Battle Monuments Commission**	Garches - 68 r. du 19-Janvier	47 01 19 76
31	G13	**American Center**	29 r. de La Sourdière, 1ᵉʳ	40 15 00 88
18	F12	**American Express**	11 r. Scribe, 9ᵉ	42 00 09 99
17	G9	**American Legion**	49 r. Pierre-Charron, 8ᵉ	42 25 41 93
28	J7	**Association France Etats-Unis**	6 bd de Grenelle, 15ᵉ	45 77 48 92
28	H8	**Bibliothèque Américaine**	10 r. du Général-Camou, 7ᵉ	45 51 46 82
30	G11	**Centre de Documentation B. Franklin**	2 r. St-Florentin, 1ᵉʳ	42 96 33 10
28	G8	**Chambre de Commerce Américaine**	21 av. George-V, 8ᵉ	47 23 80 26
		Office de tourisme *(uniquement par*	Ambassade des États-Unis	42 60 57 15
		téléphone ou par courrier)	75382 Paris Cedex 08	
14	D3	**International Herald Tribune**	Neuilly - 181 av. Ch.-de-Gaulle	46 37 93 00
		Librairies : voir Grande-Bretagne		
17	F9	**National Broadcasting** (NBC News)	73 av. Champs-Élysées, 8ᵉ	43 59 11 71
17	F9	**Newsweek Magazine**	162 r. du Fg-St-Honoré, 8ᵉ	42 56 06 81
18	F12	**Pan American World Airways** (PAN AM)	1 r. Scribe, 9ᵉ	42 66 45 45
17	F10	**Time**	17 av. Matignon, 8ᵉ	43 59 05 39
16	F8	**Trans World Airlines** (TWA)	101 av. Champs-Élysées, 8ᵉ	47 20 62 11

Ethiopie - Cap. Addis Abeba

28	J8	**Ambassade**	35 av. Charles-Floquet, 7ᵉ	47 83 83 95
18	F12	**Ethiopian Airlines**	25 r. des Mathurins, 8ᵉ	42 66 16 26

Finlande - Cap. Helsinki

29	H10	**Ambassade**	2 r. Fabert, 7ᵉ	47 05 35 45
18	F11	**Consulat Général**	18 bis r. d'Anjou, 8ᵉ	42 65 33 65
19	F13	**Chambre de Commerce**	19 bd. Haussmann, 9ᵉ	42 47 13 00
		Franco-Finlandaise		
18	F12	**Finnair** (Cie aérienne)	11 r. Auber, 9ᵉ	47 42 33 33
18	F12	**Office National du Tourisme**	13 r. Auber, 9ᵉ	42 66 40 13

Gabon - Cap. Libreville

26	J4	**Ambassade**	26 bis av. Raphaël, 16ᵉ	42 24 79 60
17	F10	**Air Gabon**	4 av. F.-D.-Roosevelt, 8ᵉ	43 59 20 63
17	F9	**Association France-Gabon**	11 r. Lincoln, 8ᵉ	42 56 20 12
		(Renseignements et Informations Touristiques)	—	—

Ghana - Cap. Accra

15	F5	**Ambassade**	8 villa Saïd, 16ᵉ	45 00 09 50

Grande-Bretagne et Irlande du Nord - Cap. Londres

18	G11	**Ambassade**	35 r. du Fg-St-Honoré, 8ᵉ	42 66 91 42
18	F11	**Consulat**	16 r. d'Anjou, 8ᵉ	42 66 91 42
18	F11	**Services des visas**	—	42 66 38 10
16	F8	**British Airways**	91 av. Champs-Élysées, 8ᵉ	49 03 93 00
17	F9	**British Broadcasting Corporation** (BBC)	155 r. du Fg-St-Honoré, 8ᵉ	45 61 97 00
18	G12	**British Caledonian Airways**	5 r. de la Paix, 2ᵉ	42 61 12 68
29	H10	**The British Council**	11 r. de Constantine, 7ᵉ	45 55 95 95
31	G13	**BritRail Voyages**	55-57 r. St-Roch, 1ᵉʳ	42 61 85 40
16	G7	**Chambre de Commerce et d'Industrie**	8 r. Cimarosa, 16ᵉ	45 05 13 08
		franco-britannique		
29	H10	**Institut Britannique**	11 r. de Constantine, 7ᵉ	45 55 71 99
43	K14	**Librairie Attica**	34 r. des Ecoles, 5ᵉ	43 26 09 53
31	G13	**— Brentano's**	37 av. de l'Opéra, 2ᵉ	42 61 52 50
30	G12	**— Galignani**	224 r. de Rivoli, 1ᵉʳ	42 60 76 07
43	L13	**— Nouveau Quartier Latin**	78 bd. St-Michel, 6ᵉ	43 26 42 70
32	K15	**— Shakespeare and Company**	37 r. de la Bûcherie, 5ᵉ	43 26 96 50
30	G12	**— W.H. Smith France**	248 r. de Rivoli, 1ᵉʳ	42 60 37 97
18	F12	**North Sea Ferries** (Transports et Voyages)	8 r. Auber, 9ᵉ	42 66 91 91
17	G9	**Office Britannique de Tourisme** (BTA)	63 r. Pierre Charron, 8ᵉ	42 89 11 11
18	F11	**P. & O. European Ferries**	9 pl. de la Madeleine, 8ᵉ	42 66 40 17
18	F12	**Royal British Legion**	8 r. Boudreau, 9ᵉ	47 42 19 26
18	F12	**Sealink**	16 bd des Capucines, 9ᵉ	47 42 00 26
19	F13	**The Times**	8 r. Halévy, 9ᵉ	47 42 73 21
18	F11	**Maison du Tourisme de Jersey**	19 bd Malesherbes, 8ᵉ	47 42 93 68

Grèce - Cap. Athènes

16	F8	Ambassade	17 r. Auguste-Vacquerie, 16e	47 23 72 28
16	G7	Consulat	23 r. Galilée, 16e	47 23 72 23
42	M11	Librairie hellénique Desmos	14 r. Vandamme, 14e	43 20 84 04
31	H13	Office Nat. Hellénique du Tourisme	3 av. de l'Opéra, 1er	42 60 65 75
18	F12	Olympic Airways	3 r. Auber, 9e	47 42 87 99
27	G6	Bureau de Presse	6 pl. de Mexico, 16e	45 53 89 99

Guatemala - Cap. Guatemala

17	E9	Ambassade	73 r. de Courcelles, 8e	42 27 78 63

Guinée - Cap. Conakry

15	G5	Ambassade	24 r. Émile-Ménier, 16e	45 53 72 25

Guinée Équatoriale - Cap. Malabo

17	E9	Ambassade	6 r. Alfred de Vigny, 8e	47 66 44 33

Haïti - Cap. Port-au-Prince

16	E8	Ambassade	10, r. Théodule-Ribot, 17e	47 63 47 78

Honduras - Cap. Tegucigalpa

30	G12	Ambassade	6 pl. Vendôme, 1er	42 61 34 75

Hong Kong - Cap. Victoria

16	G8	Office de Tourisme *(uniquement par téléphone ou par courrier)*	53, r. François-1er, 8e	47 20 39 54

Hongrie - Cap. Budapest

15	F5	Ambassade	5 bis sq. Avenue Foch, 16e	45 00 00 29
43	K13	Consulat	92 bis r. Bonaparte, 6e	43 54 66 96
43	K13	Institut Hongrois	92 r. Bonaparte, 6e	43 26 06 44
43	K13	Presse et Documentation	—	—
18	G12	Malèv (Cie aérienne)	7 r. de la Paix, 2e	42 61 57 90
19	G13	Tourisme Hongrois/Ibusz	27 r. du 4-Septembre, 2e	47 42 50 25

Inde - Cap. New Delhi

26	H4	Ambassade	15 r. Alfred-Dehodencq, 16e	45 20 39 30
18	F12	Air India	1 r. Auber, 9e	42 66 90 60
41	L10	Chambre de Commerce et d'Industrie franco-indienne	4 av. Daniel Lesueur, 7e	43 06 88 97
18	G12	Office National de Tourisme	8 bd de la Madeleine, 9e	42 65 83 86

Indonésie - Cap. Jakarta

27	H5	Ambassade	47-49 r. Cortambert, 16e	45 03 07 60
17	F9	Garuda Indonesia (Cie aérienne)	75 av. Champs-Élysées, 8e	45 62 45 45

Irak - Cap. Bagdad

15	G5	Ambassade	53 r. de la Faisanderie, 16e	45 01 51 00
15	G5	Centre Culturel	6-8 r. du Gal-Appert, 16e	47 04 66 87
16	F8	Iraqi Airways	144 av. Champs-Élysées, 8e	45 62 62 25

Iran - Cap. Téhéran

28	H7	Ambassade	4 av. d'Iéna, 16e	47 23 61 22
28	H8	Consulat	16 r. Fresnel, 16e	47 23 61 22
17	G9	Iran Air	33 av. Champs-Elysées, 8e	43 59 01 20

Irlande - Cap. Dublin

16	F7	Ambassade	4 r. Rude, 16e	45 00 20 87
19	G13	Aer Lingus (Cie aérienne)	4/ av. de l'Opéra, 2e	47 42 12 50
18	F12	Irish Continental Line (Transports et Voyages)	8 r. Auber, 9e	42 66 90 90
17	F10	Office du Commerce Extérieur Irlandais	33 rue de Miromesnil, 8e	42 65 98 05
18	G12	Office National du Tourisme	9 bd de la Madeleine, 1er	42 61 84 26

Islande - Cap. Reykjavik

18	F11	**Ambassade**	124 bd Haussmann, 8^e	45 22 81 54
19	F13	**Office National du Tourisme -**	9 bd des Capucines, 2^e	47 42 52 26
19	F13	**Icelandair** (Cie aérienne)	—	—

Israël - Cap. Jérusalem

17	F10	**Ambassade**	3 r. Rabelais, 8^e	42 56 47 47
18	G11	**Chambre de Commerce France-Israël**	47 r. du Fg-St-Honoré, 8^e	42 25 34 56
18	F12	**El Al** (Cie aérienne)	24 bd des Capucines, 9^e	47 42 45 19
32	H15	**France-Israël** (Alliance Gal Koenig)	63 bd de Sébastopol, 1er	42 33 36 82
18	G12	**Office National de Tourisme**	14 r. de la Paix, 2^e	42 61 01 97

Italie - Cap. Rome

30	J11	**Ambassade**	51 r. de Varenne, 7^e	45 44 38 90
27	H5	**Consulat**	5 bd Émile-Augier, 16^e	45 20 78 22
19	G13	**Alitalia** (Cie aérienne)	43-45 av. de l'Opéra, 2^e	40 15 01 40
17	F10	**Chambre de Commerce Italienne**	134 r. du Fg-St-Honoré, 8^e	42 25 41 88
19	F13	**Compagnie Italienne de Tourisme** (CIT)	3 bd des Capucines, 2^e	42 66 00 90
30	H11	**Corriere della Sera**	280 bd St-Germain, 7^e	45 50 42 10
28	J8	**Dante Alighieri** (Société culturelle)	12 r. Sédillot, 7^e	47 05 16 26
30	J11	**Institut Culturel**	50 r. de Varenne, 7^e	42 22 12 78
19	F13	**La Stampa**	5 r. des Italiens, 9^e	42 47 97 27
32	J16	**Librairie Tour de Babel**	10 r. du Roi-de-Sicile, 4^e	42 77 32 40
30	J11	**Maison du Livre Italien**	54 r. de Bourgogne, 7^e	47 05 03 99
18	G12	**Office national de Tourisme** (ENIT)	23 r. de la Paix, 2^e	42 66 66 68
16	F8	**Radiotelevisione Italiana** (RAI) 1re chaîne	96 av. d'Iéna, 16^e	47 20 60 40
16	F8	— 2e chaîne	—	47 20 37 67
16	F8	— 3e chaîne	—	47 20 95 06

Japon - Cap. Tokyo

17	E9	**Ambassade**	7 av. Hoche, 8^e	47 66 02 22
17	F9	**Centre Japonais de Commerce extérieur**	50 av. Champs-Élysées, 8^e	42 25 35 82
17	F9	**Chambre de Commerce et d'Industrie Japonaise**	1 av. de Friedland, 8^e	45 63 43 33
18	F11	**Chemins de Fer du Japon**	24-26 r. de la Pépinière, 8^e	45 22 60 48
31	G13	**Espace Japon** (bibliothèque)	12 r. Ste-Anne, 1er	42 60 69 30
16	G7	**Fondation du Japon**	42 av. Kléber, 16^e	47 04 28 63
17	F9	**Japan Air Lines**	75 av. Champs-Élysées, 8^e	42 25 55 01
31	H13	**Librairie Japonaise Junku**	262 r. St-Honoré, 1er	42 60 89 12
31	G13	— — **Tokyo-Do**	4 r. Ste-Anne, 1er	42 61 08 71
16	G7	**Office Franco-Japonais d'Etudes Économiques**	14 r. Cimarosa, 16^e	42 27 30 90
31	G13	**Office National du Tourisme**	4-8 r. Ste-Anne, 1er	42 96 07 94
29	H9	**Radio Télévision japonaise** (N.H.K.)	174 r. de l'Université, 7^e	47 05 80 36
16	F8	**Service culturel et d'information**	7 r. de Tilsitt, 17^e	47 66 02 22

Jordanie - Cap. Amman

14	E4	**Ambassade du Royaume Hachémite**	Neuilly - 80 bd M.-Barrès	46 24 51 38
18	G12	**Royal Jordanian** (Cie aérienne)	12 r. de la Paix, 2^e	42 61 57 45

Kenya - Cap. Nairobi

16	G7	**Ambassade**	3 r. Cimarosa, 16^e	45 53 35 00
18	G12	**Kenya Airways**	8 r. Daunou, 2^e	42 61 82 93
18	G12	**Office du Tourisme**	5 r. Volney, 2^e	42 60 66 88

Koweït - Cap. Koweït

28	G8	**Ambassade**	2 r. de Lübeck, 16^e	47 23 54 25
16	G8	**Consulat**	1 pl. des Etats-Unis, 16^e	47 23 54 25
18	G12	**Kuwait Airways**	6 r. de la Paix, 2^e	42 60 30 60

Laos - Cap. Vientiane

15	G6	**Ambassade**	74 av. Raymond-Poincaré, 16^e	45 53 02 98

Liban - Cap. Beyrouth

16	G7	**Ambassade**	3 villa Copernic, 16^e	45 00 22 25
16	F8	**Services Consulaires et Culturels**	47 r. Dumont-d'Urville, 16^e	45 00 03 30
43	L13	**Librairie Synonyme**	82 bd St-Michel, 6^e	46 33 98 50
18	F12	**Middle East Airlines**	6 r. Scribe, 9^e	42 66 06 77
17	F10	**Office National du Tourisme**	124 r. du Fg-St-Honoré, 8^e	43 59 10 36
67		**Trans Mediterranean Airways**	Orly-Sud aérogare	48 84 02 93

Libéria - Cap. Monrovia

| 17 | D10 | Ambassade | 8 r. Jacques-Bingen, 17ᵉ | 47 63 58 55 |

Libye - Cap. Tripoli

| 15 | G5 | Ambassade | 2 r. Charles-Lamoureux, 16ᵉ | 47 04 71 60 |
| 17 | F9 | Libyan Arab Airlines | 90 av. Champs-Élysées, 8ᵉ | 45 62 33 00 |

Luxembourg - Cap. Luxembourg

28	H8	Ambassade	33 av. Rapp, 7ᵉ	45 55 13 37
17	F9	Chambre de Commerce Belgo-Luxemb.	174 bd Haussmann, 8ᵉ	45 62 44 87
16	F8	Luxair (Air France)	119 av. Champs-Élysées, 8ᵉ	45 62 44 87
18	F12	Office de Tourisme	21 bd des Capucines, 2ᵉ	47 42 90 56

Madagascar - Cap. Antananarivo

| 26 | H4 | Ambassade | 4 av. Raphaël, 16ᵉ | 45 04 62 11 |
| 31 | H13 | Air Madagascar | 7 av. de l'Opéra, 1ᵉʳ | 42 60 30 51 |

Malaisie - Cap. Kuala Lumpur

| 15 | G5 | Ambassade | 2 bis r. Benouville, 16ᵉ | 45 53 11 85 |
| 18 | F12 | Malaysian Airlines System | 12 bd des Capucines, 9ᵉ | 47 42 26 00 |

Mali - Cap. Bamako

| 42 | L11 | Ambassade | 89 r. du Cherche-Midi, 6ᵉ | 45 48 58 43 |
| 31 | G13 | Air Mali | 14 r. des Pyramides, 1ᵉʳ | 42 60 31 13 |

Malte - Cap. La Valette

17	F9	Ambassade	92 av. Champs-Elysées, 8ᵉ	45 62 53 01
42	K11	Air Malta	82 r. Vaneau, 7ᵉ	45 49 06 50
42	K11	Office national du Tourisme	—	45 49 15 33

Maroc - Cap. Rabat

27	H6	Ambassade	5 r. Le Tasse, 16ᵉ	45 20 69 35
19	F14	Consulat	19 r. Saulnier, 9ᵉ	45 23 37 40
18	E12	Compagnie Marocaine de Navigation	56 r. de Londres, 8ᵉ	43 87 42 06
30	G11	Maghreb Arabe Presse	4 pl. de la Concorde, 8ᵉ	42 65 40 45
31	H13	Office National du Tourisme	161 r. St-Honoré, 1ᵉʳ	42 60 63 50
19	G13	Royal Air Maroc	34 av. de l'Opéra, 2ᵉ	47 42 10 36

Maurice (Ile) - Cap. Port-Louis

| 17 | E10 | Ambassade | 68 bd de Courcelles, 17ᵉ | 42 27 30 19 |
| 2 | C3 | Bureau d'Information Touristique (uniquement par téléphone ou par courrier) | Neuilly - 41 r. Ybry | 46 40 37 42 |

Mauritanie - Cap. Nouakchott

| 15 | G5 | Ambassade | 5 r. de Montevideo, 16ᵉ | 45 04 88 54 |
| 42 | L11 | Consulat | 89 r. du Cherche-Midi, 6ᵉ | 45 48 23 88 |

Mexique - Cap. Mexico

28	G7	Ambassade	9 r. de Longchamp, 16ᵉ	45 53 76 43
31	G14	Consulat	4 r. N.-D.-des-Victoires, 2ᵉ	42 61 51 80
18	F12	Aeromexico (Cie aérienne)	12 r. Auber, 9ᵉ	47 42 40 50
30	K12	Centre culturel	28 bd Raspail, 7ᵉ	45 49 16 26
31	G14	Office de Tourisme	4 r. N.-D. des Victoires, 2ᵉ	42 61 51 80
31	G14	Service commercial	—	40 20 07 31

Monaco - Cap. Monaco

| 26 | H4 | Ambassade | 22 bd Suchet, 16ᵉ | 45 04 74 54 |
| 18 | G12 | Office du Tourisme et des Congrès | 9 r. de la Paix, 2ᵉ | 42 96 12 23 |

Mongolie - Cap. Oulan-Bator

| 37 | L2 | Ambassade | Boulogne - 5 av. R.-Schuman | 46 05 28 12 |

Nepal - Cap. Katmandu

| 17 | F9 | Ambassade | 7 r. Washington, 8ᵉ | 43 59 28 61 |

Nicaragua - Cap. Managua

| 15 | F6 | Ambassade | 11 r. de Sontay, 16ᵉ | 45 00 35 42 |

Niger - Cap. Niamey

27	G5	**Ambassade**	154 r. de Longchamp, 16ᵉ	45 04 80 60

Nigeria - Cap. Lagos

27	G5	**Ambassade**	173 av. Victor-Hugo, 16ᵉ	47 04 68 65

Norvège - Cap. Oslo

29	G9	**Ambassade**	28 r. Bayard, 8ᵉ	47 23 72 78
14	D4	**Chambre Commerce Franco-Norvégienne**	Neuilly - 88 av. Ch.-de-Gaulle	47 45 14 90
14	D4	**Office National du Tourisme**	—	47 45 14 90
18	F12	**Scandinavian Airlines System** (SAS)	30 bd des Capucines, 9ᵉ	47 42 06 14

Nouvelle-Zélande - Cap. Wellington

15	F6	**Ambassade**	7 ter r. Léonard-de-Vinci, 16ᵉ	45 00 24 11

Oman- Cap. Mascate

28	G8	**Ambassade**	50 av. d'Iéna, 16ᵉ	47 23 01 63

Ouganda - Cap. Kampala

27	G6	**Ambassade**	13 av. Raymond-Poincaré, 16ᵉ	47 27 46 80

Pakistan - Cap. Islamabad

16	F8	**Ambassade**	18 r. Lord-Byron, 8ᵉ	45 62 23 32
16	F8	**Pakistan International Airlines**	152 av. Champs-Élysées, 8ᵉ	45 62 92 41

Panama - Cap. Panama

41	L9	**Ambassade**	145 av. de Suffren, 15ᵉ	47 83 23 32

Paraguay - Cap. Asuncion

18	L16	**Ambassade**	Courbevoie -15 r. Carle-Hébert	47 88 19 12

Pays-Bas - Cap. Amsterdam

41	K10	**Ambassade**	7 r. Eblé, 7ᵉ	43 06 61 88
41	K10	**Consulat**	9 r. Eblé, 7ᵉ	43 06 61 88
17	D10	**Chambre de Commerce Franco-Néerlandaise**	109 bd Malesherbes, 8ᵉ	45 63 54 30
30	H11	**Institut Néerlandais**	121 r. de Lille, 7ᵉ	47 05 85 99
19	G13	**Lignes Aériennes Royales Néerlandaises** (KLM)	36 bis av. de l'Opéra, 2ᵉ	47 42 57 29
17	G9	**Office Néerlandais du Tourisme**	31-33 av. Champs Élysées, 8ᵉ	42 25 41 25

Pérou - Cap. Lima

16	G7	**Ambassade**	50 av. Kléber, 16ᵉ	47 04 34 53
17	G9	**Consulat**	30 r. Marbeuf, 8ᵉ	42 89 30 13
16	F8	**Office de Tourisme**	116 Bis av. Champs-Élysées, 8ᵉ	42 25 10 04

Philippines - Cap. Manille

27	H6	**Ambassade**	39 av. Georges-Mandel,16ᵉ	47 04 65 50
5	C9	**Philippine Airlines**	118 r. de Tocqueville, 17ᵉ	42 27 06 93
27	H6	**Services culturels**	39 av. Georges-Mandel, 16ᵉ	45 53 34 92

Pologne - Cap. Varsovie

29	J10	**Ambassade**	1 r. de Talleyrand, 7ᵉ	45 51 60 80
29	J10	**Consulat**	5 r. de Talleyrand, 7ᵉ	45 51 82 22
32	K15	**Bibliothèque Polonaise**	6 quai d'Orléans, 4ᵉ	43 54 35 61
29	G9	**Institut Culturel Polonais**	31 r. Jean-Goujon, 8ᵉ	42 25 10 57
31	K13	**Librairie Polonaise**	123 bd St-Germain, 6ᵉ	43 26 04 42
19	G13	**Lignes Aériennes Polonaises** (LOT)	18 r. Louis-le-Grand, 2ᵉ	47 42 05 60
19	G13	**Office du Tourisme Polonais Orbis**	49 av. de l'Opéra, 2ᵉ	47 42 07 42

Portugal - Cap. Lisbonne

15	G5	**Ambassade**	3 r. de Noisiel, 16ᵉ	47 27 35 29
45	N17	**Consulat**	187 r. du Chevaleret, 13ᵉ	45 85 03 60
16	F8	**Centre Culturel - Fondation C. Gulbenkian**	51 av. d'Iéna, 16ᵉ	47 20 86 84
18	F11	**Chambre de Com. Franco-Portugaise**	97 bd Haussmann, 8ᵉ	42 66 38 32
17	F10	**Office Commercial du Portugal**	135 bd Haussmann, 8ᵉ	45 63 93 30
18	F12	**Office de Tourisme**	7 r. Scribe, 9ᵉ	47 42 55 57
18	G12	**TAP Air Portugal**	9 bd de la Madeleine, 1ᵉʳ	42 96 15 65

Qatar - Cap. Doha

29	H9	Ambassade	57 quai d'Orsay, 7e	45 51 90 71

Roumanie - Cap. Bucarest

29	J9	Ambassade	5 r. de l'Exposition, 7e	47 05 49 54
29	J9	Consulat	5 r. de l'Exposition, 7e	47 05 84 99
19	G13	Office de Tourisme - Tarom (Cie aérienne)	38 av. de l'Opéra, 2e	47 42 27 14
29	J9	Section Commerciale	5 r. de l'Exposition, 7e	47 05 57 64

Rwanda - Cap. Kigali

17	E9	Ambassade	12 r. Jadin, 17e	42 27 36 31

Saint-Marin - Cap. Saint-Marin

17	F10	Ambassade	6 av. Franklin-Roosevelt, 8e	43 59 22 28
17	F10	Consulat	50 r. du Colisée, 8e	43 59 82 89

Saint-Siège - Cité du Vatican

28	G8	Nonciature Apostolique	10 av. du Prés.-Wilson, 16e	47 23 58 34

El Salvador - Cap. San Salvador

16	G7	Ambassade	12 r. Galilée, 16e	47 20 42 02
16	G7	Consulat	–	47 23 98 03

Sénégal - Cap. Dakar

29	H9	Ambassade	14 av. Robert-Schuman, 7e	47 05 39 45
28	G7	Consulat	22 r. Hamelin, 16e	45 53 75 86
38	K4	Office National de Tourisme	15 r. de Remusat, 16e	40 50 07 90

Seychelles - Cap. Port-Victoria

16	G8	Ambassade	53 bis, r. François-Ier, 8e	47 23 98 11
16	G18	Consulat (uniquement par courrier ou par téléphone)	53 r. François-Ier, 8e	47 20 26 26
17	F9	Office de Tourisme	32 r. de Ponthieu, 8e	42 89 85 33

Sierra Leone - Cap. Freetown

16	E8	Consulat	16 av. Hoche, 8e	42 56 14 73
17	E9	La Maison de la Sierra Leone	6 r. Médéric, 17e	42 67 54 39

Singapour - Cap. Singapour

15	F5	Ambassade	12 square de l'av.-Foch, 16e	45 00 33 61
31	H13	Office national du Tourisme	168 r. de Rivoli, 1er	42 97 16 16
19	G13	Singapore Airlines	35 av. de l'Opéra, 2e	42 61 53 09

Somalie - Cap. Mogadiscio

16	F8	Ambassade	26 r. Dumont-d'Urville, 16e	45 00 76 51

Soudan - Cap. Khartoum

29	G9	Ambassade	56 av. Montaigne, 8e	47 20 07 34

Sri Lanka - Cap. Colombo

18	F11	Ambassade	15 r. d'Astorg, 8e	42 66 35 01
19	G13	Air Lanka	9 r. du 4-Septembre, 2e	42 97 43 44
19	G13	Office du Tourisme	19 r. du 4-Septembre, 2e	42 60 49 99

Suède - Cap. Stockholm

30	J11	Ambassade	17, r. Barbet-de-Jouy, 7e	45 55 92 15
32	J16	Centre Culturel	11 r. Payenne, 3e	42 71 82 20
18	F12	Centre Suédois du Commerce Extérieur	67 bd Haussmann, 8e	42 66 08 88
32	J16	Office du Tourisme	146-150 av. Ch.-Élysées, 8e	42 25 65 52
18	F12	Scandinavian Airlines System (SAS)	30 bd des Capucines, 9e	47 42 06 14

Suisse - Cap. Berne

29	J10	Ambassade	142 r. de Grenelle, 7e	45 50 34 46
32	J16	Centre Culturel	32 r. Francs Bourgeois, 3e	42 71 44 50
31	G13	Chambre de Commerce Suisse	16 av. de l'Opéra, 1er	42 86 14 17
18	F12	Office National du Tourisme-Chemins de fer fédéraux	11 bis r. Scribe, 9e	47 42 45 45
19	G13	Swissair	38 av. de l'Opéra, 2e	45 81 11 01

Syrie - Cap. Damas

30	J11	**Ambassade**	20 r. Vaneau, 7ᵉ	45 50 26 91
29	J9	**Centre culturel arabe syrien**	12 av. de Tourville, 7ᵉ	47 05 30 11
17	F9	**Office de tourisme**	103 r. La Boétie, 8ᵉ	45 62 56 32
18	F12	**Syrian Arab Airlines** (Syrianair)	1 r. Auber, 9ᵉ	47 42 11 06

Tanzanie Cap. Dar es-Salam

5	C9	**Ambassade**	70 bd Péreire, 17ᵉ	47 66 21 77

Tchad - Cap. N'Djamena

15	G6	**Ambassade**	65 r. Belles-Feuilles, 16ᵉ	45 53 36 75

Tchécoslovaquie - Cap. Prague

28	J8	**Ambassade**	15 av. Charles-Floquet, 7ᵉ	47 34 29 10
31	J13	**—** (Section Consulaire)	18 r. Bonaparte, 6ᵉ	43 54 26 18
19	G13	**Ceskoslovenske Aerolinie** (CSA)	32 av. de l'Opéra, 2ᵉ	47 42 38 45
27	G6	**Chambre de Commerce Franco-Tchécoslovaque**	28 av. d'Eylau, 16ᵉ	47 04 45 78
19	G13	**Office Tchécoslovaque de Tourisme - Cedok**	32 av. de l'Opéra, 2ᵉ	47 42 38 45

Thaïlande - Cap. Bangkok

27	H6	**Ambassade**	8 r. Greuze, 16ᵉ	47 04 32 22
17	F9	**Office National du Tourisme**	90 av. Champs-Elysées, 8ᵉ	45 62 86 56
16	F8	**Thai Airways International**	123 av. Champs-Elysées, 8ᵉ	47 20 64 50

Togo - Cap. Lomé

4	C8	**Ambassade**	8 r. Alfred-Roll, 17ᵉ	43 80 12 13

Tunisie - Cap. Tunis

30	K11	**Ambassade**	25 r. Barbet-de-Jouy, 7ᵉ	45 55 95 98
28	G7	**Consulat**	17-19 r. de Lübeck, 16ᵉ	45 53 50 94
19	G13	**Office National du Tourisme**	32 av. de l'Opéra, 2ᵉ	47 42 72 67
18	G12	**Tunis Air**	17 r. Daunou, 2ᵉ	42 96 10 45

Turquie - Cap. Ankara

27	J6	**Ambassade**	16 av. de Lamballe, 16ᵉ	45 24 52 24
5	C9	**Consulat**	184 bd Malesherbes, 17ᵉ	42 27 32 72
17	F9	**Bureau de Tourisme**	102 av. Champs-Élysées, 8ᵉ	45 62 78 68
19	G13	**Turkish Airlines**	34 av. de l'Opéra, 2ᵉ	47 42 60 85

Unions des Républ. Socialistes Soviétiques (URSS) - Cap. Moscou

26	G4	**Ambassade**	40-50 bd Lannes, 16ᵉ	45 04 05 50
17	E9	**Consulat**	8 r. de Prony, 17ᵉ	47 63 50 20
17	G9	**Aeroflot** (Cie aérienne)	33 av. Champs-Élysées, 8ᵉ	42 25 43 81
29	G10	**Chambre de Commerce Franco-Soviétique**	22 av. Franklin-Roosevelt, 8ᵉ	42 25 97 10
19	F13	**Intourist**	7 bd des Capucines, 2ᵉ	47 42 47 40
31	J13	**Librairie du Globe**	2 r. de Buci, 6ᵉ	43 26 54 99
15	G5	**Représentation Commerciale**	49 r. de la Faisanderie, 16ᵉ	47 27 41 39

Uruguay - Cap. Montevideo

16	F7	**Ambassade**	15 r. Le Sueur, 16ᵉ	45 00 91 50

Vatican - (Voir Saint-Siège)

Venezuela - Cap. Caracas

16	G7	**Ambassade**	11 r. Copernic, 16ᵉ	45 53 29 98
28	H7	**Consulat**	42 av. du Prés.-Wilson, 16ᵉ	45 53 00 88
19	F13	**Viasa** (Cie aérienne)	5 bd des Capucines, 2ᵉ	47 42 20 07

Vietnam - Cap. Hanoï

38	L3	**Ambassade**	62 r. Boileau, 16ᵉ	45 24 50 63
14	D3	**Section commerciale**	Neuilly - 44 av. de Madrid	46 24 85 77

Yémen - (Républ. Arabe-RAY) - Cap. Sanaa

28	J8	**Ambassade**	21 av. Charles-Floquet, 7ᵉ	43 06 66 22
17	F9	**Yemenia (Yemen Airways)**	52 av. Champs-Élysées, 8ᵉ	42 56 06 00

		Yemen (Républ. Démocratique) - Cap. Aden		
28	G8	Ambassade	25 r. Georges Bizet, 16ᵉ	47 23 61 76
		Yougoslavie - Cap. Belgrade		
15	G5	Ambassade	54 r. de la Faisanderie, 16ᵉ	45 04 05 05
15	G5	Consulat	152 bis r. de Longchamp, 16ᵉ	45 04 56 78
32	H15	Centre Culturel	123 r. St-Martin, 4ᵉ	42 72 50 50
27	G6	Chambre économique	69 av. Raymond-Poincaré, 16ᵉ	47 04 92 76
45	K18	Librairie Yougofranc	55 r. Traversière, 12ᵉ	43 43 59 29
19	F13	Office de Tourisme	31 bd des Italiens, 2ᵉ	42 68 07 07
19	F13	Yugoslav Airlines (JAT)	—	42 68 06 06
		Zaïre - Cap. Kinshasa		
29	G9	Ambassade	32 cours Albert-1ᵉʳ, 8ᵉ	42 25 57 50
18	G12	Air Zaïre	7 bd de la Madeleine, 1ᵉʳ	47 03 91 65
		Zambie - Cap. Lusaka		
16	F8	Ambassade	76 av. d'Iéna, 16ᵉ	47 23 43 52
		Zimbabwe - Cap. Harare		
16	F8	Ambassade	5 r. de Tilsitt, 8ᵉ	47 63 48 31

*Pour vous diriger dans la banlieue de Paris,
utilisez les plans Michelin au 15 000ᵉ :*

   *n° 17 **Nord-Ouest** en 1 feuille*
   *n° 18 **Nord-Ouest** avec répertoire des rues*

   *n° 19 **Nord-Est** en 1 feuille*
   *n° 20 **Nord-Est** avec répertoire des rues*

   *n° 21 **Sud-Ouest** en 1 feuille*
   *n° 22 **Sud-Ouest** avec répertoire des rues*

   *n° 23 **Sud-Est** en 1 feuille*
   *n° 24 **Sud-Est** avec répertoire des rues*

*Pour visiter les **Environs de Paris**,
utilisez le **guide Vert Michelin***

Ces ouvrages se complètent utilement.

BIBLIOTHÈQUES - CENTRES CULTURELS
LIBRARIES, BIBLIOTHEKEN, BIBLIOTECAS

32	H15	**Centre Georges-Pompidou**	pl. Georges-Pompidou, 4e	42 77 12 33
33	K17	**Arsenal**	bd Henri IV, 4e	42 77 44 21
31	H13	**Arts Décoratifs**	109 r. de Rivoli, 1er	42 60 32 14
32	G16	**Conservatoire Nat. des Arts et Métiers**	292 r. St-Martin, 3e	42 71 24 14
🔞	K12	**Documentation Internat. Contemporaine**	Nanterre - 6 allée de l'Université	47 21 40 22
23	G21	**Documentation Scientifique et Technique**	25 r. du Retrait, 20e	43 58 35 59
42	K12	**Documentation Sciences Humaines**	54 bd Raspail, 6e	45 44 38 49
32	J16	**Forney**	1 r. du Figuier, 4e	42 78 14 60
32	J16	**Historique de la Ville de Paris**	24 r. Pavée, 4e	42 74 44 44
44	K16	**Institut du Monde Arabe**	r. des Fossés St-Bernard, 5e	46 34 25 25
32	H15	**Maison de la Poésie**	101 r. Rambuteau, 1er	42 36 27 53
31	J13	**Mazarine**	23 quai de Conti, 6e	43 54 89 48
44	M16	**Muséum Nat. d'Histoire Naturelle**	38 r. Geoffroy-St-Hilaire, 5e	43 31 71 24
31	G13	**Nationale** (BN)	58 r. de Richelieu, 2e	47 03 81 26
43	K14	**Nordique**	6 r. Valette, 5e	43 29 61 00
30	J12	**Protestantisme**	54 r. des Saints-Pères, 7e	45 48 62 07
43	L14	**Ste-Geneviève**	10 pl. du Panthéon, 5e	43 29 61 00
31	H14	**Vidéothèque de Paris**	Forum des Halles Porte Saint-Eustache, 1e	40 26 34 30

Paris compte de nombreuses bibliothèques d'études et 55 bibliothèques municipales de prêt. Outre les plus connues, générales ou spécialisées, indiquées ci-dessus, citons-en quelques autres, très spécialisées, comme les bibliothèques des Arts du spectacle (à l'Arsenal), du Saulchoir (religion), de la Préfecture de Police, de l'Observatoire de Meudon...

Les bibliothèques de prêt et de consultation, qui offrent parfois un département discothèque ou cassettothèque, sont ouvertes au public dans la plupart des Mairies et divers autres centres ; la liste des bibliothèques pour la jeunesse y est disponible.

Pour connaître les adresses des bibliothèques et Centres Culturels étrangers, voir p. 57 à 68.

Salles d'expositions

29	G10	**Galeries Nationales du Grand Palais**	av. du Gén.-Eisenhower, 8e	42 89 54 10
28	G8	**Palais de Tokyo**	13 av. Président-Wilson, 16e	47 23 36 53
31	H14	**Pavillon des Arts**	101 r. Rambuteau, 1er	42 33 82 50
29	G10	**Petit Palais**	av. Winston-Churchill, 8e	42 65 12 73

CIMETIÈRES
CEMETERIES, FRIEDHÖFE, CEMENTERIOS

38	M3	**Auteuil**	57 r. Claude-Lorrain, 16e	46 51 20 83
5	B10	**Batignolles**	8 r. St-Just, 17e	46 27 03 18
23	F22	**Belleville**	40 r. du Télégraphe, 20e	46 36 66 23
47	N21	**Bercy**	329 r. de Charenton, 12e	43 48 28 93
60	R23	**Charenton**	av. de Gravelle, 12e	43 68 62 60
35	H22	**Charonne**	pl. St. Blaise, 20e	43 71 40 66
56	S15	**Gentilly**	5 r. de Ste-Hélène, 13e	45 88 38 80
39	M6	**Grenelle**	174 r. St-Charles, 15e	45 57 13 43
6	C12	**Montmartre**	av. Rachel, 18e	43 87 64 24
42	M12	**Montparnasse**	3 bd Edgar-Quinet, 14e	43 20 68 52
54	R11	**Montrouge**	18 av. Pte-de-Montrouge, 14e	46 56 52 52
27	H6	**Passy**	2 r. du Cdt-Schlœsing, 16e	47 27 51 42
35	H21	**Père-Lachaise**	16 r. du Repos, 20e	43 70 70 33
47	L22	**Picpus**	35 r. de Picpus, 12e	43 42 24 22
48	M23	**St-Mandé (Sud)**	r. du Général-Archinard, 12e	43 46 03 06
7	C14	**St-Pierre** (cim. du Calvaire)	2 r. du Mont-Cenis, 18e	
7	C13	**St-Vincent**	6 r. Lucien-Gaulard, 18e	46 06 29 78
59	P21	**Valmy**	av. Pte-de-Charenton, 12e	43 68 62 60
39	M6	**Vaugirard**	320 r. Lecourbe, 15e	45 57 26 30
22	D20	**La Villette**	46 r. d'Hautpoul, 19e	42 08 05 45

Hors des limites de Paris se situent les cimetières parisiens de Bagneux (🞐🞐 F21), la Chapelle (9 A17), Ivry (🞐🞐 F2-F3), Pantin (12 A23), St-Ouen (🔞 K24) et Thiais (🞐🞐 L3-M3).

COMMERCE
BUSINESS, GESCHÄFT, COMERCIO

Salons, Foires, Expositions
Fairs, Exhibitions, Messen, Ausstellungen, Salones, Ferias, Exposiciones

22	B13	Comité des Expositions de Paris	Boulogne Billancourt - 55 quai Alphonse Le Gallo	49 09 60 91
45	M18	Espace Austerlitz	24 quai d'Austerlitz, 13e	47 20 37 36
4	C7	Espace Champerret	r. Jean Ostreicher, 17e	47 20 37 36
10	C20	Grande Halle de la Villette	211 av. Jean-Jaurès, 19e	42 49 77 22
19	F14	Hôtel des Ventes	9 r. Drouot, 9e	42 46 17 11
15	E6	Palais des Congrès	2 pl. de la Pte-Maillot, 17e	46 40 22 22
51	N6	Parc des Expositions (S.E.P.E)	Pte-de-Versailles, 15e	48 42 87 00
20	B16	Parc d'Expositions de Paris-Nord	Villepinte - ZAC Paris-Nord II	48 63 30 30

Grands Magasins et Centres commerciaux
Department stores and shopping centres, Kaufhäuser, Einkaufszentren, Grandes Almacenes y Centros Comerciales

32	J15	Bazar de l'Hôtel-de-Ville Rivoli	52 r. de Rivoli, 4e	42 74 90 00
10	C19	— Flandre	119 r. de Flandre, 19e	40 34 71 69
39	K6	Beaugrenelle	36 r. Linois, 15e	45 75 71 31
30	K11	Au Bon Marché	38 r. de Sèvres, 7e	45 49 21 22
42	L11	C & A Maine Montparnasse	1 r. de l'Arrivée, 15e	45 38 52 76
31	H14	— Rivoli	122-124 r. de Rivoli, 1er	42 33 71 95
16	E8	FNAC Etoile	26 av. de Wagram, 8e	47 66 52 50
31	H14	— Forum des Halles	1-7 r. Pierre-Lescot, 1er	42 61 81 18
42	L12	— Montparnasse	136 r. de Rennes, 6e	45 44 39 12
32	H15	Forum des Halles	1 r. Pierre-Lescot, 1er	42 96 68 74
56	P16	Galaxie	30 av. d'Italie, 13e	45 80 09 09
18	F12	Galeries Lafayette Haussmann	40 bd Haussmann, 9e	42 82 34 56
42	L11	— Montparnasse	22 r. du Départ, 15e	45 38 52 87
42	M11	Inno Montparnasse	35 r. du Départ, 14e	43 20 69 30
47	K21	— Nation	20 bd de Charonne, 20e	43 73 17 59
27	J5	— Passy	53 r. de Passy, 16e	45 24 52 32
42	L11	Maine-Montparnasse	66 bd du Montparnasse, 15e	45 38 52 54
18	F12	Marks & Spencer	35-41 bd Haussmann, 9e	47 42 42 91
15	E6	Palais des Congrès	2 pl. de la Pte-Maillot, 17e	46 40 22 22
18	F12	Au Printemps Haussmann	64 bd Haussmann, 9e	42 82 50 00
56	P16	— Italie	30 av. d'Italie, 13e	45 81 11 50
47	K22	— Nation	25 cours Vincennes, 20e	43 71 12 41
33	G17	— République	pl. de la République, 11e	43 55 39 09
16	E8	— Ternes	30 av. des Ternes, 17e	43 80 20 00
31	H14	Samaritaine	19 r. de la Monnaie, 1er	45 08 33 33
18	G12	Aux Trois Quartiers	17 bd de la Madeleine, 1er	42 60 39 30

Marchés, Markets, Märkte, Mercados

33	G17	Carreau du Temple	r. Dupetit-Thouars, 3e	42 71 08 80
46	N20	Entrepôts de Bercy	1 cour Chamonard, 12e	43 43 15 41
31	H13	Le Louvre des Antiquaires	2 pl. du Palais-Royal, 1er	42 97 27 00
7	A14	Marché aux Puces	St-Ouen - 85 r. des Rosiers	40 11 59 69
68		Marché d'Intérêt Nat. de Paris-Rungis	Rungis - 1 r. de la Tour	46 87 35 35
28	K8	Le Village Suisse	54 av. Motte-Picquet, 15e	43 06 69 90

Nombreuses sont les artères commerçantes de Paris :

- *les unes pour leur choix d'articles de luxe et la haute couture : avenue Montaigne et Champs Elysées aux diverses galeries ; place et avenue de l'Opéra, rue Tronchet, rue Royale, rue du Fbg St-Honoré.*
- *les autres pour leur activité principale : rue de la Paix et place Vendôme (joaillerie-bijouterie) ; rue St-Lazare et boulevard St-Michel (chaussures et sacs) ; rue de Passy et de Sèvres (habillement) ; rue du Fbg-St-Antoine (bois et meubles), rue de Paradis (cristaux et porcelaines).*

Sur quelques places se tiennent des marchés de plein air : marchés aux fleurs et aux oiseaux.

CULTES (¹)

CHURCHES,
KIRCHEN UND ANDERE KULTSTÄTTEN, CULTOS

Églises et chapelles catholiques
Catholic churches and chapels
Katholische Kirchen und Kapellen, Iglesias y Capillas Católicas

18	F11	**Archevêché** (Maison Diocésiane)	8 r. de la Ville-l'Evêque, 8ᵉ	42 66 90 15
32	K15	**Notre-Dame** (cathédrale)	6 Parvis Notre-Dame, 4ᵉ	43 26 07 39
17	E9	**Annonciation** (égl. Dominicains)	222 r. du Fg-St-Honoré, 8ᵉ	45 63 63 04
34	J20	**Bon Pasteur** (égl.)	177 r. de Charonne, 11ᵉ	43 71 05 24
23	G22	**Cœur Eucharistique de Jésus** (égl.)	22 r. du Lt-Chauré, 20ᵉ	43 60 74 55
16	F8	**Corpus Christi** (chap.)	23 av. Friedland, 8ᵉ	42 25 20 62
56	N16	**Deux Moulins** (chap.)	185-187 r. du Château-des-Rentiers, 13ᵉ	45 70 94 75
54	P12	**Franciscains** (chap.)	7 r. Marie-Rose, 14ᵉ	45 40 74 98
55	R13	**Franciscaines Missionnaires de Marie** (chap.)	32-34 av. Reille, 14ᵉ	45 89 15 51
47	L22	**Immaculée Conception** (égl.)	34 r. du Rendez-Vous, 12ᵉ	43 07 75 29
21	D17	**Mission Belge** (chap.)	228 r. La Fayette, 10ᵉ	46 07 95 76
30	K11	**Missions Etrangères de Paris** (chap.)	128 r. du Bac, 7ᵉ	45 48 19 92
42	L11	**N.-D. des Anges** (chap.)	102 bis r. de Vaugirard, 6ᵉ	42 22 97 57
26	J4	— **de l'Assomption de Passy** (égl.)	90 r. de l'Assomption, 16ᵉ	42 24 41 50
38	L4	— **d'Auteuil** (égl.)	Place Théodore Rivière, 16ᵉ	45 25 30 17
23	G21	— **Auxiliatrice** (chap.)	15 r. du Retrait, 20ᵉ	46 36 97 67
32	H16	— **des Blancs Manteaux** (égl.)	12 r. des Blancs-Manteaux, 4ᵉ	42 72 09 37
41	K9	— **du Bon Conseil** (chap.)	6 r. A.-de-Lapparent, 7ᵉ	47 83 56 68
8	B15	— **du Bon Conseil** (égl.)	140 r. de Clignancourt, 18ᵉ	46 06 39 80
20	G15	— **de Bonne-Nouvelle** (égl.)	25 r. de la Lune, 2ᵉ	42 33 65 74
22	D19	— **des Buttes-Chaumont** (égl.)	80 r. de Meaux, 19ᵉ	42 06 16 86
27	H6	— **de Chaldée** (rite oriental cathol.)	4 r. Greuze, 16ᵉ	45 53 23 09
42	L12	— **des Champs** (égl.)	91 bd du Montparnasse, 6ᵉ	43 22 03 06
7	B14	— **de Clignancourt** (égl.)	2 pl. Jules-Joffrin, 18ᵉ	42 54 39 13
15	D6	— **de la Compassion** (chap.)	pl. du Général-Kœnig, 17ᵉ	45 74 83 31
5	C9	— **de Confiance** (chap.)	164 r. de Saussure, 17ᵉ	47 66 87 72
22	G20	— **de la Croix** (égl.)	3 pl. de Ménilmontant, 20ᵉ	46 36 74 88
33	J18	— **d'Espérance**	4 r. du Cdt Lamy, 11ᵉ	47 00 12 11
9	C18	— **des Foyers** (chap.)	18 r. de Tanger, 19ᵉ	40 34 93 75
57	P17	— **de la Gare** (égl.)	pl. Jeanne d'Arc, 13ᵉ	45 83 35 75
40	K7	— **de Grâce** (égl.)	4-6 r. Fondary, 15ᵉ	45 77 46 50
27	J6	— **de Grâce de Passy** (égl.)	10 r. de l'Annonciation, 16ᵉ	45 25 76 32
43	L14	— **du Liban** (rite maronite)	17 r. d'Ulm, 5ᵉ	43 29 47 60
19	E13	— **de Lorette** (égl.)	18 bis r. Châteaudun, 9ᵉ	48 78 92 72
23	F21	— **de Lourdes** (égl.)	130 r. Pelleport, 20ᵉ	43 62 61 60
41	L9	— **du Lys** (chap.)	7 r. Blomet, 15ᵉ	45 67 81 81
20	D16	— **des Malades** (chap.)	15 r. Ph.-de-Girard, 10ᵉ	46 07 92 87
30	K11	— **de la Médaille Miraculeuse** (chap.)	140 r. du Bac, 7ᵉ	45 48 10 13
46	N20	— **de la Nativité de Bercy** (égl.)	9 pl. Lachambeaudie, 12 ᵉ	43 07 86 51
39	N6	— **de Nazareth** (égl.)	351 r. Lecourbe, 15ᵉ	45 58 50 26
23	F22	— **des Otages** (égl.)	81 r. Haxo, 20ᵉ	43 64 62 84
43	M13	— **de Paix** (chap.)	32 r. Boissonade, 14ᵉ	43 22 42 03
34	H20	— **du Perpétuel Secours** (basilique)	55 bd Ménilmontant, 11ᵉ	48 05 94 93
53	P9	— **du Rosaire** (égl.)	194 r. R.-Losserand, 14ᵉ	45 43 13 16
27	H6	— **du St-Sacrement** (chap.)	20 r. Cortambert, 16ᵉ	45 03 34 12
40	N8	— **de la Salette** (égl.)	27 r. de Dantzig, 15ᵉ	45 31 12 16
41	N10	— **du Travail** (égl.)	59 r. Vercingétorix, 14ᵉ	43 20 09 51
31	G14	— **des Victoires** (basilique)	pl. des Petits-Pères, 2ᵉ	42 60 90 47
27	J5	**Religieuses de l'Assomption** (chap.)	17 r. de l'Assomption, 16ᵉ	46 47 84 56
7	C14	**Sacré-Cœur** (basilique)	pl. Parvis Sacré-Cœur, 18ᵉ	42 51 17 02
55	P14	**St-Albert le Grand** (égl.)	122 r. de la Glacière, 13ᵉ	45 89 19 76
33	H18	— **Ambroise** (égl.)	2 r. St-Ambroise, 11ᵉ	43 55 56 18
18	D12	— **André de l'Europe** (égl.)	24 bis r. de Leningrad, 8ᵉ	45 22 27 29
52	P7	— **Antoine de Padoue** (égl.)	52 bd Lefebvre, 15ᵉ	45 31 12 84
45	K18	— **Antoine des Quinze-Vingts** (égl.)	66 av. Ledru-Rollin, 12ᵉ	43 43 93 94

(1) Un centre d'information et de documentation religieux est à votre service, 8 rue Massillon, 75004 PARIS ; ☎ 46 33 01 01. Informations religieuses téléphonées 43 29 11 22.

18	E11	**St-Augustin** (égl.)	pl. St-Augustin, 8ᵉ	45 22 23 12
42	M11	**— Bernard** (chap.)	34 av. du Maine, 15ᵉ	43 21 50 76
8	D16	**— Bernard de la Chapelle** (égl.)	11 r. Affre, 18ᵉ	42 64 52 12
36	J23	**— Charles de la Croix-St-Simon** (chap.)	16 bis r. Croix-St-Simon, 20ᵉ	43 70 77 96
17	D10	**— Charles de Monceau** (égl.)	22 bis r. Legendre, 17ᵉ	47 63 05 84
39	L5	**— Christophe de Javel** (égl.)	4 r. St-Christophe, 15ᵉ	45 77 63 78
8	C16	**— Denys de la Chapelle** (égl.)	16 r. de la Chapelle, 18ᵉ	46 07 35 52
33	H17	**— Denys du St-Sacrement** (égl.)	68 r. de Turenne, 3ᵉ	42 72 28 96
55	N13	**— Dominique** (égl.)	20 r. Tombe-Issoire, 14ᵉ	45 65 20 25
46	L20	**— Éloi** (égl.)	1 pl. M.-de-Fontenay, 12ᵉ	43 07 55 65
47	M21	**— Esprit** (égl.)	186 av. Daumesnil, 12ᵉ	43 07 52 84
44	L15	**— Étienne du Mont** (égl.)	pl. Ste-Geneviève, 5ᵉ	43 54 11 79
19	F14	**— Eugène** (égl.)	4 bis r. Ste-Cécile, 9ᵉ	48 24 70 25
31	H14	**— Eustache** (égl.)	r. du Jour, 1ᵉʳ	42 36 31 05
16	E7	**— Ferdinand-Ste-Thérèse** (égl.)	27 r. d'Armaillé, 17ᵉ	45 74 00 32
38	L3	**— François** (chap.)	44 r. Molitor, 15ᵉ	46 51 37 54
22	E20	**— François d'Assise** (égl.)	9 r. de Mouzaïa, 19ᵉ	46 07 32 57
17	D9	**— François de Sales** (égl.)	6 r. Brémontier, 17ᵉ	47 66 75 90
29	K10	**— François-Xavier** (égl.)	bd des Invalides, 7ᵉ	47 83 32 12
47	K22	**— Gabriel** (égl.)	5 r. des Pyrénées, 20ᵉ	43 72 59 73
21	E18	**— Georges** (égl.)	114 av. Simon-Bolivar, 19ᵉ	46 07 26 88
26	K4	**— Georges** (rite byzantin-roumain)	38 r. Ribera, 18ᵉ	45 27 22 59
31	H14	**— Germain l'Auxerrois** (égl.)	2 pl. du Louvre, 1ᵉʳ	42 60 13 96
35	H22	**— Germain de Charonne** (égl.)	4 pl. St-Blaise, 20ᵉ	43 71 42 04
31	J13	**— Germain-des-Prés** (égl.)	3 r. St-G.-des-Prés, 6ᵉ	43 25 41 71
32	J15	**— Gervais-St-Protais** (égl.)	pl. St-Gervais, 4ᵉ	48 87 32 02
57	R17	**— Hippolyte** (égl.)	27 av. de Choisy, 13ᵉ	45 85 12 05
15	G6	**— Honoré d'Eylau** (nouvelle église)	66 bis av. R.-Poincaré, 16ᵉ	45 01 96 00
30	K12	**— Ignace** (égl.)	33 r. de Sèvres, 6ᵉ	45 48 25 25
43	L14	**— Jacques du Haut Pas** (égl.)	252 r. St-Jacques, 5ᵉ	43 25 91 70
10	C19	**— Jacques-St-Christophe** (égl.)	6 pl. de Bitche, 19ᵉ	40 34 93 75
22	E20	**— Jean-Baptiste de Belleville** (égl.)	139 r. de Belleville, 19ᵉ	42 08 54 54
40	L7	**— Jean-Baptiste de Grenelle** (égl.)	23 pl. Etienne-Pernet, 15ᵉ	48 28 64 34
41	M10	**— Jean-Baptiste de la Salle** (égl.)	9 r. du Dr-Roux, 15ᵉ	47 34 19 95
35	J21	**— Jean Bosco** (égl.)	79 r. Alexandre-Dumas, 20ᵉ	43 70 29 27
19	D13	**— Jean de Montmartre** (égl.)	19 r. des Abbesses, 18ᵉ	46 06 43 96
32	H16	**— Jean-St-François** (égl.)	13 r. du Perche, 3ᵉ	42 78 31 93
21	G18	**— Joseph** (égl.)	161 r. St-Maur, 11ᵉ	43 57 58 50
21	D17	**— Joseph Artisan** (égl.)	214 r. La Fayette, 10ᵉ	46 07 92 87
42	K12	**— Joseph des Carmes** (égl.)	70 r. de Vaugirard, 6ᵉ	42 22 41 80
6	B11	**— Joseph des Epinettes** (chap.)	2 impasse des Epinettes, 17ᵉ	46 27 89 70
6	B11	**— — —**	40 r. Pouchet, 17ᵉ	46 27 11 24
31	K14	**— Julien le Pauvre** (rite grec-byzantin)	1 r. St-Julien-le-Pauvre, 5ᵉ	43 54 20 41
40	M8	**— Lambert de Vaugirard** (égl.)	Pl. Gerbert, 15ᵉ	48 28 56 90
20	F16	**— Laurent** (égl.)	68 bd Magenta, 10ᵉ	46 07 24 65
28	K8	**— Léon** (égl.)	1 pl. du Card.-Amette, 15ᵉ	45 67 01 32
32	H15	**— Leu-St-Gilles** (égl.)	92 bis r. St-Denis, 1ᵉʳ	42 33 50 22
18	F12	**— Louis d'Antin** (égl.)	63 r. Caumartin, 9ᵉ	45 26 65 34
29	K9	**— Louis-Ecole Militaire** (chap.)	13 pl. Joffre, 7ᵉ	
32	K16	**— Louis en l'Ile** (égl.)	19 bis r. St-L.-en-l'Ile, 4ᵉ	46 34 11 60
29	J10	**— Louis des Invalides** (égl.)	Hôtel des Invalides, 7ᵉ	45 55 92 30
44	M16	**— Marcel** (égl.)	80 bd de l'Hôpital, 13ᵉ	47 07 27 43
C6	D6	**— Martin-de-Porrès** (chap.)	41 r. Jacques-Ibert, 17ᵉ	40 55 01 12
21	F17	**— Martin des Champs** (égl.)	36 r. Albert-Thomas, 10ᵉ	42 08 36 60
44	M15	**— Médard** (égl.)	141 r. Mouffetard, 5ᵉ	43 36 14 92
32	H15	**— Merry** (égl.)	78 r. St-Martin, 4ᵉ	42 71 93 93
6	C11	**— Michel des Batignolles** (égl.)	12 bis r. St-Jean, 17ᵉ	43 87 33 94
32	G15	**— Nicolas des Champs** (égl.)	252 bis r. St-Martin, 3ᵉ	42 72 92 54
32	K15	**— Nicolas Hors les Murs** (égl.)	15 r. des Bernardins, 5ᵉ	43 54 21 00
32	J16	**— Paul-St-Louis** (égl.)	99 r. St-Antoine, 4ᵉ	42 72 30 32
17	F10	**— Philippe du Roule** (égl.)	154 r. du Fg-St-Honoré, 8ᵉ	43 59 24 56
41	L9	**— Pie X** (Italie)	36 r. Miollis, 15ᵉ	47 83 58 65
28	G8	**— Pierre de Chaillot** (égl.)	33 av. Marceau, 16ᵉ	47 20 12 33
29	H9	**— Pierre du Gros Caillou** (égl.)	92 r. St. Dominique, 7ᵉ	45 55 22 38
7	C14	**— Pierre de Montmartre** (égl.)	2 r. du Mont-Cenis, 18ᵉ	46 06 57 63
54	P12	**— Pierre de Montrouge** (égl.)	Pl. Victor Basch, 14ᵉ	45 40 66 08
9	A17	**— Pierre-St-Paul** (chap.)	44 r. Charles-Hermite, 18ᵉ	40 38 08 11
31	G13	**— Roch** (égl.)	296 r. St-Honoré, 1ᵉʳ	42 60 81 69
31	K14	**— Séverin** (égl.)	1 r. des Prêtres-St-Séverin, 5ᵉ	43 25 96 63
31	K13	**— Sulpice** (égl.)	pl. St-Sulpice, 6ᵉ	46 33 21 78

30	J12	**St-Thomas d'Aquin** (égl.)	pl. St-Thomas-d'Aquin, 7ᵉ	42 22 59 74
20	E15	**— Vincent de Paul** (égl.)	pl. Franz-Liszt, 10ᵉ	48 78 47 47
42	K11	**— Vincent de Paul**	95 r. de Sèvres, 6ᵉ	42 22 63 70
		(chap. Pères Lazaristes)		
30	J12	**— Vladimir le Grand**	51 r. des Saints-Pères, 6ᵉ	45 48 48 65
		(rite oriental ukrainien)		
56	P15	**Ste-Anne Maison Blanche** (égl.)	188 r. de Tolbiac, 13ᵉ	45 89 34 73
48	L23	**— Bernadette** (chap.)	12 av. Pte-de-Vincennes, 12ᵉ	43 07 75 29
38	L4	**— Bernadette** (chap.)	4 r. d'Auteuil, 16ᵉ	45 25 30 17
11	C21	**— Claire** (égl.)	179 bd Sérurier, 19ᵉ	42 05 42 35
30	J11	**— Clotilde** (égl.)	23 bis, r. Las-Cases, 7ᵉ	47 05 22 46
22	D20	**— Colette** (chap.)	41 r. d'Hautpoul, 19ᵉ	46 07 32 57
32	H16	**— Croix-St-Jean** (rite arménien)	13 r. du Perche, 3ᵉ	42 78 31 93
32	G16	**— Elisabeth** (égl.)	195 r. du Temple, 3ᵉ	48 87 56 77
7	B13	**— Geneviève-des-Gdes Carrières** (égl.)	174 r. Championnet, 18ᵉ	46 27 84 43
7	B14	**— Hélène** (égl.)	4 r. Esclangon, 18ᵉ	46 06 16 99
55	R13	**— Jeanne d'Arc** (chap. Franciscaines)	32 av. Reille, 14ᵉ	45 89 15 51
37	M2	**— Jeanne de Chantal** (égl.)	96 bd Murat, 16ᵉ	46 51 03 30
34	K19	**— Marguerite** (égl.)	36 r. St-Bernard, 11ᵉ	43 71 34 24
26	K4	**— Marie** (Abbaye bénédictine)	3 r. de la Source, 16ᵉ	45 25 30 07
6	C11	**— Marie des Batignolles** (égl.)	77 pl. Dr-F.-Lobligeois, 17ᵉ	46 27 57 67
18	G11	**— Marie-Madeleine** (égl.)	pl. de la Madeleine, 8ᵉ	42 65 52 17
4	C7	**— Odile** (égl.)	2 av. Stéph.-Mallarmé, 17ᵉ	42 27 18 37
18	D12	**— Rita** (chap.)	65 bd de Clichy, 9ᵉ	48 74 99 23
56	P15	**— Rosalie** (égl.)	50 bd Auguste-Blanqui, 13ᵉ	43 31 36 83
26	K4	**— Thérèse** (chap.)	40 r. La Fontaine, 16ᵉ	45 24 43 04
18	E12	**— Trinité** (égl.)	pl. d'Estienne-d'Orves, 9ᵉ	48 74 12 77
38	K4	**— Trinité** (rite byzantin-russe)	39 r. François-Gérard, 16ᵉ	45 20 05 53
43	M14	**Val de Grâce** (égl.)	1 pl. Laveran, 5ᵉ	43 29 12 31

Services in foreign languages, Gottesdienste in Fremdsprachen, Cultos en idiomas extranjeros

27	H5	**Cœur Immaculé de Marie** (Espagnol)	51 bis r. de la Pompe, 16ᵉ	45 04 23 34
30	G12	**N.D. de l'Assomption** (Polonais)	pl. M. Barrès, 1ᵉʳ	42 60 93 85
29	G9	**— de la Consolation** (Italien)	23 r. Jean-Goujon, 8ᵉ	42 25 61 84
23	E22	**— de Fatima-Marie Médiatrice** (Sanctuaire)	48 bd Serurier, 19ᵉ	
		(Portugais)		
15	G5	**St-Albert le Grand** (Allemand)	38 r. Spontini, 16ᵉ	47 04 31 49
16	E8	**St-Joseph** (Anglophone)	50 av. Hoche, 8ᵉ	47 27 28 56
34	K20	**Ste-Famille** (Italien)	46 r. de Montreuil, 11ᵉ	43 72 49 30

Églises issues de la Réforme

Protestant churches, Protestantische Kirchen, Iglesias Reformistas

18	E12	**Fédération Protestante de France**	47 r. de Clichy, 9ᵉ	48 74 15 08

Reformed churches, Reformierte Kirchen, Culto Reformado

18	E12	**Eglise Réformée de France** (Bureau National)	47 r. de Clichy, 9ᵉ	48 74 90 92
27	H6	**Annonciation** (de l')	19 r. Cortambert, 16ᵉ	45 03 43 10
38	L3	**Auteuil** (d')	53 r. Erlanger, 16ᵉ	42 51 72 85
18	D11	**Batignolles** (des)	44 bd des Batignolles, 17ᵉ	43 87 69 49
22	F19	**Belleville** (de)	97 r. Julien-Lacroix, 20ᵉ	43 66 15 39
35	H22	**Béthanie** (de)	185 r. des Pyrénées, 20ᵉ	46 36 25 58
15	E6	**Étoile** (de l')	54 av. de la Grande-Armée, 17ᵉ	45 74 41 79
33	J17	**Foyer de l'Ame**	7 bis r. Pasteur-Wagner, 11ᵉ	47 00 47 33
40	K8	**— de Grenelle**	17 r. de l'Avre, 15ᵉ	45 79 81 49
42	L12	**Luxembourg** (du)	58 r. Madame, 6ᵉ	45 48 13 50
7	C14	**Maison Verte** (Montmartre)	127 r. Marcadet, 18ᵉ	42 54 61 25
31	H14	**Oratoire du Louvre**	145 r. St-Honoré, 1ᵉʳ	42 60 21 64
30	J11	**Pentemont** (de)	106 r. de Grenelle, 7ᵉ	42 22 07 69
41	N10	**Plaisance** (de)	95 r. de l'Ouest, 14ᵉ	45 43 91 11
44	N15	**Port-Royal** (de)	18 bd Arago, 13ᵉ	45 35 30 56
20	E15	**Rencontre** (de la)	17 r. des Petits-Hôtels, 10ᵉ	48 24 96 43
18	F11	**St-Esprit** (du)	5 r. Roquépine, 8ᵉ	42 65 43 58
33	J17	**Ste-Marie**	17 r. St-Antoine, 4ᵉ	43 79 82 59

Culte Luthérien, *Lutheran churches, Lutherische Kirchen, Culto Luterano*

56	N16	**Égl. Évangélique Luthérienne de Paris**	13 r. Godefroy, 13ᵉ	45 82 19 99
5	D10	— Ascension (de l')	47 r. Dulong, 17ᵉ	47 63 90 10
32	J16	— Billettes (des)	24 r. des Archives, 4ᵉ	42 72 38 79
34	K20	— Bon Secours (du)	20 r. Titon, 11ᵉ	43 73 04 57
19	F14	— Rédemption (de la)	16 r. Chauchat, 9ᵉ	47 70 80 30
40	L8	— Résurrection (de la)	8 r. Quinault, 15ᵉ	
29	J9	— St-Jean	147 r. de Grenelle, 7ᵉ	47 05 85 66
43	M13	—˙ St Marcel	24 r. Pierre-Nicole, 5ᵉ	43 36 03 89
8	C15	— St-Paul	90 bd Barbès, 18ᵉ	46 06 91 18
22	D19	— St-Pierre	55, r. Manin, 19ᵉ	42 08 45 56
56	N16	— Trinité (de la)	174 bd Vincent-Auriol, 13ᵉ	43 36 03 89

Culte Baptiste, *Baptist churches, Baptistische Kirchen, Culto Bautista*

30	J12	**Égl. Évangélique Baptiste**	48 r. de Lille, 7ᵉ	42 61 13 95
47	M22	— —	32 r. Victor-Chevreuil, 12ᵉ	43 43 45 10
42	N11	— —	123 av. du Maine, 14ᵉ	43 22 51 57
22	B14	— du Point du Jour	Boulogne - 133 route de la Reine	46 47 69 60
6	B12	**Égl. du Tabernacle**	163 bis r. Belliard, 18ᵉ	46 27 43 12

Cultes en langues étrangères
Services in foreign languages, Gottesdienste in Fremdsprachen, Cultos en idiomas extranjeros

16	G8	**American Cathedral in Paris**	23 av. George-V, 8ᵉ	47 20 17 92
29	G9	**Church of Scotland** (Écosse)	17 r. Bayard, 8ᵉ	48 78 47 94
18	E12	**Deutsche Evangelische Christus-Kirche**	25 r. Blanche, 9ᵉ	45 26 79 43
56	N16	**Eglise Réformée néerlandaise**	172 bd Vincent-Auriol, 13ᵉ	47 02 36 21
16	F8	**Frederikscircken** (Danemark)	17 r. Lord-Byron, 8ᵉ	42 56 12 84
29	G9	**Reformatus Templom** (Hongrie)	17 r. Bayard, 8ᵉ	48 57 60 71
16	F8	**St George's Anglican Church**	7 r. A.-Vacquerie, 16ᵉ	47 20 22 51
18	F11	**St Michael's English Church**	5 r. d'Aguesseau, 8ᵉ	47 42 70 88
17	E9	**Svenska Kyrkan** (Suède)	9 r. Médéric, 17ᵉ	47 63 70 33
29	H9	**The American Church in Paris**	65 quai d'Orsay, 7ᵉ	47 05 07 99

Églises Orthodoxes

38	L3	**Apparition de la Ste-Vierge** (Russe)	87 bd Exelmans, 16ᵉ	46 51 92 25
44	K15	**N.-D. Joie des Affligés et Ste-Geneviève**	4 r. St-Victor, 5ᵉ	45 82 67 70
52	N7	**Présentation de la Ste-Vierge** (Russe)	91 r. O.-de-Serres, 15ᵉ	42 50 53 66
16	E8	**St-Alexandre Newski** (cathédrale) Russe	12 r. Daru, 8ᵉ	42 27 37 34
28	G8	**St-Etienne** (cathédrale) Grecque	7 r. Georges-Bizet, 16ᵉ	47 20 82 35
29	G9	**St-Jean-Baptiste** (cathédrale) rite arménien	15 r. Jean-Goujon, 8ᵉ	43 59 67 03
8	B15	**St-Sava** (Serbe)	23 r. du Simplon, 18ᵉ	42 55 31 05
41	L9	**St-Séraphin de Sarov** (Russe)	91 r. Lecourbe, 15ᵉ	42 73 05 03
22	D19	**St-Serge** (Russe)	93 r. de Crimée, 19ᵉ	42 08 12 93
22	E20	**St-Simon** (Ukrainien)	6 r. de Palestine, 19ᵉ	42 05 93 62
40	L7	**Ste-Nino** (Géorgien)	6 r. de la Rosière, 15ᵉ	42 02 25 29
32	H15	**Ste-Trinité**	30 bd de Sébastopol, 4ᵉ	47 39 86 84
43	K14	**Sts-Archanges** (Roumain)	9 bis, r. J.-de-Beauvais, 5ᵉ	43 54 67 47
19	E13	**Sts-Constantin et Hélène** (Grecque)	2 bis, r. Laferrière, 9ᵉ	48 78 35 53
38	M3	**Tous les Saints de la Terre Russe** (Russe)	19 r. Claude-Lorrain, 16ᵉ	45 27 24 82
40	M8	**Les Trois Sts-Hiérarques**	5 r. Pétel, 15ᵉ	45 32 92 65

Synagogues, *Synagogen, Sinagogas*

19	E13	**Association Consistoriale Israélite de Paris**	17 r. St-Georges, 9ᵉ	42 85 71 09
19	F14	**Centre Communautaire — Maison des Jeunes**	19 bd Poissonnière, 2ᵉ	42 33 80 21
16	G7	**Union Libérale Israélite de France**	24 r. Copernic, 16ᵉ	47 04 37 27
		Synagogues et Oratoires :		
32	G16	**Synagogue**	15 r. N.-D.-Nazareth, 3ᵉ	42 78 00 30

32	J16	Oratoire Fleishman	18 r. des Écouffes, 4e	48 87 97 86
32	J16	Syn. « Agoudas Hakehilos » (Orthodoxe)	10 r. Pavée, 4e	48 87 21 54
32	J16	Syn. Adath Yechouroun	25 r. des Rosiers, 4e	
33	J17	Synagogue	21 bis r. des Tournelles, 4e	42 74 32 80
33	J17	Synagogue	14 pl. des Vosges, 4e	48 87 79 45
44	M15	Synagogue	30 bd de Port Royal, 5e	43 31 98 20
44	M15	Synagogue	9 r. Vauquelin, 5e	47 07 21 22
20	F15	Syn. Rachi	6 r. Ambroise-Thomas, 9e	48 24 86 94
19	E14	Synagogue Portugaise	28 r. Buffault, 9e	45 26 80 87
19	E14	Synagogue	8 r. Lamartine, 9e	45 26 87 60
19	F14	Syn. Adath Yereim	10 r. Cadet, 9e	42 46 36 47
19	E13	Synagogue Berith Chalom	18 r. St-Lazare, 9e	48 78 45 32
19	F13	Synagogue et oratoire	44 r. de la Victoire, 9e	45 26 95 36
19	F14	Synagogue	3 r. Saulnier, 9e	47 70 09 23
19	F14	Synagogue Beth Israël	4 r. Saulnier, 9e	
20	F15	Synagogue	4 r. Martel, 10e	
20	D15	Synagogue	9 r. Guy-Patin, 10e	42 85 12 74
33	J18	Syn. Don Isaac Abravanel	84 r. de la Roquette, 11e	47 00 75 95
34	J19	Synagogue	18 r. Basfroi, 11e	
34	J19	Syn. Adath Israël	36 r. Basfroi, 11e	43 67 89 20
47	M21	Orat. Beth Yaakov	15 r. Lamblardie, 12e	43 47 36 78
57	P18	Synagogue	19 r. Domrémy, 13e	45 85 25 56
55	P14	Syn. Sidi Fredj Halimi	61 r. Vergniaud, 13e	45 88 93 84
41	N10	Synagogue	121 r. de l'Ouest, 14e	
53	P9	Oratoire	223 r. Vercingétorix, 14e	45 45 03 43
41	L9	Synagogue	14 r. Chasseloup-Laubat, 15e	42 73 36 29
39	K6	Synagogue	11 r. Gaston-de-Caillavet, 15e	45 75 38 01
40	K7	Oratoire	13 r. Fondary, 15e	45 78 25 07
27	G5	Syn. Ohel Abraham	31 r. de Montevideo, 16e	45 04 66 73
16	D7	Synagogue	19-21 r. Galvani, 17e	45 74 51 81
7	B14	Syn. de Montmartre	13 r. Ste-Isaure, 18e	42 64 48 34
7	C14	Oratoire	42 r. des Saules, 18e	46 06 71 39
10	B19	Synagogue	11-13 r. Curial, 19e	42 45 65 16
21	E18	Oratoire	70 av. Secrétan, 19e	
22	F19	Oratoire	120 bd de Belleville, 20e	47 97 46 96
22	F19	Synagogue et oratoire	75 r. Julien-Lacroix, 20e	43 58 28 39
22	F19	Synagogue-Temple Guez	19 r. de Tourtille, 20e	43 57 62 39
36	J23	Syn. Bet Yaacov Yossef	5 square des Cardeurs, 20e	43 56 03 11

Culte Musulman, *Islam, Islamische Kultstätten, Culto Musulmán*

| 44 | L16 | Institut Musulman | pl. du Puits-de-l'Ermite, 5e | 45 35 97 33 |
| 44 | M16 | Mosquée | pl. du Puits-de-l'Ermite, 5e | 45 35 97 33 |

Culte Bouddhique, *Buddhism, Buddhistische Kultstätten, Culto Budista*

| 48 | L20 | Institut Internat. Bouddhique | 20 cité Moynet, 12e | 43 41 54 48 |
| 60 | P24 | Centre Cultuel et culturel Bouddhique | 40 bis rte de ceinture du Lac Daumesnil, 12e | |

Autres cultes, *Other churches, Andere Kultstätten, Cultos diversos*

23	E22	Église de Jésus Christ des Saints des Derniers jours (Mormons)	66 r. de Romainville, 19e	42 45 28 57
44	N16	Église Adventiste du 7e jour	130 bd de l'Hôpital, 13e	43 31 33 91
20	F15	—	63 r. du Fg Poissonnière, 9e	47 70 68 23
35	K22	—	96 r. des Grands-Champs, 20e	43 50 36 44
55	N14	Église catholique orthodoxe de France	96 bd Auguste-Blanqui, 13e	45 42 44 12
44	K15	Église catholique St-Nicolas du Chardonnet	30 r. St-Victor, 5e	46 34 28 33
40	M8	Église protestante évangélique luthérienne	105 r. de l'Abbé-Groult, 15e	48 42 58 09
18	K17	Fédération Evangélique de France (Région parisienne)	Courbevoie 40 r. du 22 Septembre	43 33 77 24

*Sports et loisirs de plein air en Ile-de-France,
consultez la **carte Michelin** détaillée n° 170 à 1/100 000.*

ENSEIGNEMENT SUPÉRIEUR

HIGHER EDUCATION
UNIVERSITÄTEN, HOCHSCHULEN
ENSEÑANZA SUPERIOR

Institut de France
Institute of France, Instituto de Francia

31	J13	Institut de France	23 quai de Conti, 6ᵉ	43 29 55 10
		Académie Française	–	43 26 85 15
		Académie des Inscriptions et Belles Lettres	–	43 26 92 82
		Académie des Sciences	–	43 26 66 21
		Académie des Beaux-Arts	–	43 26 22 47
		Académie des Sciences Morales et Politiques	–	43 26 31 35

Académies et Institutions, *Academies and institutions,*
Akademien und staatliche Institutionen, Academias e Instituciones

30	H11	Académie Agriculture	18 r. de Bellechasse, 7ᵉ	47 05 10 37
30	K12	— Chirurgie	26 bd Raspail, 7ᵉ	45 48 22 54
15	G5	— Nat. Chirurgie dentaire	22 r. Émile-Ménier, 16ᵉ	47 04 65 40
28	J7	— Marine	3 av. Octave-Gréard, 7ᵉ	42 60 33 30
31	J13	— Nat. Médecine	16 r. Bonaparte, 6ᵉ	43 26 96 80
43	L13	— Nat. Pharmacie	4 av. de l'Observatoire, 6ᵉ	43 25 54 49
16	F7	— Sciences d'Outre-Mer	15 r. La Pérouse, 16ᵉ	47 20 87 93
29	J10	— Vétérinaire de France	60 bd La Tour-Maubourg, 7ᵉ	43 68 68 37
43	N13	Bureau des Longitudes	77 av. Denfert-Rochereau, 14ᵉ	40 51 21 21
30	H11	Centre National de la Recherche Scientifique (CNRS)	15 q. Anatole-France, 7ᵉ	45 55 92 25
43	K14	Collège de France	11 pl. M.-Berthelot, 5ᵉ	43 29 12 11
29	L14	Institut Curie	26 r. d'Ulm, 5ᵉ	43 29 12 42
43	J10	Institut Géographique National	136 bis r. Grenelle, 7ᵉ	45 50 34 95
44	N15	Manufacture des Gobelins	42 av. des Gobelins, 13ᵉ	48 87 24 14
44	L16	Museum National d'Histoire Naturelle	57 r. Cuvier, 5ᵉ	43 36 00 28
43	N13	Observatoire de Paris	61 av. de l'Observatoire, 14ᵉ	40 51 21 21
19	G13	Phonothèque Nationale et Audiovisuel	2 r. de Louvois, 2ᵉ	47 03 88 20
30	J11	Société Nat. d'Horticulture de France	84 r. de Grenelle, 7ᵉ	45 48 81 00

Services et Organismes para-universitaires
University organizations, Universitäre Einrichtungen,
Servicios y Organismos para-universitarios

43	M13	Centre Régional des Œuvres Universitaires et Scolaires (CROUS) (Information et accueil pour étudiants)	39 av. G.-Bernanos, 5ᵉ	43 29 12 43
55	S13	Cité Internationale Universitaire de Paris	19 bd Jourdan, 14ᵉ	45 89 68 52
55	R13	Fondation Santé des Etudiants de France	8 r. Emile-Deutsch-de-la Meurthe, 14ᵉ	45 89 43 39
22	F23	Service Interacadémique des Examens et Concours	Arcueil - 7 r. Ernest-Renan	46 57 11 90

La Cité Internationale Universitaire de Paris (S13) occupe, au Sud du Parc Montsouris, un quadrilatère de 40 ha, autour duquel s'ordonnent :

- la Maison Internationale, qui offre des activités culturelles (théâtre) et sportives (piscine) dans le cadre de la Fondation Nationale, à laquelle se rattachent un Hôpital International et trois restaurants universitaires.

- des Maisons d'étudiants et Fondations, vivant chacune de façon autonome, les unes françaises (Fondation Deutsch-de-la-Meurthe, Pavillon Honnorat, etc.), les autres étrangères, regroupant plus de cent nationalités.

Universities, Universitäten, Universidades

43	K14	**Académie de Paris** (Rectorat).	47 r. des Ecoles, 5ᵉ	40 46 22 11	
43	L14	**Paris I** Panthéon-Sorbonne	12 pl. du Panthéon, 5ᵉ	46 34 97 00	
43	L14	**Paris II** Droit, Économie et Sciences sociales . . .	12 pl. du Panthéon, 5ᵉ	46 34 97 00	
43	K14	**Paris III** Sorbonne Nouvelle.	17 r. de la Sorbonne, 5ᵉ	46 34 01 10	
43	K14	**Paris IV** Paris-Sorbonne	1 r. Victor-Cousin, 5ᵉ	40 46 22 11	
31	K14	**Paris V** René Descartes.	12 r. de l'Éc.-Médecine, 6ᵉ	40 46 16 16	
44	L16	**Paris VI** Pierre et Marie Curie	4 pl. Jussieu, 5ᵉ	43 36 25 25	
44	L16	**Paris VII**	2 pl. Jussieu, 5ᵉ	43 36 25 25	
20	E2	**Paris VIII**	St-Denis - 8 r. de la Liberté	48 21 63 64	
15	F5	**Paris IX** Paris-Dauphine	pl. du Mar.-de-Lattre de-Tassigny, 16ᵉ	45 05 14 10	
18	K12	**Paris X** Paris-Nanterre	Nanterre - 200 av. de la République	40 97 72 00	
101	pli 33	**Paris XI** Paris-Sud	Orsay - 15 av. G.-Clemenceau	69 41 67 50	
24	H9	**Paris XII** Paris-Val-de-Marne	Créteil - av. du Gén.-de-Gaulle	48 98 91 44	
18	D23	**Paris XIII** Paris-Nord	Villetaneuse - av. J.-B.-Clément	49 40 30 00	

Teaching hospitals, Universitätskliniken, Facultades de Medicina

43	M14	**U.E.R. Cochin-Port-Royal**	**Paris V**	24 r. du Fg St-Jacques, 14ᵉ	43 20 12 40
41	L10	**— Necker-Enfants Malades**	**—**	156 r. de Vaugirard, 15ᵉ	47 83 33 03
22	B8	**— Paris-Ouest**		Garches - 104 bd R. Poincaré	47 41 81 18
31	K14	**— Broussais-Hôtel-Dieu**	**Paris VI**	15 r. de l'École de Médecine, 6ᵉ	43 29 29 29
45	M17	**— Pitié-Salpétrière**	**—**	91 bd. de l'Hôpital, 13ᵉ	45 84 11 84
46	K19	**— Saint-Antoine**	**—**	27, rue Chaligny, 12ᵉ	43 41 71 00
20	E16	**— Lariboisière**	**Paris VII**	10, av. de Verdun, 10ᵉ	42 03 94 26
7	A13	**— Xavier-Bichat**	**—**	16 r. Henri Huchard, 18ᵉ	42 63 84 20
24	F1	**U.F.R. Paris-Sud**	**Paris XI**	Kremlin-Bicêtre - 63 r. G. Péri	46 70 11 85
24	H10	**— Paris-Val-de-Marne** (H. Mondor)	**Paris XII**	Créteil - 8 r. du Gal Sarrail	49 81 21 11
20	J7	**— Paris-Nord** (Avicenne)	**Paris XIII**	Bobigny - 74 r. Marcel Cachin	48 38 91 76

Institutes of Technology, Technische Hochschulen, Institutos Universitarios de Tecnología

38	M4	**Paris V**	143 av. de Versailles, 16ᵉ	45 24 46 02
22	D11	**Paris X**	Ville-d'Avray - 1 chemin Desvallières	47 09 05 70
101	pli 2	**—**	Cergy - Allée des Chênes-Pourpres	30 32 66 44
22	J22	**Paris XI**	Cachan - 9 av. Div.-Leclerc	46 64 10 32
101	pli 33	**—**	Orsay - Plateau du Moulon	69 41 00 40
22	K19	**—**	Sceaux - 8 av. Cauchy	46 60 06 83
24	H9	**Paris XII**	Créteil - av. du Gén.-de-Gaulle	48 98 91 44
101	pli 37	**—**	Évry - Quartier Les Passages 22 Allée Jean Rostand	60 78 03 63
20	F1	**Paris XIII**	St-Denis - pl. du 8-Mai-1945	48 21 61 55
18	D23	**—**	Villetaneuse - av. J.-B.-Clément	49 40 30 00

Visite des églises, monuments et musées

*Le **guide Vert Michelin PARIS** décrit les monuments les plus intéressants : leur histoire, leur architecture, les œuvres d'art qu'ils referment.*

Pour les monuments les plus importants, ces descriptions sont accompagnées d'illustrations ou de plans mettant en évidence les grandes étapes de leur construction et la situation des œuvres d'art.

Les horaires et tarifs de visite y figurent, ainsi que les jours et périodes de fermeture.

30	J12	**Administration** (Éc. Nat.) ENA	13 r. de l'Université, 7ᵉ	42 61 55 35
43	L14	**Administration et Direction** des affaires (École) EAD	15 r. Soufflot, 5ᵉ	43 29 97 60
39	L6	**Administration des Entreprises** (Inst.)	162 rue St-Charles, 15ᵉ	45 54 97 24
43	L13	**Administration Publique** (Inst. Internat.)	2 av. de l'Observatoire, 6ᵉ	43 26 49 00
17	D10	École Européenne des **Affaires** EAP	108 bd Malesherbes, 17ᵉ	47 54 65 00
44	M15	Institut National **Agronomique Paris-Grignon**	16 r. Cl.-Bernard, 5ᵉ	43 37 15 50
42	L12	**Alliance Française**	101 bd Raspail, 6ᵉ	45 44 38 28
		(École de langue et civilisation françaises)		
42	M12	**Architecture** (École Spéciale)	254 bd Raspail, 14ᵉ	43 22 83 70
19	F14	**Art Dramatique** (Conserv. Nat. Sup.)	2 bis r. Conservatoire, 9ᵉ	42 46 12 91
46	L20	**Arts Appliqués** BOULLE (École Sup.)	9 r. Pierre-Bourdan, 12ᵉ	43 46 67 34
40	N8	**Arts Appliqués et Métiers d'Art** (École Nationale Supérieure)	63 r. Olivier-de-Serre, 15ᵉ	45 30 20 66
43	L14	**Arts Décoratifs** (Éc. Nat. Sup.)	31 r. d'Ulm, 5ᵉ	43 29 86 79
30	K12	**Arts Graphiques et d'Architecture Intérieure** (École Supérieure)	31 r. du Dragon, 6ᵉ	42 22 55 07
		Atelier MET de PENNINGHEN et J. D'ANDON		
56	P15	**Arts et Industries Graphiques** ESTIENNE (École Supérieure)	18 bd Auguste-Blanqui, 13ᵉ	43 36 96 19
22	L19	**Arts et Manufactures** (École Centrale)	Châtenay-Malabry - Grande Voie des Vignes	46 61 33 10
32	G16	**Arts et Métiers** (Conserv.Nat)	292 r. St-Martin, 3ᵉ	42 71 24 14
44	N16	**Arts et Métiers** (Éc. Nat. Sup)	151 bd de l'Hôpital, 13ᵉ	43 36 49 55
18	E12	**Arts et Techniques du Théâtre** (Éc. Nat. Sup)	21 r. Blanche, 9ᵉ	48 74 44 30
33	J17	Les **Ateliers** (Éc. Nat. Sup. de Création Industrielle)	48 r. St-Sabin, 11ᵉ	43 38 09 09
31	J13	**Beaux-Arts** (Éc. Nat. Sup)	14 r. Bonaparte, 6ᵉ	42 60 34 57
47	L21	**Bois** (Éc. Supérieure)	6 av. de St-Mandé, 12ᵉ	46 28 09 33
42	K12	**Carmes** (Séminaire)	21 r. d'Assas, 6ᵉ	45 48 05 16
42	K12	Institut **Catholique de Paris**	21 r. d'Assas, 6ᵉ	42 22 41 80
43	K14	**Chartes** (École Nationale)	19 r. de la Sorbonne, 5ᵉ	46 33 41 82
43	L14	**Chimie** (Éc. Nat. Sup)	11 r. P.-et-M.-Curie, 5ᵉ	43 36 25 25
44	N16	**Chimie, Physique, Biologie** (École Nationale)	11 r. Pirandello, 13ᵉ	43 31 90 94
34	G19	**Commerce de Paris** (Éc. Sup.)	79 av. République, 11ᵉ	43 55 39 08
101	pli 33	**Électricité** (Éc. Sup.) SUPELEC	Gif-sur-Yvette - plateau de Moulon	69 41 80 40
101	pli 2	**Électronique et ses Applications** (École Nationale Supérieure) ENSEA	Cergy - allée des Chênes- Pourpres	30 30 92 44
42	K12	**Électronique de Paris** (Inst. Sup) I.S.E.P.	21 r. d'Assas, 6ᵉ	45 48 24 87
30	J12	**Études Politiques** (Inst.)	27 r. St-Guillaume, 7ᵉ	45 49 50 50
43	M13	**Faculté Libre Autonome et Cogérée** d'Économie et de Droit (FACO)	115 r. N.-D.-des-Champs, 6ᵉ	43 29 89 09
28	H8	**Fondation des Métiers de l'Image et du Son** (FEMIS)	13 av. du Prés.-Wilson, 16ᵉ	47 23 36 53
42	L11	**Génie Rural des Eaux et Forêts** (Éc. Nat.)	19 av. du Maine, 15ᵉ	45 49 88 00
27	G5	**Gestion** (Institut Supérieur)	8 r. de Lota, 16ᵉ	45 53 60 00
29	K9	**Guerre** (École Supérieure)	1 pl. Joffre, 7ᵉ	45 50 32 80
43	L14	École Pratique des **Hautes Études** (Inst. H. Poincaré)	11 r. P.-et-M.-Curie, 5ᵉ	43 54 83 57
22	M8	**Hautes Études Commerciales** (HEC) (jusqu'à juin 88)	Jouy-en-Josas - 1 r. de la Libération	39 56 70 00
30	K12	**Hautes Études en Sciences Sociales** (Éc.)	54 bd Raspail, 6ᵉ	45 44 39 79
31	J13	**Hautes Études Sociales** (École Libre)	4 pl St-Germain-des-Prés, 6ᵉ	42 22 68 06
		Hautes Études Internationales (École Libre)	—	42 22 68 06
64	DU	**Horticulture et Technique du** **Paysage** (École du Breuil)	Rte de la Ferme - Bois de Vincennes, 12ᵉ	43 28 28 94
22	G4	**Horticulture** (École Nationale Supérieure) et du Paysage (École Nat. Supérieure)	Versailles - 4 r. Hardy — 6 bis r. Hardy	39 50 60 87 39 53 98 89
24	G3	**Industries du Caoutchouc** (Éc. Sup.) IFOCA	Vitry - 60 r. Auber	46 71 91 22
20	S9	**Informatique** (École Supérieure)	Montreuil - 98 r. Carnot	48 59 69 69
24	B21-B22	**Ingénieurs en Électrotechnique et** **Électronique** (École Supérieure)	Noisy-le-Grand - 2 bd Blaise-Pascal	45 92 65 00
44	N15	**Institut Français de Restauration** des Œuvres d'Art (IFROA)	1 r. Berbier-du-Mets, 13ᵉ	43 37 93 37

42	K12	**Interprétariat et Traduction** (Institut Supérieur) ISIT	21 r. d'Assas, 6ᵉ	42 22 33 16
15	G5	**Interprètes et Traducteurs** (École Supérieure) ESIT	bd Lannes, 16ᵉ Centre Universitaire Dauphine	45 05 14 10
44	M15	Séminaire **Israélite de France**	9 r. Vauquelin, 5ᵉ	47 07 21 22
31	J13	**Journalisme** (École Supérieure)	4 pl. St-Germain-des-Prés, 6ᵉ	42 22 68 06
31	J13	**Langues et Civilisations Orientales** (Institut National)	2 r. de Lille, 7ᵉ	42 60 34 58
44	L15	**Louis Lumière** (École Nationale) Photo-Cinéma-Son	8 r. Rollin, 5ᵉ	43 29 01 70
31	H13	**Louvre** (École)	34 quai du Louvre, 1ᵉ	42 60 39 26
1	D2	**Management** (Centre d'Enseignement) CNOF	Puteaux - 10 r. Jean-Jaurès - Imm. Litwin	47 76 43 79
42	L11	**Mécanique et Électricité** (SUDRIA) École	4 r. Blaise-Desgoffe, 6ᵉ	45 48 03 70
43	L13	**Mines** (École Nationale Supérieure)	60 bd Saint-Michel, 6ᵉ	42 34 90 00
30	K11	**Missions Etrangères** (Séminaire)	128 r. du Bac, 7ᵉ	45 48 19 92
18	E11	**Musique de Paris** (Conserv. Nat. Sup.)	14 r. de Madrid, 8ᵉ	42 93 15 20
17	D9	**Musique de Paris** (École Normale)	114 bis bd Malesherbes, 17ᵉ	47 63 85 72
43	M14	**Normale Supérieure** (mixte)	45 r. d'Ulm, 5ᵉ	43 29 12 25
🖂22	H19	— (mixte)	Fontenay-aux-Roses - 31 av. Lombart	47 02 60 50
🖂22	B13	— (garçons)	St-Cloud - Grille d'Honneur du Parc	46 02 41 03
54	R12	**Normale Supérieure** (Jeunes filles)	48 bd Jourdan, 14ᵉ	45 89 08 33
53	R10	—	Montrouge - 1 r. M.-Arnoux	46 57 12 86
🖂22	H22	**Normale Supérieure** (technologie)	Cachan - 61 av. du Prés.-Wilson	47 40 20 00
🖂18	N9	**Pétrole et Moteurs** (École Nationale Supérieure) IFP	Rueil Malmaison - 4 av. de Bois-Préau	47 49 02 14
43	M14	**Physique et Chimie Industrielles** (École Sup.)	10 r. Vauquelin, 5ᵉ	43 37 77 00
🖂101	pli 34	**Polytechnique** (École)	Palaiseau - Route de Saclay	69 41 82 00
🖂22	K20	**Polytechnique Féminine** (École)	Sceaux - 3 bis r. Lakanal	46 60 33 31
30	J12	**Ponts et Chaussée** (École Nationale)	28 r. des Sts-Pères, 7ᵉ	42 60 34 13
53	P9	**Puériculture** (Institut)	26 bd Brune, 14ᵉ	45 39 22 15
42	K12	**Saint-Sulpice** (Séminaire)	6, r. du Regard, 6ᵉ	42 22 38 45
51	R5	—	Issy-les-Moulineaux - 33 r. du Gén.-Leclerc	46 44 78 40
43	M14	**Schola Cantorum**	269 r. St-Jacques, 5ᵉ	43 54 56 74
🖂101	pli 2	**Sciences Économiques et Commerciales** (École Supérieure) Groupe ESSEC	Cergy-Pontoise - Av. de la Grande-École	30 38 38 00
63	BT	**Sciences Géographiques** (École Nationale)	St-Mandé - 2 av. Pasteur	43 74 12 15
38	L4	**Sciences et Techniques Humaines** (Inst. Privé)	6 av. Léon-Heuzey, 16ᵉ	42 24 10 72
56	R16	—	83 av. d'Italie, 13ᵉ	45 85 59 35
🖂101	pli 33	**Sciences et Techniques Nucléaires** (Institut National)	Gif-sur-Yvette - Bât. 395 Centre d'Ét. Nucl. de Saclay	69 08 21 59
53	R9	**Statistique et Administration Économique** (École Nationale) E.N.S.A.E.	Malakoff - 3 av. P.-Larousse	45 40 04 16
🖂101	pli 33	**Techniques Aérospatiales** (École Supérieure) E.S.T.A.	Orsay - Bât. 502 bis Complexe scientifique	69 28 68 57
39	N6	**Techniques Avancées** (Éc. Nat. Sup.)	32 bd Victor, 15ᵉ	45 52 44 08
55	P14	**Télécommunications** (Éc. Nat. Sup)	46 r. Barrault, 13ᵉ	45 81 77 77
🖂101	pli 37	**Télécommunications** (Institut Nat.)	Evry - 9 r. Ch.-Fourier	60 76 40 40
43	N13	**Théologie** (Institut Protestant)	83 bd Arago, 14ᵉ	43 31 61 64
31	K14	**Travaux Publics, du Bâtiment et de l'Industrie** (École Spéciale)	57 bd St-Germain, 5ᵉ	46 34 21 99
🖂24	E7-F7	**Vétérinaire d'Alfort** (École Nationale)	Maisons-Alfort - 7 av. du Gén.-de.-Gaulle	43 96 71 00

Participez à notre effort permanent de mise à jour.
Adressez-nous vos remarques et vos suggestions.
Cartes et Guides Michelin
46, avenue de Breteuil, 75341 PARIS CEDEX 07.

INFORMATION, *INFORMACIÓN*

19	G14	**Agence France-Presse**	13 pl. de la Bourse, 2ᵉ	42 33 44 66
19	G14	— **Centrale Parisienne de Presse**	26 r. du Sentier, 2ᵉ	40 26 11 11
19	F14	— **Parisienne de Presse**	18 r. St-Fiacre, 2ᵉ	42 36 95 59

Radio-Télévision, *Rundfunk - Fernsehen*

27	K5	**Radio-France**	116 av. P.-Kennedy, 16ᵉ	42 30 22 22
29	H9	**Télévision Française** (TF1)	19 r. Cognacq-Jay, 7ᵉ	42 75 12 34
42	L11	— (Relations Publiques)	17 r. de l'Arrivée, 15ᵉ	45 38 67 67
29	G9	**Antenne 2**	22 av. Montaigne, 8ᵉ	42 99 42 42
29	G9	**France Régions 3** (FR3)	28 cours Albert-Iᵉʳ, 8ᵉ	42 25 59 59
27	K5	(Renseignements aux Téléspectateurs)	116 av. P.-Kennedy, 16ᵉ	42 30 17 68
40	N7	**Canal Plus**	78 r. Olivier-de-Serres, 15ᵉ	45 30 10 10
29	G9	**La Cinq**	21 r. Jean-Goujon, 8ᵉ	42 89 60 00
29	G9	**M6**	16 cours Albert-Iᵉʳ, 8ᵉ	42 56 66 66
29	G9	**EDIRADIO** (RTL)	22 r. Bayard, 8ᵉ	40 70 40 70
29	G9	**Europe Nº 1 - Télécompagnie**	26 bis r. François-Iᵉʳ, 8ᵉ	42 32 90 00
16	F8	**Radio Monte-Carlo**	12 r. Magellan, 8ᵉ	47 23 00 01

Grands quotidiens
Main daily newspapers, *Größere Tageszeitungen, Grandes diarios*

29	G9	**La Croix-l'Evénement**	3 r. Bayard, 8ᵉ	45 62 51 51
17	G9	**Les Echos**	37 av. Champs-Elysées, 8ᵉ	45 62 19 68
49	R2	**L'Équipe**	Issy-les-Moulineaux - 4 r. Rouget-de-l'Isle	40 93 20 20
17	F10	**Le Figaro** (Administr-Publicité)	25 av. Matignon, 8ᵉ	42 21 62 00
31	G14	— (Rédaction) et **Figaro-l'Aurore**	37 r. du Louvre, 2ᵉ	42 21 62 00
32	G15	**France-Soir**	100 r. Réaumur, 2ᵉ	42 21 20 00
20	F15	**L'Humanité**	5 r. Fg-Poissonnière, 9ᵉ	42 46 82 69
33	G17	**Libération**	11 r. Béranger, 3ᵉ	42 76 17 89
19	F13	**Le Monde**	7 r. des Italiens, 9ᵉ	42 47 97 27
18	J24	**Le Parisien**	St-Ouen - 25 av. Michelet	42 52 82 15
14	D4	**Le Quotidien de Paris**	Neuilly-sur-Seine - 2 r. Ancelle	47 47 12 32
39	M5	**La Tribune de l'Expansion**	2 5 r. Leblanc, 15ᵉ	40 60 40 60

Journaux de Province
Main regional newspapers, *Größere regionale Tageszeitungen, Periódicos de Provincia*

33	J17	**L'Auvergant de Paris**	13 bd Beaumarchais, 4ᵉ	42 77 70 05
32	G15	**Le Dauphiné Libéré**	100 r. Réaumur, 2ᵉ	42 86 05 43
28	H8	**La Dépêche du Midi**	7 r. de Monttessuy, 7ᵉ	45 55 91 71
18	F11	**Les Dernières Nouvelles d'Alsace**	3 r. de Rigny, 8ᵉ	43 87 12 30
19	F13	**L'Est Républicain**	24 r. du 4-Septembre, 2ᵉ	47 42 51 00
22	B15	**Midi Libre**	Boulogne - 83 r. du Château	46 05 05 06
19	F13	**La Montagne**	27 r. de La Michodière, 2ᵉ	42 65 55 04
19	G14	**La Nouvelle République du Centre Ouest**	17 r. de la Banque, 2ᵉ	42 96 99 39
16	F8	**Ouest-France**	114 av. Champs-Elysées, 8ᵉ	45 62 29 93
31	G14	**Paris-Normandie**	62 r. du Louvre, 2ᵉ	45 08 59 66
31	H13	**Le Républicain Lorrain**	8 r. de l'Echelle, 1ᵉ	42 60 67 88
19	F13	**Sud-Ouest**	27 r. de la Michodière, 2ᵉ	42 66 17 52
17	F9	**La Voix du Nord**	73 av. Champs-Elysées, 8ᵉ	43 59 10 38

Renseignements par téléphone
Information by telephone, *Telefonische Auskunft, Información por teléfonó*

Horloge des neiges	42 66 64 28	Information Météo	43 69 00 00
Horloge parlante	36 99	Météo Ile-de-France	43 69 02 02
Informations téléphonées	36 69 10 00	Météo France	43 69 01 01
Information Bourse	42 60 84 00		
(jours ouvr., 12 h 15-18 h)			

LES JEUNES A PARIS

THE YOUNG IN PARIS, JUGEND IN PARIS, LOS JÓVENES EN PARÍS

32	H15	**Accueil des Jeunes en France**	119 r. St-Martin, 4ᵉ	42 77 87 80
32	J16	—	16 r. du Pont-L.-Philippe, 4ᵉ	42 78 04 82
43	M13	—	139 bd St-Michel, 5ᵉ	43 54 95 86
32	J15	**Bureau d'Accueil des Jeunes**	12 quai de Gesvres, 4ᵉ	48 87 97 67
28	J7	**Centre d'Information et Documentation Jeunesse** (CIDJ)	101 quai Branly, 15ᵉ	45 67 35 85
29	K9	**Commission Armées-Jeunesse**	1 pl. Joffre, 7ᵉ	45 50 32 80
57	P18	**Direction départementale Jeunesse et sports** (bureau Information-Documentation)	6 r. Eugène-Oudiné, 13ᵉ	40 77 55 98
33	K17	**Direction de la Jeunesse et des Sports de la Ville de Paris**	r. Bassompierre, 4ᵉ	42 76 40 40

Hébergement
Accommodation, Unterkunft, Alojamiento

48	M23	**Centre International de Séjour de Paris**	6 av. Maurice-Ravel, 12ᵉ	43 43 19 01
56	S16	—	17 bd Kellermann, 13ᵉ	45 80 70 76
55	P13	**Foyer International d'Accueil de Paris**	30 r. Cabanis, 14ᵉ	45 89 89 15
18	L13	— la Défense	**Nanterre -** 19 r. Salvador-Allende	47 25 91 34
18	K20	**Léo-Lagrange** (Centre Intern. de Séjour)	**Clichy -** 107 r. Martre	42 70 03 22
32	J16	**Maisons Internationales de la Jeunesse et des Etudiants** (MIJE)	11 r. du Fauconnier, 4ᵉ	42 74 23 45
32	J16	—	6 r. de Fourcy, 4ᵉ	42 74 23 45
32	J16	—	12 r. des Barres, 4ᵉ	42 74 23 45
34	J19	**Résidence AJF-Bastille**	151 av. Ledru-Rollin, 11ᵉ	43 79 53 86
18	E11	**Union Chrétienne de Jeunes Filles**	22 r. de Naples, 8ᵉ	45 22 23 49
23	G21	—	65 r. Orfila, 20ᵉ	46 36 82 80
40	M7	—	168 r. Blomet, 15ᵉ	45 33 48 21
12	F14	**Union Chrétienne de Jeunes Gens**	14 r. de Trévise, 9ᵉ	46 70 90 94
22	L15	**Auberges de Jeunesse**	**Châtenay-Malabry -** 3 chemin du Loup-Pendu	46 32 17 43
24	M7-M8	—	**Choisy-le-Roi -** 125 av. de Villeneuve-St-Georges	48 90 92 30

Loisirs éducatifs
Cultural associations, Kulturelle Vereinigungen, Asociaciones Educativas

45	K17	**Centres d'animation de la Ville de Paris Direction de la Jeunesse et des Sports**	17 bd Morland, 4ᵉ	42 77 15 50
18	D11	**Fédération Régionale des Maisons des Jeunes et de la Culture**	54 bd des Batignolles, 17ᵉ	43 87 66 83
32	J16	**Jeunesses Musicales de France**	56 r. de l'Hôtel-de-Ville, 4ᵉ	42 78 19 54
34	K20	**Maison Internationale des Jeunes**	4 r. Titon, 11ᵉ	43 71 99 21
55	N14	**Union Nationale des Centres Sportifs de Plein Air** (UCPA)	62 r. de la Glacière, 13ᵉ	43 36 05 20
32	H15		28 bd de Sébastopol, 4ᵉ	48 04 76 76

Mouvements de Jeunesse
Youth organizations, Jugendorganisationen, Organizaciones Juveniles

21	D18	**Scouts de France**	54 av. Jean-Jaurès, 19ᵉ	42 38 37 37
19	F13	**Eclaireuses et Eclaireurs de France**	66 r. Chaussée-d'Antin, 9ᵉ	48 74 51 40
29	K10	**Éclaireuses et Éclaireurs Israélites de France**	27 av. de Ségur, 7ᵉ	47 83 60 33
5	A10	**Fédération Éclaireuses et Éclaireurs Unionistes de France**	**Clichy -** 15 r. Klock	42 70 52 20

29	J10	**Armée** (Hôtel des Invalides)	129 r. de Grenelle, 7ᵉ	45 55 92 30
15	F6	**Arménien**	59 av. Foch, 16ᵉ	45 56 15 88
7	C14	**Art Juif**	42 r. des Saules, 18ᵉ	42 57 84 15
32	H15	**Art moderne**	Centre G.-Pompidou, 4ᵉ	42 77 12 33
28	G8-H8	**Art moderne de la ville de Paris**	11 av. Prés.-Wilson, 16ᵉ	47 23 61 27
48	N23	**Arts Africains et Océaniens**	293 av. Daumesnil, 12ᵉ	43 43 14 54
31	H13	**Arts Décoratifs**	107 r. de Rivoli, 1ᵉʳ	42 60 32 14
31	H13	**Arts de la Mode**	109 r. de Rivoli, 1ᵉʳ	42 60 32 14
31	G13	**Arts du Spectacle**	Galerie Colbert, 2ᵉ	
14	E4	**Arts et Traditions Populaires**	6 rte du Mahatma-Gandhi, 16ᵉ	40 67 90 00
32	K15	**Assistance Publique**	47 quai de la Tournelle, 5ᵉ	46 33 01 43
27	J6	**Balzac** (Maison de)	47 r. Raynouard, 16ᵉ	42 24 56 38
26	J4	**Bouchard**	25 r. de l'Yvette, 16ᵉ	46 47 63 46
18	G11	**Bouilhet-Christofle**	12 r. Royale, 8ᵉ	42 60 34 07
42	L11	**Bourdelle**	16 r. A.-Bourdelle, 15ᵉ	45 48 67 27
31	G13	**Cabinet des Médailles et Antiques**	58 r. de Richelieu, 2ᵉ	47 03 83 30
33	J17	**Carnavalet**	23 r. de Sévigné, 3ᵉ	42 72 21 13
17	E10	**Cernuschi**	7 av. Velasquez, 8ᵉ	45 63 50 75
31	G13	**Charles-Cros**	Galerie Colbert, 2ᵉ	42 61 83 19
32	H16	**Chasse et nature**	60 r. des Archives, 3ᵉ	42 72 86 43
64	CT	**Chasseurs à pied, mécanisés et alpins**	Vincennes - Château de Vincennes	43 74 11 55
28	H7	**Cinéma-Henri Langlois**	pl. du Trocadéro, 16ᵉ	45 53 74 39
27	H6	**Clemenceau**	8 r. Franklin, 16ᵉ	45 20 53 41
31	K14	**Cluny**	6 pl. Paul-Painlevé, 5ᵉ	43 25 62 00
18	F12	**Cognacq-Jay** *(transfert en cours)*	25 bd des Capucines, 2ᵉ	42 61 94 54
15	F5	**Contrefaçon**	16 r. de la Faisanderie, 16ᵉ	45 01 51 11
20	F15	**Cristal**	30 bis r. Paradis, 10ᵉ	47 70 64 30
31	J13	**Delacroix**	6 r. de Furstemberg, 6ᵉ	43 54 04 87
15	F6	**D'Ennery**	59 av. Foch, 16ᵉ	45 53 57 96
19	E13	**Frédéric Masson**	27 pl. St-Georges, 9ᵉ	48 78 14 33
19	F14	**Grand Orient de France** et Franc Maçonnerie Européenne	16 r. Cadet, 9ᵉ	45 23 20 92
31	H14	**Grévin** (nouveau)	Niv.-1 Forum des Halles, 1ᵉʳ	42 61 28 50
19	F14	**Grévin**	10 bd Montmartre, 9ᵉ	47 70 85 05
28	G7	**Guimet**	6 pl. d'Iéna, 16ᵉ	47 23 61 65
19	E13	**Gustave-Moreau**	14 r. de La Rochefoucauld, 9ᵉ	48 74 38 50
42	L11	**Hébert**	85 r. du Cherche-Midi, 6ᵉ	42 22 23 82
32	H16	**Histoire de France**	60 r. des Fr.-Bourgeois, 3ᵉ	42 77 11 30
44	L16	**Histoire Naturelle** (Museum Nat.)	57 r. Cuvier, 5ᵉ	45 87 00 28
7	D13	**Historial de Montmartre**	11 r. Poulbot, 18ᵉ	46 06 78 92
31	H14	**Holographie**	Niv.-1 Forum des Halles, 1ᵉʳ	42 96 96 83
28	H7	**Homme**	17 pl. du Trocadéro, 16ᵉ	45 53 70 60
24	B8	**Insigne de l'armée de terre**	Vincennes - Château de Vincennes	43 74 11 55
44	K16	**Institut du Monde Arabe**	r. Fossés St-Bernard, 5ᵉ	46 34 25 25
18	E11	**Instrumental** (Conservatoire de Musique)	14 r. de Madrid, 8ᵉ	42 93 15 20
32	H15	**Instruments de Musique Mécanique**	Impasse Berthaud, 3ᵉ	42 71 99 54
17	F10	**Jacquemart-André**	158 bd Haussmann, 8ᵉ	45 62 39 94
17	D9	**Jean-Jacques Henner**	43 av. de Villiers, 17ᵉ	47 63 42 73
32	J16	**Kwok On** (Asie)	41 r. des Francs-Bourgeois, 4ᵉ	42 72 99 42
30	H11	**Légion d'Honneur**	2 r. de Bellechasse, 7ᵉ	45 55 95 16
31	H13	**Louvre**	Cour Napoléon, 1ᵉʳ	42 86 99 00
27	J5	**Lunettes et lorgnettes**	2 av. Mozart, 16ᵉ	45 27 21 05
28	H7	**Marine**	17 pl. du Trocadéro, 16ᵉ	45 53 31 70
26	H4	**Marmottan**	2 r. Louis-Boilly, 16ᵉ	42 24 07 02
32	J16	**Martyr Juif Inconnu** (Mémorial)	17 r. Geoffroy-l'Asnier, 4ᵉ	42 77 44 72
43	L14	**de la Mer et des Eaux** (Centre)	195 r. St-Jacques, 5ᵉ	46 33 08 61
32	K16	**Mickiewicz**	6 quai d'Orléans, 4ᵉ	43 54 35 61
43	L13	**Minéralogie** (École des Mines)	60 bd St-Michel, 6ᵉ	42 34 91 39
44	L16	**Minéralogie** (Université Paris VI)	Tour 25, 4 pl. Jussieu, 5ᵉ	43 36 25 25
28	G8	**Mode et Costume** (Palais Galliera)	10 av. Pierre-1ᵉʳ-de-Serbie, 16ᵉ	47 20 85 23
31	J13	**Monnaie** (Hôtel des Monnaies)	11 quai de Conti, 6ᵉ	40 46 56 66
7	C14	**Montmartre**	12 r. Cortot, 18ᵉ	46 06 61 11
28	H7	**Monuments Français**	1 pl. du Trocadéro, 16ᵉ	47 27 35 74
17	E10	**Nissim de Camondo**	63 r. de Monceau, 8ᵉ	45 63 26 32
32	K15	**Notre-Dame**	10 r. Cloître-N.-U., 4ᵉ	43 25 42 92
18	E12	**Opéra**	pl. de l'Opéra	42 66 50 22
30	H11	**Orangerie des Tuileries**	pl. de la Concorde, 1ᵉʳ	42 97 48 16
29	J10	**Ordre Nat. de la Libération**	51 bis bd La Tour-Maubourg, 7ᵉ	47 05 04 10

30	H12	**Orsay**	1 r. de Bellechasse, 7ᵉ	45 49 48 14
29	G10	**Palais de la Découverte**	av. Franklin-D.-Roosevelt, 8ᵉ	43 59 18 21
41	M10	**Pasteur**	25 r. du Dr.-Roux, 15ᵉ	45 68 82 82
29	G10	**Petit-Palais**	av. Winston-Churchill, 8ᵉ	42 65 12 73
29	J10	**Plans-Reliefs**	Hôtel des Invalides, 7ᵉ	47 05 11 07
33	H16	**Picasso**	5 r. de Thorigny, 3ᵉ	42 71 25 21
41	M10	**Poste**	34 bd de Vaugirard, 15ᵉ	43 20 15 30
44	K15	**Préfecture de Police** (Collections historiques)	1 bis r. Basse-des-Carmes, 5ᵉ	43 29 21 57
20	F15	**Publicité**	18 r. de Paradis, 10ᵉ	42 46 13 09
19	E13	**Renan-Scheffer**	16 r. Chaptal, 9ᵉ	48 74 95 38
29	J10	**Rodin**	77 r. de Varenne, 7ᵉ	47 05 01 34
10	B20	**Sciences et de l'industrie** (cité)	30 av. Corentin-Cariou, 19ᵉ	40 05 70 00
45	L17	**Sculpture en plein air**	quai St-Bernard, 5ᵉ	43 26 91 90
29	H9	**SEITA** (Galerie)	12 r. Surcouf, 7ᵉ	45 56 60 17
32	H16	**Serrure** (Bricard)	1 r. de la Perle, 3ᵉ	42 77 79 62
37	M2	**Sport**	24 r. du Cdt Guilbaud, 16ᵉ	46 51 39 26
32	G15	**Techniques**	270 r. St-Martin, 3ᵉ	40 27 22 20
33	J17	**Victor Hugo** (Maison de)	6 pl. des Vosges, 4ᵉ	42 72 16 65
27	J6	**Vin**	5-7 square Charles-Dickens, 16ᵉ	45 25 63 26
43	L13	**Zadkine**	100 bis r. d'Assas, 6ᵉ	43 26 91 90

PARCS ET JARDINS, *PARKS AND GARDENS,*
PARKS UND GÄRTEN, PARQUES Y JARDINES

32	J16	**Albert-Schweitzer** (sq.)	r. de l'Hôtel de Ville, 4ᵉ
44	L15	**Arènes de Lutèce** (sq.)	r. des Arènes, 5ᵉ
5	C10	**Batignolles** (sq.)	pl. Charles-Fillion, 17ᵉ
22	F19,F20	**Belleville** (parc)	r. Piat, 20ᵉ
46	M19	**Bercy** (parc)	r. et quai de Bercy, 12ᵉ
30	K12	**Boucicaut** (sq.)	r. de Sèvres, 7ᵉ
23	D21	**Butte du Chapeau Rouge** (sq.)	bd d'Algérie, 19ᵉ
22	E19	**Buttes Chaumont** (parc)	r. Botzaris, 19ᵉ
6	C12	**Carpeaux** (sq.)	r. Carpeaux, 18ᵉ
30	H12	**Carrousel** (jardin)	pl. du Carrousel, 1ᵉ
28	J8	**Champ de Mars** (parc)	quai Branly, 7ᵉ
56	P16	**Choisy** (sq.)	128-160 av. de Choisy, 13ᵉ
31	K14	**Cluny** (Jardin du Musée)	bd St-Germain, 5ᵉ
52	P8	**Docteur Calmette** (sq.)	bd Lefèbvre, 15ᵉ
35	G22	**Édouard-Vaillant** (sq.)	r. du Japon, 20ᵉ
24	F23	**Emmanuel Fleury** (sq.)	r. Le Vau, 20ᵉ
6	B12	**Epinettes** (sq.)	r. Maria-Deraismes, 17ᵉ
52	N8	**Georges Brassens** (parc)	r. des Morillons, 15ᵉ
31	H14	**Halles** (jardin)	r. Berger, 1ᵉʳ
29	J10	**Intendant** (jardin)	pl. Vauban, 7ᵉ
32	K15	**Jean XXIII** (sq.)	quai de l'Archevéché, 4ᵉ
56	S15	**Kellermann** (parc)	r. Poterne des Peupliers, 13ᵉ
18	F11	**Louis XVI** (sq.)	bd Haussmann, 8ᵉ
43	L13	**Luxembourg** (jardin)	pl. André-Honnorat, 6ᵉ
43	M13	**Marco-Polo** (jardin)	av. de l'Observatoire, 6ᵉ
34	H19	**Maurice Gardette** (sq.)	r. du Général-Blaise, 11ᵉ
17	E9	**Monceau** (parc)	bd de Courcelles, 8ᵉ
55	R13	**Montsouris** (parc)	bd Jourdan, 14ᵉ
31	G13	**Palais Royal** (jardin)	r. de Valois, 1ᵉʳ
44	L16	**Plantes** (jardin)	quai St-Bernard, 5ᵉ
26	H4-J4	**Ranelagh** (jardin)	av. Raphaël, 16ᵉ
56	N15	**René Le Gall** (sq.)	r. Corvisart, 13ᵉ
43	L13	**Robert Cavelier de La Salle** (jardin)	av. de l'Observatoire, 6ᵉ
40	L8-M8	**Saint-Lambert** (sq.)	r. Jean-Formigé, 15ᵉ
35	H21	**Samuel de Champlain** (sq.)	av. Gambetta, 20ᵉ
47	K22	**Sarah Bernhardt** (sq.)	r. de Lagny, 20ᵉ
54	R11	**Serment de Koufra** (sq.)	av. Ernest Reyer, 14ᵉ
36	G23	**Séverine** (sq.)	pl. de la Pte-de-Bagnolet, 20ᵉ
32	G16	**Temple** (sq.)	r. du Temple, 3ᵉ
44-45	K16,L17	**Tino Rossi** (jardin)	44-45 Port St-Bernard, 5ᵉ
28	H7	**Trocadéro** (jardins)	av. de New York, 16ᵉ
30	H12	**Tuileries** (jardin)	pl. de la Concorde, 8ᵉ
31	J14	**Vert-Galant** (sq.)	pl. du Pont-Neuf, 1ᵉʳ
40	L7	**Violet** (sq.)	place Violet, 15ᵉ
10	B20	**Villette** (parc)	av. Jean-Jaurès, 19ᵉ

Pa. At. 6

A Paris, 163 **bureaux de poste** sont à la disposition du public. Ces bureaux sont identifiés et localisés sur les plans *(p. ▮ à ▮▮)* par le signe bleu ▣. La vente des timbres-poste courants est pratiquée dans tous les bureaux de tabac.

Service normal : Les **bureaux des P. & T.** sont ouverts au public du lundi au vendredi de 8 h à 19 h, le samedi de 8 h à 12 h.
Toutes les opérations peuvent y être pratiquées.

Ouvertures exceptionnelles et services réduits : **Horaires et opérations**

31	G14	**Paris 1er Recette Principale**	52 r. du Louvre	40 28 20 00
32	H15	**Paris 1er RP Annexe 1 — Forum des Halles**	Centre Commercial, niveau 4	40 26 83 24
17	F9	**Paris 8 - Annexe 1**	71 av. des Champs-Élysées	43 59 55 18
28	J7	**Tour Eiffel (1er étage) - Paris 7 - Annexe 2**	av. Gustave-Eiffel	45 51 05 78
15	E6	**Paris 17 - Annexe 2**	Palais des Congrès	47 57 61 83
10	D19	**Paris 19 Belvédère**	118 av. Jean-Jaurès	42 06 31 45

Recette Principale. — *Ouvert jour et nuit.*
Aux heures de service normal *(voir ci-dessus)* : toutes opérations ;
Samedi (à partir de 12 h), les dimanches et jours fériés et la nuit (℡ 40 26 32 34) : vente de timbres-poste ; téléphone, télégraphe ; dépôt des objets recommandés et chargés ; paiement des chèques postaux de dépannage, des mandats-lettres, des Postchèques étrangers ; remboursements sans préavis sur livrets de C.N.E. ; retrait des objets (sauf les mandats) adressés en Poste Restante à Paris RP.

Recette Principale Annexe 1 — Forum des Halles (Porte Lescot). — *Ouvert du lundi au vendredi (10 h à 18 h) et samedi (9 h à 12 h).*

Paris 7 - Annexe 2. — *Ouvert tous les jours de 10 h 45 à 18 h 30.*

Paris 8 - Annexe 1. — *Ouvert en semaine, de 8 h à 22 h ; les dimanches et jours fériés, voir ci-dessous.*
Aux heures de service normal *(voir ci-dessus)* : toutes opérations.
Lundi au samedi (à partir de 19 h) et les dimanches et jours fériés (10 h à 12 h et 14 h à 20 h) : téléphone, télégraphe ; vente des timbres-poste ; affranchissement des correspondances (sauf dimanches et jours fériés) ; délivrance des objets en Poste Restante.

Paris 17 - Annexe 2. — *Ouvert du lundi au vendredi (8 h à 19 h) et samedi (8 h à 12 h).*

Paris 19 Belvédère. — *Ouvert du lundi au vendredi (11 h à 12 h 30 et 18 h à 19 h 30) et samedi (11 h à 12 h 30).*

Poste restante : Tous les bureaux de Paris assurent le service Poste Restante. Mais le courrier adressé **« Poste Restante - Paris »** sans spécification d'arrondissement est à retirer à la Recette Principale, 52, rue du Louvre.

Centre des Chèques Postaux (C.C.P.) : Le **C.C.P.** 16 rue des Favorites, 15e (M 9) ℡ 45 30 77 77 *(renseignements par téléphone du lundi au vendredi de 7 h à 19 h et samedi de 7 h à 12 h)* est ouvert au public du lundi au vendredi de 8 h à 19 h et le samedi de 8 h à 12 h.

Télex

18	E12	**Agence Commerciale**	8 r. d'Amsterdam, 9e	42 68 14 14
		Paris St-Lazare *(lundi au vendredi 8 h 30 à 18 h, samedi 8 h 30 à 12 h)*		
31	G14	**Bureau Télégraphique Internat.**	9 pl. de la Bourse, 2e	42 33 44 11
		(jour et nuit)		
19	G14	**Paris Bourse** *(8 h à 20 h)*	5-7 r. Feydeau, 2e	42 47 12 12

Divers services P. & T.

Renseignements téléphoniques	12	**Télégrammes téléphonés :**		
Réclamations	13	—	métropole	36 55
Réveil par téléphone	36 88	—	étranger (sauf anglais)	42 33 44 11
Renseignements postaux	42 80 87 89	—	— (en anglais)	42 33 21 11

P. & T. : POSTAL SERVICES

Normal opening times and services. — **Post offices** provide the full range of services from Mondays to Fridays 8am to 7pm, Saturdays 8am to noon.

Additional opening times with a limited service

General Post Office. — 52 rue du Louvre (G14) ☎ 40 28 20 00. *Open 24 hours. Outwith normal hours a limited service only is provided* (☎ 40 26 32 34).

Paris 1st - Forum des Halles. — 4th level, Porte Lescot (H15) ☎ 40 26 83 24. *Open Mondays to Fridays 10am to 6pm and Saturdays 9am to noon.*

Paris 7th - Tour Eiffel. — 1st floor, avenue Gustave Eiffel (28J7) ☎ 45 51 05 78. *Open daily, including Sundays and holidays, 10.45am to 6.30pm.*

Paris 8th. — 71 avenue des Champs-Élysées (F9) ☎ 43 59 55 18. *Open Mondays to Saturdays 8am to 11.30pm. A limited service only is available from 7pm Mondays to Saturdays and from 10am to noon and 2 to 8pm on Sundays and holidays.* Apply in advance for full details.

Paris 17th. — Palais des Congrès, place Porte Maillot (E6) ☎ 47 57 61 83. *Open Mondays to Fridays 8am to 7pm and Saturdays 8am to noon.*

Paris 19th Belvédère. — 118 avenue Jean-Jaurès (D19). *Open Mondays to Fridays 11am to 12.30pm and 6 to 7.30pm and Saturdays 11am to 12.30pm.*

Poste Restante. — All Parisian post offices have Poste Restante. Letters sent « **Poste Restante Paris** » with no arrondissement number go to the General Post Office.

P. & T. : POST

Öffnungszeiten. — Die **Postämter** sind montags bis freitags von 8-19 Uhr und samstags von 8-12 Uhr geöffnet. Sie versehen dann alle Postdienste.

Besondere Schalterstunden, nur begrenzte Postdienste

Hauptpostamt. — 52, rue du Louvre (G14) ☎ 40 28 20 00. *Tag und Nacht geöffnet. Samstags ab 12 Uhr, an Sonn- und Feiertagen sowie nachts (☎ 40 26 32 34) nur bestimmte Dienstleistungen.*

Paris 1e - Postamt 1 — Forum des Halles, Niveau 4 (Porte Lescot) (H15) ☎ 40 26 83 24. *Geöffnet : montags-freitags 10-18 Uhr ; samstags 9-12 Uhr.*

Paris 7e - Eiffelturm — 1. Etage, Avenue Gustave-Eiffel (28 J7) ☎ 45 51 05 78. *Geöffnet : täglich, auch an Sonn- und Feiertagen, von 10.45-18.30 Uhr.*

Paris 8e - Postamt 1. — 71 avenue des Champs-Élysées (F9) ☎ 43 59 55 18. *Geöffnet : 8-23.30 Uhr. Montags-samstags ab 19 Uhr und an Sonn- und Feiertagen (10-12, 14-20 Uhr) nur bestimmte Dienstleistungen.*

Paris 17e - Postamt 2. — Palais des Congrès (E6) ☎ 47 57 61 83. *Geöffnet : montags-freitags 8-19 Uhr, samstags 8-12 Uhr.*

Paris 19e - Belvédère. — 118 avenue Jean-Jaurès (D19). *Geöffnet : montags-freitags 11-12.30 Uhr und 18-19.30 Uhr ; samstags 11-12.30 Uhr.*

Postlagernde Sendungen. — Mit Angabe des Arrondissements können postlagernde Sendungen *(poste restante)* an alle Pariser Postämter geschickt werden. Falls als Adresse jedoch nur « **Poste Restante - Paris** » vermerkt ist, muß die Post bei der Hauptpost, 52 rue du Louvre, *(s. oben)* abgeholt werden.

P. & T. : SERVICIOS POSTALES

Servicio normal. — Para todas las operaciones, las **oficinas de los P.T.T.** están abiertas al público de lunes a viernes de 8 h a 19 h, los sábados de 8 h a 12 h.

Aperturas excepcionales y servicios reducidos

Paris 1º - Oficina Principal. — 52 rue du Louvre (G14) ☎ 40 28 20 00. *Abierta día y noche. Sábados (desde 12 h), domingos, festivos y durante la noche : sólo son posibles algunas operaciones.* Informarse. ☎ 40 26 32 34.

Paris 1º - Forum des Halles. — Piso 4, porte Lescot (H15) ☎ 40 26 83 24. *Abierta de lunes a viernes de 10 h a 18 h. Sábados de 9 h a 12 h.*

Paris 7º - Tour Eiffel. — Piso 1, avenue Gustave-Eiffel (28J7) ☎ 45 51 05 78. *Abierta todos los días de 10 h 45 a 18 h 30.*

Paris 8º. — 71 avenue des Champs-Élysées (F9) ☎ 43 59 55 18. *Abierta de 8 h a 22 h. De lunes a sábados (desde 19 h), domingos y festivos : lólo son posibles algunas operaciones.* Informarse.

Paris 17º. — Palais des Congrès, place Porte Maillot (E6) ☎ 47 57 61 83. *Abierta de lunes a viernes de 8 h a 19 h. Sábados de 8 h a 12 h.*

Paris 19º. — 118 avenue Jean-Jaurès (D19). *Abierta de lunes a viernes de 11 h a 12 h 30 y de 18 h a 19 h 30. Sábados de 11 h a 12 h 30.*

Lista de Correos. — Todas las oficinas mantienen el servicio de Lista de Correos (Poste Restante). Pero la correspondencia a « **Poste Restante - Paris** » sin especificación de distrito, debe de ser retirada en la Oficina Principal, 52 rue du Louvre.

Grands Hôpitaux, Cliniques, Maisons de Santé,
Hospitals, Krankenhäuser, Grandes Hospitales

Paris

22	E19	**Adolphe de Rothschild** (Fond. ophtalmologique)	25 r. Manin, 19ᵉ	48 03 65 65
29	H9	**Alma** (Clinique)	166 r. de l'Université, 7ᵉ	45 55 95 10
32	K16	**Banque Française des Yeux**	6 quai des Célestins, 4ᵉ	42 77 19 21
43	M13	**Baudelocque** (Clinique)	123 bd de Port-Royal, 14ᵉ	42 34 11 40
6	A12	**Bichat** (Hôpital)	46 r. Henri-Huchard, 18ᵉ	40 25 80 80
28	G8	**Bizet** (Clinique)	23 r. Georges-Bizet, 16ᵉ	47 23 78 26
39	M6	**Boucicaut** (Hôpital)	78 r. de la Convention, 15ᵉ	45 54 92 92
44	N15	**Broca** (Hôp.)	54-56 r. Pascal, 13ᵉ	45 35 20 10
53	P10	**Broussais** (Hôpital)	96 r. Didot, 14ᵉ	45 41 95 41
9	A18	**Claude-Bernard** (Hôpital)	10 av. Pte-d'Aubervilliers, 19ᵉ	40 25 80 80
43	M14	**Cochin** (Groupe Hosp.)	27 r. du Fg-St-Jacques , 14ᵉ	42 34 12 12
36	J23	**Croix-St-Simon** (Hôp.)	125 r. d'Avron, 20ᵉ	43 71 12 01
43	L14	**Curie** (Institut-Section Hospit.)	26 r. d'Ulm, 5ᵉ	43 29 12 42
46	L20	**Diaconesses** (Hôp.)	18 r. du Sergent-Bauchat, 12ᵉ	43 41 72 00
20	D16	**Fernand-Widal** (Hôp.)	200 r. du Fg-St-Denis, 10ᵉ	42 80 62 33
44	M16	**Gardien de la Paix** (Fond.)	35 bd St-Marcel, 13ᵉ	43 31 88 60
44	L16	**Geoffroy-St-Hilaire** (Clin.)	59 r. Geoffroy-St-Hilaire, 5ᵉ	43 37 66 00
38	M3	**Henry-Dunant** (Hôp.)	95 r. Michel-Ange, 16ᵉ	46 51 52 46
32	J15	**Hôtel-Dieu de Paris** (Hôp.)	1 pl. Parvis-Notre-Dame, 4ᵉ	42 34 82 34
57	P17	**Jeanne d'Arc** (Clin.)	11-13 r. Ponscarme, 13ᵉ	45 84 15 75
41	N9	**Labrouste** (Clin.chirurg.)	64 r. Labrouste, 15ᵉ	48 56 57 58
42	K11	**Laennec** (Hôp.)	42 r. de Sèvres, 7ᵉ	45 44 39 39
20	D15	**Lariboisière** (Hôp.)	2 r. Ambroise-Paré, 10ᵉ	42 80 62 33
33	G18	**Léonard de Vinci** (Clin.)	95 av. Parmentier, 11ᵉ	43 55 39 33
42	M11	**Léopold-Bellan** (Hôp.)	19-21 r. Vercingétorix, 14ᵉ	43 20 13 23
16	E7	**Marmottan** (Centre médical)	17-19 r. d'Armaillé, 17ᵉ	45 74 00 04
23	E22	**Maussins** (Clin.des)	67 r. de Romainville, 19ᵉ	42 03 94 76
34	J20	**Mont-Louis** (Clin.)	8-10 r. de la Folie-Regnault, 11ᵉ	43 71 11 00
41	L10	**Necker-Enfants Malades** (Groupe hospitalier)	149 r. de Sèvres, 15ᵉ	42 73 80 00
54	P11	**N.-D. de Bon-Secours** (Hôp.)	66 r. des Plantes, 14ᵉ	40 52 40 52
41	M10	**Pasteur** (Institut-Hôp.)	211 r. de Vaugirard, 15ᵉ	45 67 35 09
43	M14	**Péan** (Clin.chirurg.)	11 r. de la Santé, 13ᵉ	45 87 68 68
56	R15	**Peupliers** (Hôp.)	8 pl. Abbé-G.-Hénocque, 13ᵉ	45 65 15 15
45	M17	**Pitié-Salpêtrière** (Groupe hospitalier)	47 bd de l'Hôpital, 13ᵉ	45 70 21 12
43	M13	**Port-Royal** (Maternité)	123 bd de Port-Royal, 14ᵉ	42 34 12 12
33	K18	**Quinze-Vingts** (Hôp.)	28 r. de Charenton 12ᵉ	43 46 15 20
23	E22	**Robert-Debré** (Hôp.)	48 bd Sérurier, 19ᵉ	40 03 20 00
19	E13	**La Rochefoucauld** (Institut de psychiatrie)	23 r. de La Rochefoucauld, 9ᵉ	42 80 61 51
47	L22	**Rothschild** (Hôp.)	33 bd de Picpus, 12ᵉ	43 41 72 72
48	K19	**St-Antoine** (Hôp.)	184 r. du Fg-St-Antoine, 12ᵉ	43 44 33 33
41	M9	**St-Jacques** (Hôp.)	37 r. des Volontaires, 15ᵉ	45 66 93 09
42	K11	**St-Jean-de-Dieu** (Clin.)	19 r. Oudinot, 7ᵉ	43 06 94 06
53	P10	**St-Joseph** (Fond.-Hôp.)	7 r. Pierre-Larousse, 14ᵉ	40 52 33 33
20	E15	**St-Lazare** (Hôp.)	107 bis r. du Fg-St-Denis, 10ᵉ	42 80 62 33
21	F17	**St-Louis** (Hôp.)	1 av. Claude-Vellefaux, 10ᵉ	42 49 49 49
40	N8	**St-Michel** (Hôp.)	33 r. Olivier-de-Serres, 15ᵉ	48 28 40 80
43	M13	**St-Vincent-de-Paul** (Hôp.)	74 av. Denfert-Rochereau, 14ᵉ	40 48 81 11
55	P13	**Ste-Anne** (Centre hosp.)	1 r. Cabanis, 14ᵉ	45 65 80 00
40	M7	**Ste-Félicité** (Maternité)	37 r. St-Lambert, 15ᵉ	45 32 72 83
44	M16	**Sport** (clin.)	36 bd St-Marcel, 13ᵉ	45 35 36 52
43	M13	**Tarnier** (Hôp.)	89 r. d'Assas, 6ᵉ	42 34 12 12
35	G22	**Tenon** (Hôp.)	4 r. de la Chine, 20ᵉ	40 30 70 00
47	M22	**Trousseau** (Hôp.)	26 av. Dr.-A.-Netter, 12ᵉ	43 46 13 90
55	R13	**Université de Paris** (Hôp. internat.)	42 bd Jourdan, 14ᵉ	45 89 47 89
43	M14	**Val-de-Grâce** (Hôp.)	74 bd de Port-Royal, 5ᵉ	43 29 12 31
18	D12	**Vintimille** (Clin.)	58 r. de Douai, 9ᵉ	45 26 89 69

24	H10-H11	**Albert-Chenevier** (Hôp.)	Créteil - 40 r. de Mesly	49 81 31 31
61	AZ	**Ambroise-Paré** (Hôp.)	Boulogne - 9 av. Ch.-de-Gaulle	46 04 91 09
3	B5	**Américain (Hôp.)**	Neuilly-sur-Seine - 63 bd Victor-Hugo	47 47 53 00
22	H16	**Antoine-Beclère** (Hôp.)	Clamart - 157 r. Porte-de-Trivaux	45 37 44 44
24	C12	**Armand-Brillard** (Clin.)	Nogent-sur-Marne - 3-5 av. Watteau	43 94 81 00
20	J7	**Avicenne** (Hôp.)	Bobigny - 125 r. de Stalingrad	48 95 55 55
18	K21	**Beaujon** (Hôp.)	Clichy - 100 bd Général-Leclerc	47 39 33 40
24	B8	**Bégin** (Hôp. Instr. Armées)	St-Mandé - 69 av. de Paris	43 74 12 40
24	F1	**Bicêtre** (Centre hosp.)	Le Kremlin-Bicêtre - 78 r. du Gén-Leclerc	45 21 21 21
22	N19	**Bois de Verrières** (Clin.)	Antony - 66 r. du Colonel-Fabien	46 66 21 50
2	C3	**Centre Hospitalier**	Neuilly-sur-Seine - 36 bd Gén.-Leclerc	47 47 11 44
18	N15	**Centre Hospitalier**	Puteaux - 1 bd Richard-Wallace	47 72 51 44
22	B13	**Centre Hospitalier**	Saint-Cloud - 3 pl. Silly	46 02 70 92
20	F3	**Centre Hosp. Général**	Saint-Denis - 2 r. du Dr-Delafontaine	42 35 61 40
24	G11	**Centre Hosp. Intercomm.**	Créteil - 40 av. de Verdun	48 98 91 80
20	N10	**Centre Hosp. Intercomm.**	Montreuil - 56 bd de la Boissière	48 58 90 80
24	S10	**Centre Hosp. Intercomm.**	Villeneuve-St-Georges - 40 allée de la Source	43 82 39 40
24	H1-H2	**Centre Hosp. spécialisé**	Villejuif - 54 av. de la République	46 77 81 04
24	F5	**Charles-Foix** (Groupe hosp.)	Ivry-sur-Seine - 7 av. de la République	46 70 15 92
51	P5	**Corentin-Celton** (Hôp.)	Issy-les-Moulineaux - 37 bd Gambetta	45 54 95 33
20	P7	**Dhuys** (Clin.)	Bagnolet - 1 r. Pierre-Curie	43 60 01 50
24	N13	**Emile-Roux** (Centre Hosp.)	Limeil-Brévannes - Pl. Le Naourès	45 69 96 33
24	E8	**Esquirol** (Hôp.)	Saint-Maurice - 12 r. du Val d'Osne	43 75 92 33
20	N8	**Floréal** (Clin.)	Bagnolet - 40 r. Floréal	43 61 44 90
18	13	**Foch** (Centre médico-chirurg.)	Suresnes - 40 r. Worth	47 72 91 91
5	A10	**Gouin** (Hôp. chirurg.)	Clichy - 2 r. Gaston-Paymal	47 30 30 30
24	G1-H1	**Gustave-Roussy** (Inst.)	Villejuif - 39 r. Camille-Desmoulins	45 59 49 09
22	K16	**Hauts-de-Seine** (Clin.)	Châtenay-Malabry - 17 av. du Bois	46 30 22 50
3	D6	**Henri-Hartmann** (Clin.)	Neuilly-sur-Seine - 26 bd Victor-Hugo	47 58 12 10
24	G10-H10	**Henri-Mondor** (Hôp.)	Créteil - 51 av. Mar.-de-Lattre-de-Tassigny	49 81 21 11
3	C6	**Hertford** (British Hosp.)	Levallois-Perret - 3 r. Barbès	47 58 13 12
24	E3-F3	**Jean-Rostand** (Groupe hosp.)	Ivry-sur-Seine - 39-41 r. Jean-Le-Galleu	46 70 15 55
22	E11	**Jean Rostand** (Centre hosp.Intercomm.)	Sèvres - 141 Grande-Rue	45 34 75 11
20	K13	**Jean Verdier** (Hôp.)	Bondy - av. du 14-Juillet	48 47 31 03
18	H14	**Louis-Mourier** (Hôp.)	Colombes - 178 r. des Renouillers	47 60 61 62
20	R18	**Maison-Blanche** (Centre hosp. spécialisé)	Neuilly-sur-Marne - 3 av. Jean-Jaurès	43 00 96 90
18	J13	**Maison de Nanterre** (Hôp.)	Nanterre - 403 av. de la République	47 80 75 75
18	D21	**Maison de Santé**	Épinay - 6 av. de la République	48 21 49 00
1	A2	**Marcelin-Berthelot** (Centre hosp.)	Courbevoie - 30 r. Kilford	47 68 78 78
22	J17	**Marie-Lannelongue** (Centre chirurg.)	Le Plessis-Robinson - 133 av. de la Résistance	46 30 21 33
18	M8	Les **Martinets** (Clin.)	Rueil-Malmaison - 97 av.-Albert-1er	47 08 92 33
22	J14	**Meudon-la-Forêt-Vélizy** (Clin.)	Meudon-la-Forêt - 3 av. de Villacoublay	46 30 21 31
3	C5	**N.-D.-du-Perpétuel Secours** (Hôp.)	Levallois-Perret - 2 r. Kléber	47 57 31 57
24	G2-H2	**Paul-Brousse** (Groupe hosp.)	Villejuif - 12 av. P.-Vaillant-Couturier	45 59 30 00
49	S2	**Percy** (Hôp. militaire)	Clamart - 101 av. Henri-Barbusse	46 45 21 04
22	B8	**Raymond-Poincaré** (Hôp.)	Garches-104 bd R.-Poincaré	47 41 79 00
20	K4	**La Roseraie** (Centre hosp. privé)	Aubervilliers - 120 av. de la République	48 34 93 93
24	C16-C17	**Saint-Camille** (Hôp.)	Bry-sur-Marne - 2 r. des Pères-Carmilliens	48 81 11 80
18	N10	**Stell** (Hôp.départemental)	Rueil-Malmaison - 1 r. Charles-Drot	47 32 92 90
51	R5	**Suisse de Paris** (Hôp.)	Issy-les-Moulineaux - 10 r. Minard	46 45 21 36
20	L15	**Valère-Lefebvre** (Hôp.)	Le Raincy - 73 bd de l'Ouest	43 02 41 44
20	R18	**Ville-Évrard** (Centre hosp. spécialisé)	Neuilly-sur-Marne - 2 av. Jean-Jaurès	43 00 96 36

*Le **guide Vert Michelin Paris** (édition en français, anglais et allemand), est le complément indispensable du plan de Paris que vous avez en main.*

Institutions socio-médicales,
Entraide, Secours, Retraite, Maisons d'accueil
Social and medical institutions, Assistance,
Sozialversicherung, Fürsorge, Sociedades Médicas, Mutuas y Seguros

23	E21	**Affaires Sanitaires et Sociales** d'Ile de France	58-62 r. de Mouzaïa, 19e	42 00 33 00
28	K7	**Allocations Familiales Rég. Parisienne** (Caisse)	18 r. Viala, 15e	45 71 34 56
40	L7	**Anselme Payen** (Maison d'accueil)	75 r. Violet, 15e	45 78 65 20
18	E11	**Armée du Salut**	76 r. de Rome, 8e	43 87 41 19
32	J15	**Assistance Publique-Hôpitaux de Paris**	3 av. Victoria, 4e	42 77 11 22
29	J9	**Aveugles de France** (Fédération)	58 av. Bosquet, 7e	45 51 20 08
6	A12	**Bichat** (Long séjour)	170 bd Ney, 18e	40 25 79 02
10	C19	**Caisse Nat. Ass. Vieillesse Trav. Salariés**	110 r. de Flandre, 19e	42 03 30 30
20	D15	**Caisse Primaire Assur. Maladie de Paris**	69 bis r. de Dunkerque, 9e	42 80 63 67
16	F8	**Croix-Rouge Française**	1 pl. Henri-Dunant, 8e	40 70 10 10
20	D16	**Fernand-Widal** (Long séjour)	200 r. Fg St-Denis, 10e	42 80 62 33
35	H22	**Fondation Alquier Debrousse** (Maison d'accueil)	26 r. des Balkans, 20e	43 67 69 69
47	M21	**Fondation de Rothschild** (Maison de retraite)	76 r. de Picpus, 12e	43 44 78 10
29	J10	**Institution Nat. des Invalides**	6 bd des Invalides, 7e	45 50 32 66
45	L17	**Institut Médico-Légal**	2 pl. Mazas, 12e	43 43 78 53
41	L10	**Institut Nat. des Jeunes Aveugles**	56 bd des Invalides, 7e	45 67 35 08
43	L14	**Institut Nat. de Jeunes Sourds**	254 r. St-Jacques, 5e	43 54 82 80
57	P17	**Inst. Nat. Santé et Recherche Médicale**	101 r. de Tolbiac, 13e	45 84 14 41
54	N11	**Julie Siegfried** (Maison d'accueil)	88 r. de Gergovie, 14e	45 43 86 00
41	K10	**Ma Maison** (Maison de retraite)	62 av. de Breteuil, 7e	45 67 97 05
		—	13 r. Philippe de Girard, 10e	42 02 22 20
47	L21	—	71 r. de Picpus, 12e	43 43 43 40
38	M3	—	23 r de Varize, 16e	46 51 36 25
47	L21	**La Muette** (Maison de retraite)	43 r. du Sergent Bauchat, 12e	43 43 12 15
42	N12	**La Rochefoucauld** (Maison de retraite)	15 av. Gal Leclerc, 14e	43 27 23 56
56	P15	**Paralysés de France** (Association)	17 bd Auguste Blanqui, 13e	45 80 82 40
45	M17	**Pitié-Salpétrière** (Long séjour)	47 bd de l'Hôpital, 13e	45 70 21 12
51	R6	**Rosier Rouge** (Foyer d'accueil)	**Vanves** - 16 av. du Général de Gaulle	46 45 61 94
38	L4	**Sainte Périne** (Maison de retraite et long séjour)	11 r. Chardon-Lagache, 16e	45 20 00 09
33	H17	**Secours Populaire Français**	9-11 r. Froissart, 3e	42 78 50 48

Services médicaux d'urgence
Medical emergency numbers, Notruf,
Teléfonos de Urgencia

		SAMU (Paris)		45 67 50 50
		S.O.S. Médecin		47 07 77 77
		S.O.S. Docteurs 92		46 03 77 44
		Urgences médicales de Paris (Jour et Nuit)		48 28 40 04
59	R22	**Ambulances Assistance Publique**	**Charenton** - 28 r. de l'Entrepôt	43 78 26 26
		Radio-Ambulances		47 07 37 39
18	P13	**Centre de soins aux brûlés** (Hôpital Foch)	**Suresnes** - 40 r. Worth	47 72 91 91
16	E7	**Centre anti-drogue** (Hôpital Marmottan)	17-19 r. d'Armaillé, 17e	45 74 00 04
20	D16	**Centre anti-poison** (Hôpital Fernand-Widal)	200 r. du Fg-St-Denis, 10e	42 05 63 29
		Transfusions d'urgence		43 07 47 28
		S.O.S. Vétérinaire (Paris et Région Parisienne) (nuit et dimanches)		48 32 93 30

*Deux **guides Verts Michelin** sur Paris et sa région :*

– Paris
– Ile-de-France

SPECTACLES

ENTERTAINMENTS, VERANSTALTUNGEN, ESPECTÁCULOS

Théâtres, *Theatres, Theater, Teatros*

20	F16	**Antoine-Simone Berriau**	14 bd de Strasbourg, 10ᵉ	42 08 77 71
18	D11	**Arts Hébertot**	78 bis bd des Batignolles, 17ᵉ	43 87 23 23
19	D14	**Atelier**	1 pl. Charles-Dullin, 18ᵉ	46 06 49 24
18	F12	**Athénée**	4 sq. de l'Opéra-L.-Jouvet, 9ᵉ	47 42 67 27
20	D16	**Bouffes-du-Nord**	209 r. du Fg-St-Denis, 10ᵉ	42 39 34 50
19	G13	**Bouffes-Parisiens**	4 r. Monsigny, 2ᵉ	42 96 60 24
52	P8	**Carré Silvia-Monfort**	106 r. Brancion, 15ᵉ	45 31 28 34
28	H7	**Chaillot** (Th. Nat.)	1 pl. du Trocadéro, 16ᵉ	47 27 81 15
29	G9	**Champs-Elysées**	15 av. Montaigne, 8ᵉ	47 20 30 88
55	S13	**Cité Internat. Universitaire**	21 bd Jourdan, 14ᵉ	45 89 38 69
35	G21-H21	**Colline** (Th. Nat.)	15 r. Malte Brun, 20ᵉ	43 66 03 00
18	F12	**Comédie Caumartin**	25 r. Caumartin, 9ᵉ	47 42 43 41
19	D13	**Comédie de Paris**	42 r. Fontaine, 9ᵉ	42 81 00 11
29	G9	**Comédie des Champs-Elysées**	15 av. Montaigne, 8ᵉ	47 23 37 21
31	H13	**Comédie-Française**	2 r. de Richelieu, 1ᵉʳ	40 15 00 15
18	G12	**Daunou**	7 r. Daunou, 2ᵉ	42 61 69 14
18	F12	**Édouard-VII-Sacha Guitry**	10 pl. Édouard-VII, 9ᵉ	47 42 57 49
30	G11	**Espace Pierre Cardin**	1 av. Gabriel, 8ᵉ	42 66 17 30
32	H15	**Essaïon**	6 r. Pierre-au-Lard, 4ᵉ	42 78 46 42
19	E13	**Fontaine**	10 r. Fontaine, 9ᵉ	48 74 74 40
42	M11	**Gaîté-Montparnasse**	26 r. de la Gaîté, 14ᵉ	43 22 16 18
20	F15	**Gymnase-Marie Bell**	38 bd Bonne-Nouvelle, 10ᵉ	42 46 79 79
31	K14	**Huchette**	23 r. de la Huchette, 5ᵉ	43 26 38 99
19	E13	**La Bruyère**	5 r. La Bruyère, 9ᵉ	48 74 76 99
19	G13	**La Michodière**	4 bis r. de La Michodière, 9ᵉ	47 42 95 22
42	L12	**Lucernaire-Berthommé-Le Guillochet**	53 r. N.-D. des-Champs, 6ᵉ	45 44 57 34
18	F11	**Madeleine**	19 r. de Surène, 8ᵉ	42 65 07 09
32	G16	**Marais**	37 r. Volta, 3ᵉ	42 78 03 53
17	G10	**Marigny**	Carré Marigny, 8ᵉ	42 56 04 41
18	F12	**Mathurins**	36 r. des Mathurins, 8ᵉ	42 65 90 00
18	F12	**Michel**	38 r. des Mathurins, 8ᵉ	42 65 35 02
18	F12	**Mogador**	25 r. Mogador, 9ᵉ	42 85 45 30
42	M11	**Montparnasse**	31 r. de la Gaîté, 14ᵉ	43 22 77 74
19	F14	**Nouveautés**	24 bd Poissonnière, 9ᵉ	47 70 52 76
43	K13	**Odéon** (Th. Nat.)	pl. de l'Odéon, 6ᵉ	43 25 70 32
18	E12	**Œuvre**	55 r. de Clichy, 9ᵉ	48 74 42 52
18	F12	**Opéra de Paris** (Th.Nat.)	pl. de l'Opéra, 9ᵉ	42 66 50 22
19	F13	**Opéra de Paris** (salle Favart)	pl. Boieldieu, 2ᵉ	47 42 53 71
21	G17	**Palais des Glaces**	37 r. du Fg-du-Temple, 10ᵉ	46 07 49 93
31	G13	**Palais-Royal**	38 r. de Montpensier, 1ᵉʳ	42 97 59 81
18	E12	**Paris**	15 r. Blanche, 9ᵉ	43 59 39 39
10	C20	**Paris-Villette**	211 av. Jean-Jaurès, 19ᵉ	42 02 02 68
52	P7	**Plaine**	13 r. Gén.-Guillaumat, 15ᵉ	42 50 15 65
42	L12	**Poche Montparnasse**	75 bd du Montparnasse, 6ᵉ	45 48 92 97
20	G16	**Porte-St-Martin**	16 bd St-Martin, 10ᵉ	46 07 37 53
18	G12	**Potinière**	7 r. Louis-Le-Grand, 2ᵉ	42 61 44 16
20	G16	**Renaissance**	20 bd St-Martin, 10ᵉ	42 08 18 50
17	G10	**Renaud-Barrault**	av. Franklin-Roosevelt, 8ᵉ	42 56 60 70
19	E13	**St-Georges**	51 r. St-Georges, 9ᵉ	48 78 63 47
29	G9	**Studio des Champs-Élysées**	15 av. Montaigne, 8ᵉ	47 23 35 10
55	P14	**Théâtre 13**	24 rue Daviel, 13ᵉ	45 88 16 30
33	J18	**Théâtre de la Bastille**	76 r. de la Roquette, 11ᵉ	43 57 42 14
23	F22	**Théâtre de l'Est-Parisien** (TEP)	159 av. Gambetta, 20ᵉ	43 63 20 96
31	J14	**Théâtre Musical de Paris-Châtelet** (TMP)	1 pl. du Châtelet, 1ᵉʳ	42 33 00 00
64	CT	**Théâtre du Soleil** (Cartoucherie)	rte du Champ-de-Manœuvre, 12ᵉ Bois de Vincennes	43 74 24 08
32	J15	**Théâtre de la Ville**	2 pl. du Châtelet, 4ᵉ	42 74 22 77
18	E11	**Tristan Bernard**	64 r. du Rocher, 8ᵉ	45 22 08 40
19	F14	**Variétés**	7 bd Montmartre, 2ᵉ	42 33 09 92

Informations téléphonées sur les expositions, les dates et ouvertures des musées municipaux ☏ 42 78 73 81.

Concert halls, Konzertsäle, Salas de conciertos

17	D9	**Cortot**	78 r. Cardinet, 17ᵉ	47 63 85 72
17	F10	**Gaveau**	45 r. La Boétie, 8ᵉ	45 63 20 30
16	E8	**Pleyel**	252 r. Fg-St-Honoré, 8ᵉ	45 61 06 30

Des concerts et ballets sont fréquemment proposés à la Maison de la Radio et au Palais de Chaillot *(pl. du Trocadéro et du 11-Novembre)*, ainsi que dans les grands théâtres de la capitale (Théâtre Musical de Paris-Châtelet. Théâtre de la Ville, Théâtre des Champs-Élysées...) et à l'Université Paris II *(92 r. d'Assas)*.

Des concerts spirituels et récitals d'orgue sont régulièrement donnés à Notre-Dame, St-Germain-des-Prés, St-Séverin, St-Roch, St-Louis des Invalides, St-Eustache...

Cinéma, *Cinemas, Kinos, Cines*

Consulter la presse chaque mercredi - See newspaper on Wednesdays — Siehe Presse jeden Mittwoch - Consultar los periódicos el miércoles.

Cinémathèque Française : salle Chaillot av. Albert-de-Mun Tél. 47 04 24 24.

Music-halls, cabarets

31	J13	**Alcazar de Paris**	62 r. Mazarine, 6ᵉ	43 29 02 20
28	G8	**Crazy Horse**	12 av. George-V, 8ᵉ	47 23 32 32
19	D14	**Élysée-Montmartre**	72 bd Rochechouart, 18ᵉ	45 52 25 15
19	F14	**Folies-Bergère**	32 r. Richer, 9ᵉ	42 46 77 11
16	F8	**Lido-Normandie**	116 bis av. des Champs-Elysées, 8ᵉ	45 63 11 61
19	D13	**Moulin-Rouge** (Bal du)	82 bd de Clichy, 18ᵉ	46 06 00 19
44	K15	**Paradis Latin**	28 r. du Card.-Lemoine, 5ᵉ	43 25 28 28

Spectacles pour enfants
Children's entertainment
Veranstaltungen für Kinder, Espectáculos para niños

39	M5-N5	**Cirque Gruss** (à l'ancienne) (en hiver)	Pl. Balard, 15ᵉ	42 45 85 85
28	J8	**Marionnettes du Champ-de-Mars**	Allée du Gal Marguerite, 7ᵉ	46 37 07 87
17	G10	**Marionnettes des Champs-Élysées**	Rond-Point des Champs-Elysées, 8ᵉ	46 07 45 69
43	L13	**Marionnettes du Luxembourg**	r. Guynemer,6 ᵉ	43 26 46 47
52	N8	**Marionnettes de Vaugirard**	Square G. Brassens - r. Brancion, 15ᵉ	46 07 45 69
28	H8	**Musée des Enfants**	12 av. de New York, 16ᵉ	47 23 61 27
62	CV	**Musée en Herbe**	Jardin d'Acclimatation 16ᵉ	40 67 97 66
19	D14	— (Halle St-Pierre)	2 r. Ronsard, 18ᵉ	42 58 74 12
62	CV'	**Théâtre du Jardin**	Jardin d'Acclimatation - Bois de Boulogne, 16ᵉ	40 67 97 86

Salles diverses (réunions, variétés, ...)
Other variety halls, Andere Säle, Otras salas

18	E12	**Casino de Paris**	16 r. de Clichy, 9ᵉ	48 74 15 80
20	G16	**Caveau de la République**	1 bd St-Martin, 3ᵉ	42 78 44 45
33	H17	**Cirque d'Hiver**	110 r. Amelot, 11ᵉ	47 00 12 25
16	E8	**Espace Wagram**	39 av. Wagram, 17ᵉ	43 80 30 03
30	H11	**Maison de la Chimie**	28 r. St-Dominique, 7ᵉ	47 05 10 73
18	F12	**Olympia-Bruno-Coquatrix**	28 bd des Capucines, 9ᵉ	47 42 82 45
44	K15	**Palais de la Mutualité**	24 r. St-Victor, 5ᵉ	40 46 11 11
15	E6	**Palais des Congrès**	2 pl. de la Pte-Maillot, 17ᵉ	47 58 12 51
39	N6	**Palais des Sports**	pl. Pte de Versailles, 15ᵉ	48 28 40 90
46	M19	**Palais Omnisports de Paris-Bercy**	8 bd de Bercy, 12ᵉ	43 41 72 04
18	D12	**Théâtre des 2 Anes**	100 bd de Clichy, 18ᵉ	46 06 10 26
11	B21	**Zénith**	211 av. J.-Jaurès, 19ᵉ	42 08 60 00

18	L12	**Amandiers**	Nanterre - 7 av. Pablo-Picasso	47 21 18 81
24	F18	**Boucles de la Marne**	Champigny - 54 bd du Château	48 80 90 90
24	F18	**Centre Municipal d'Animation G.-Philipe**	Champigny - 54 bd du Château	48 80 96 28
24	A8	**Daniel-Sorano**	Vincennes - 16 r. Charles-Pathé	43 74 73 74
22	N20	**Firmin-Gémier**	Antony - pl. Firmin-Gémier	46 66 02 74
18	F24	**Gérard-Philipe**	Saint-Denis - 59 bd Jules-Guesde	42 43 17 17
18	N15	**Hauts-de-Seine**	Puteaux - 5 r. Henri-Martin	47 72 09 59
24	H4	**Jean-Vilar**	Vitry - 9 av. Youri-Gagarine	46 82 84 90
24	K10	**Maison des Arts André-Malraux** **Maison de la Culture de Créteil**	Créteil - pl. Salvador-Allende	48 99 18 88
24	L6-L7	**Paul-Éluard**	Choisy-le-Roi - 4 av. Villeneuve-St-Georges	48 90 89 79
24	H2	**Romain-Rolland**	Villejuif - 18 r. Eugène-Varlin	47 26 15 02
37	N1	**Th. de Boulogne-Billancourt** (TBB)	Boulogne - 60 r. de la Belle-Feuille	46 03 60 44
20	J4	**Th. de la Commune**	Aubervilliers - square Stalingrad	48 34 67 67
18	J20	**Th. de Gennevilliers**	Gennevilliers - 41 av. des Grésillons	47 93 26 30
24	F4	**Th. d'Ivry**	Ivry - 1 r. Simon-Dereure	46 70 21 55
18	J19	**Th. Municipal**	Asnières - 16 pl. de l'Hôtel-de-Ville	47 90 63 12
60	R23	**Th. Municipal**	Charenton-le-Pont - 107 r. de Paris	43 68 55 81
24	G13	**Théâtre Rond Point Liberté**	Saint-Maur - 20 r. de la Liberté	48 89 99 10

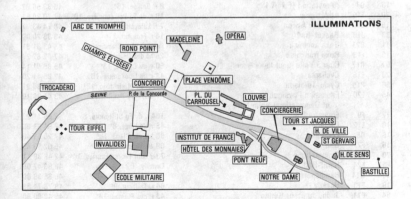

*Un kiosque-théâtre, situé sur le terre-plein Ouest de l'église
de la Madeleine, offre au public la possibilité d'acheter
tous les jours sauf le lundi, entre 12 h 30 et 20 h, des places
de théâtre à moitié prix pour des représentations le soir même.*

18	F11	**Comité National Olympique et Sportif**	23 r. d'Anjou, 8ᵉ	42 65 02 74
64	CT	**Institut Nat. du Sport et de**	11 av. du Tremblay, 12ᵉ	43 74 11 21
		l'Éducation Physique (I.N.S.E.P.)	Bois de Vincennes	
57	P18	**Jeunesse et Sports** Dir. Rég.	6-8 r. Eugène-Oudiné, 13ᵉ	45 84 12 05
45	K17	Dir. de la Ville de Paris	17 bd Morland, 4ᵉ	42 77 15 50

Clubs

44	K15	**Assoc. Sportive de la Police de Paris**	4 r. Montagne-Ste-Geneviève, 5ᵉ	43 54 59 26
53	P10	**Assoc. Sportive des PTT de Paris**	12 allée Gaston-Bachelard, 14ᵉ	45 39 69 14
22	C14	**Athlétic-Club de Boulogne-Billancourt**	Boulogne - Mairie de Boulogne	46 84 78 25
14	E3	**Bowling de Paris**	Bois de Boulogne, 16ᵉ	40 67 94 00
18	F11	**Club Alpin Français**	7 r. La Boétie, 8ᵉ	47 42 36 77
37	L2	**Club Athlétique des Sports Généraux**	av. du Général-Sarrail, 16ᵉ	46 51 55 40
48	M23	**Club des Nageurs de Paris**	34 bd Carnot, 12ᵉ	46 28 77 03
21	D18	**Club de Natation Les Mouettes de Paris**	15 av. Jean-Jaurès, 19ᵉ	42 05 73 14
19	F14	**Paris St-Germain Football-Club**	28 r. Bergère, 9ᵉ	42 46 90 84
43	M13	**Paris Université-Club** (PUC)	31 av. Georges-Bernanos, 5ᵉ	46 33 21 89
61	AX	**Polo de Paris**	Allée du Bord-de-l'Eau -	45 20 10 00
			Bois de Boulogne, 16ᵉ	
41	K10	**Racing-Club de France**	5 r. Eblé, 7ᵉ	45 67 55 86
25	G2	(Croix-Catelan)	Bois de Boulogne, 16ᵉ	45 27 55 85
17	E9	**Racing-Club de Paris**	17, av. Hoche, 8ᵉ	42 89 04 96
14	E3	**Société Bouliste du lac St-James**	Rte de la Muette à Neuilly	40 67 90 44
			Bois de Boulogne, 16ᵉ	
14	F3	**Société Équestre de l'Étrier**	Route de Madrid aux Lacs, 16ᵉ	45 01 20 02
14	E3	**Société d'Équitation de Paris**	Route de la Muette à Neuilly	45 01 20 06
			Bois de Boulogne, 16ᵉ	
37	M2	**Stade Français**	2 r. du Cdt-Guilbaud, 16ᵉ	46 51 66 53
37	N2	**Tennis Club de Paris**	15 av. Félix-d'Hérelle, 16ᵉ	46 47 73 90
21	D17	**Union Sportive Métropolitaine**	159 bd de la Villette, 10ᵉ	42 06 52 38
		des Transports		
16	G7	**Yacht-Club de France**	6 r. Galilée, 16ᵉ	47 20 89 29

Fédérations
Federations, Sportverbände, Federaciones

16	F8	**Aéronautique**	52, r. Galilée, 8ᵉ	47 20 39 75
16	G7	**Aérostation (F.F.A.)**	6 r. Galilée, 16ᵉ	46 33 56 82
20	F15	**Athlétisme**	10 r. du Fg-Poissonnière, 10ᵉ	47 70 90 61
18	E12	Sociétés d'**Aviron**	7 r. Lafayette, 9ᵉ	48 74 43 77
33	J18	**Basket-Ball**	14 r. Froment, 11ᵉ	43 38 20 00
11	B21	**Boxe anglaise**	Pantin -14 r. Scandicci	48 43 61 31
19	F13	**Boxe française**	25 bd des Italiens, 2ᵉ	47 42 82 27
57	R17	**Char à Voile** (Ligue Ile-de-France)	50 r. du Disque, 13ᵉ	45 85 91 14
20	E15	**Cyclisme**	43 r. de Dunkerque, 10ᵉ	42 85 41 20
56	P15	**Cyclo-Tourisme**	8 r. Jean-Marie-Jégo, 13ᵉ	45 80 30 21
46	L20	**Éducation Physique**	41-43, r. de Reuilly, 12ᵉ	43 41 86 10
		et Gymnastique Volontaire		
17	F9	**Équestre Française**	164 r. du Fg-St-Honoré, 8ᵉ	42 25 11 22
18	E12	**Escrime**	45 r. de Liège, 8ᵉ	42 94 91 38
16	G8	**Football**	60 bis av. d'Iéna, 16ᵉ	47 20 65 40
16	F7	**Golf**	69 av. Victor-Hugo, 16ᵉ	45 02 13 55
20	F15	**Gymnastique**	7 ter cour Petites-Écuries, 10ᵉ	42 46 39 11
22	F24	**Hand-Ball**	Gentilly - 62 r. G.-Péri	46 63 47 00
43	N14	**Handisport**	18 r. de la Glacière, 13ᵉ	45 35 39 00
19	F13	**Hockey**	64 r. Taitbout, 9ᵉ	48 78 74 88
54	P11	**Judo, Ju jitsu, Kendo**	43 r. des Plantes, 14ᵉ	45 42 80 90
54	P12	**Karaté**	122 r. de la Tombe-Issoire, 14ᵉ	45 40 65 53
20	F15	**Lutte**	2 r. Gabriel-Laumain, 10ᵉ	48 24 82 35
17	F10	**Montagne et de l'Escalade**	20 bis r. La Boétie, 8ᵉ	47 42 39 80
33	H18	**Motocyclisme**	74 av. Parmentier, 11ᵉ	47 00 94 40
27	J5	**Motonautique**	49 r. de Boulainvilliers, 16ᵉ	45 25 61 76
23	F22	**Natation**	148 av. Gambetta, 20ᵉ	48 57 64 00
19	F13	**Parachutisme**	35 r. St-Georges, 9ᵉ	48 78 45 00
38	M4	**Pelote Basque** (Ligue Ile-de-France)	2 quai Saint-Exupéry, 16ᵉ	42 88 94 99

19	D13	**Pétanque** (Ligue Ile-de-France)	9 r. Duperré, 9ᵉ	48 74 61 63
28	G8	**Randonnée Pédestre**	9 av. George-V, 8ᵉ	47 23 62 32
19	F13	**Rugby**	7 cité d'Antin, 9ᵉ	48 74 84 75
31	H14	**Rugby à Treize**	7 r. Jules-Breton, 13ᵉ	43 31 29 77
16	E7	**Ski** (Antenne parisienne)	81 av. des Ternes, 17ᵉ	45 72 64 40
17	G9	**Ski Nautique**	16 r. Clément-Marot, 8ᵉ	47 20 05 00
21	G18	**Spéléologie**	130 r. St-Maur, 11ᵉ	43 57 56 54
27	G5	**Sport Automobile**	136 r. de Longchamp, 16ᵉ	47 27 97 39
33	H17	**Sportive et Culturelle de France**	24-26 r. Oberkampf, 11ᵉ	
20	L5	**Sportive et Gymnique du Travail**	Pantin - Tour Essor 14 r. Scandicci	48 43 61 31
31	H14	**Sports de Glace**	42 r. du Louvre, 1ᵉʳ	40 26 51 38
20	S7	**Sports Sous-Marins**	Montreuil - 21 r. Voltaire	48 70 92 93
37	L2	**Tennis**	2 av. Gordon-Bennett, 16ᵉ	47 43 48 00
53	S10	**Tennis de Table**	Montrouge - 4, r. Guillot	47 46 97 97
28	G8	**Tir**	16 av. du Prés-Wilson, 16ᵉ	47 23 72 38
6	B11	**Tir à l'Arc**	7 r. des Epinettes, 17ᵉ	42 26 37 00
47	N21N	**Trampoline et Sports Acrobatiques**	4 r. de Capri, 12ᵉ	43 40 28 94
28	G7	**Voile**	55 av. Kléber, 16ᵉ	45 53 68 00
30	K12	**Vol à Voile**	29 r. de Sèvres, 6ᵉ	45 44 04 78
22	D20	**Volley-Ball**	43 bis, r. d'Hautpoul, 19ᵉ	42 00 22 34

Hippodromes
Racecourses, Pferderennbahnen, Hipódromos

26	J3	**Auteuil**	Pelouse Bois de Boulogne, 16ᵉ	45 27 12 25
		Chantilly (60)	Route de l'Aigle	44 57 21 35
18	A19	**Enghien** (95)	Soisy-sous-Montmorency - 1 pl. André-Foulon	39 89 00 12
101	Pli 36	**Évry** (91)	Rte départementale 31	60 77 82 80
61	AY	**Longchamp**	Bois de Boulogne, 16ᵉ	42 24 13 29
18	D8	**Maisons-Laffitte** (78)	av. Molière	39 62 90 95
18	S11	**St-Cloud** (92)	4 r. du Camp-Canadien	47 71 69 26
64	DU	**Vincennes**	2 route de la Ferme, 12ᵉ Bois de Vincennes	43 68 35 39

Patinoires
Skating rinks, Eisbahnen, Pistas de patinaje sobre hielo

21	E18	**Pailleron**	30 r. Édouard-Pailleron, 19ᵉ	42 08 72 26
1	B2	**Centre Olympique**	Courbevoie - pl. Ch.-de-Gaulle	47 88 03 33
18	G18	**Patinoire Olympique**	Asnières - bd P.-de-Coubertin	47 99 96 06
22	C15	**Patinoire municipale**	Boulogne - 1 r. V.-Griffuelhes	46 21 00 96
18	G14	**Patinoire**	Colombes - Ile Marante	47 81 90 09
20	S12	**Patinoire**	Fontenay-s-Bois - av. Ch.-Garcia	48 75 17 00
20	L15	**Patinoire**	Le Raincy - 72 allée du Jardin Anglais et de Finchley	43 81 41 41
18	J23	**Patinoire**	St-Ouen - 4 r. du Docteur-Bauer	40 10 89 19

Piscines
Swimming pools, Schwimmbäder, Piscinas

8	B15	**Amiraux**	6 r. Hermann-Lachapelle, 18ᵉ	46 06 46 47
42	L11	**Armand-Massard**	66 bd du Montparnasse, 15ᵉ	45 38 65 19
54	N12	**Aspirant-Dunand**	20 r. Saillard, 14ᵉ	45 45 50 37
26	J3	**Auteuil**	Rte des Lacs-à-Passy, 16ᵉ	42 24 07 59
6	B11	**Bernard Lafay**	79 r. de la Jonquière, 17ᵉ	42 26 11 05
7	A14	**Bertrand Dauvin**	12 r. René-Binet, 18ᵉ	42 54 51 55
41	L9	**Blomet**	17 r. Blomet, 15ᵉ	47 83 35 05
56	P15	**Butte-aux-Cailles**	5 pl. Paul-Verlaine, 13ᵉ	45 89 60 05
4	C8	**Champerret**	36 bd de Reims, 17ᵉ	47 66 49 98
57	P17	**Château-des-Rentiers**	184 r. Chât.-des-Rentiers, 13ᵉ	45 85 18 26
21	D17	**Château-Landon**	31 r. du Château-Landon, 10ᵉ	46 07 34 68
33	H18	**Cour des Lions**	11 r. Alphonse-Baudin, 11ᵉ	43 55 09 23
30	H11	**Deligny**	Face 25 quai Anatole-France, 7ᵉ	45 51 72 15

53	R9	**Didot**	22 av. Georges-Lafenestre, 14ᵉ	45 39 89 29
45	N17	**Dunois**	70 r. Dunois, 13ᵉ	45 85 44 81
28	J7	**Émile-Anthoine**	9 r. Jean-Rey, 15ᵉ	45 67 10 20
19	D14	**Georges-Drigny**	18 r. Bochart-de-Saron, 9ᵉ	45 26 86 93
22	D20	**Georges-Hermant**	6-10 r. David-d'Angers, 19ᵉ	42 02 45 10
35	J21	**Georges-Rigal** (centre sportif)	115-119 bd de Charonne, 11ᵉ	43 70 64 22
23	F22	**Georges-Vallerey**	148 av. Gambetta, 20ᵉ	43 64 47 00
31	H14	**Halles**	10 pl. de la Rotonde, 1ᵉʳ	42 36 98 44
9	B17	**Hébert**	2 r. des Fillettes, 18ᵉ	46 07 60 01
26	G4	**Henry-de-Montherlant**	32 bd Lannes, 16ᵉ	45 03 03 64
9	C18	**Ilot Riquet**	15, r. Mathis, 19ᵉ	42 41 51 00
44	L15	**Jean-Taris**	16 r. Thouin, 5ᵉ	43 25 54 03
39	L6	**Keller**	14 r. de l'Ing.-Robert-Keller,15ᵉ	45 77 12 12
37	L2	**Molitor**	2 av. de la Pte-Molitor, 16ᵉ	46 51 10 61
34	G19	**Oberkampf**	160 r. Oberkampf, 11ᵉ	43 57 56 19
22	E19	**Pailleron**	30 r. Edouard-Pailleron, 19ᵉ	42 08 72 26
52	P7	**Plaine**	13 r. du Général-Guillaumat, 15ᵉ	45 32 34 00
44	K15	**Pontoise**	19 r. de Pontoise, 5ᵉ	43 54 82 45
39	K6	**R. et A. Mourlon** (Beaugrenelle)	19 r. Gaston-de-Caillavet, 15ᵉ	45 75 40 02
48	M23	**Roger-Le-Gall**	34 bd Carnot, 12ᵉ	46 28 77 03
10	B19	**Rouvet**	1 r. Rouvet, 19ᵉ	40 36 40 97
31	K13	**St-Germain**	7 r. Clément, 6ᵉ	43 29 08 15
32	H15	**St-Merri**	18 r. du Renard, 4ᵉ	42 72 29 45
19	E14	**Valeyre** (Paul-Valeyre)	24 r. de Rochechouart, 9ᵉ	42 85 27 61

Stades
Stadiums, Sportpläze, Estadios

7	A14	**Bertrand-Dauvin**	12 r. René-Binet, 18ᵉ	46 06 08 43
57	S17-S18	**Carpentier**	81 bd Massena, 13ᵉ	45 85 57 43
57	P17	**Charles-Moureu**	12-36 r. Charles Moureu, 13ᵉ	45 83 40 00
53	R9	**Didot**	18 av. Marc Sangnier, 14ᵉ	45 39 89 35
54	R12	**Elisabeth**	7-15 av. Paul Appell, 14ᵉ	45 40 78 39
28	J7	**Emile-Anthoine**	9 r. Jean Rey, 15ᵉ	45 67 25 25
37	L1	**Fond des Princes**	61 av. de la Pte-d'Auteuil, 16ᵉ	46 51 82 80
38	M4	**Fronton Chiquito de Cambo**	2 quai St-Exupéry, 16ᵉ	42 88 94 99
37	M2	**Stade Français** (Centre sportif Géo André)	2 r. du Cdt-Guilbaud, 16ᵉ	46 51 66 53
37	L2	**Jean-Bouin** (CASG)	av. du Gén.-Sarrail, 16ᵉ	46 51 55 40
11	C21	**Jules-Ladoumègue**	1 pl. de la Pte-de-Pantin, 19ᵉ	48 43 23 86
53	R10	**Jules-Noël**	3, av. Maurice-d'Ocagne, 14ᵉ	45 39 54 37
47	N22	**Léo-Lagrange**	68 bd Poniatowski, 12ᵉ	46 28 31 57
36	H23-J23	**Louis-Lumière**	30 r. Louis-Lumière, 20ᵉ	43 70 86 32
6	A12	**Max-Rousie**	28 r. André-Bréchet, 17ᵉ	46 27 17 94
46	M19	**Palais omnisports de Paris-Bercy**	8 bd de Bercy, 12ᵉ	43 41 72 04
37	M2	**Parc des Princes**	24 r. du Cdt-Guilbaud, 16ᵉ	42 88 02 76
15	D6	**Paul-Faber**	17-19 av. de la Pte de Villiers, 17ᵉ	47 57 05 75
64	DU	**Pershing**	Rte du Bosquet-Mortemart, 12ᵉ	43 28 28 93
			Bois de Vincennes	
37	N2	**Pierre-de-Coubertin**	82 av. Georges-Lafont, 16ᵉ	45 27 79 12
51	N5	**Plaine de Vaugirard** (Centre sportif Suzanne Lenglen)	2 r. Louis-Armand, 15ᵉ	45 54 36 12
8	A15	**Poissonniers**	2 r. Jean-Cocteau, 18ᵉ	42 51 24 68
9	A17	**Porte de la Chapelle**	56 bd Ney, 18ᵉ	42 49 10 01
52	P8	**Porte de la Plaine**	13 r. du Général-Guillaumat, 15ᵉ	45 33 56 99
37	L1	**Roland-Garros**	2 av. Gordon-Bennett, 16ᵉ	47 43 48 00
60	P23	**Vélodrome Jacques-Anquetil**	av. de Gravelle, 12ᵉ	43 68 01 27
			Bois de Vincennes	

ALLO SPORTS   42 76 54 54

Information concernant les manifestations sportives
ainsi que les fédérations
et les équipements sportifs à Paris.

TOURISME
TOURISM, TOURISMUS, TURISMO

16	F8	Office de Tourisme de Paris-Accueil de France	127 av. des Champs-Élysées, 8e	47 23 61 72
31	G13	Maison de la France	8 av. de l'Opéra, 1er	42 96 10 23

Organismes,
Tourist associations, Touristische Organisationen, Organismos

16	E7	Association Française des Automobile-Clubs	9 r. Anatole-de-la-Forge, 17e	42 27 82 00
20	F15	Auto-Camping, Caravaning-Club de France	37 r. d'Hauteville, 10e	47 70 29 81
30	G11	Automobile-Club de France	8 pl. de la Concorde, 8e	42 65 08 26
16	F7	Automobile-Club de l'Ile-de-France	14 av. de la Gde-Armée, 17e	43 80 68 58
30	J12	Camping-Club de France	218 bd St-Germain, 7e	45 48 30 03
31	H14	Camping-Club Internat. de France	14 r. des Bourdonnais, 1er	42 36 12 40
19	G13	Compagnie Française du Thermalisme	32 av. de l'Opéra, 2e	47 42 67 91
32	J15	Féd. Franç. de Camping-Caravaning	78 r. de Rivoli, 4e	42 72 84 08
17	F10	Féd. Nat. des Logis et Auberges de France	25 r. Jean-Mermoz, 8e	43 59 86 67
8	C16	Féd. Unies des Auberges de Jeunesse	27 r. Pajol, 18e	45 05 13 14
31	G13	Havas-Voyages (Agence)	26 av. de l'Opéra, 1er	42 61 80 56
30	K12	Ligue Franç.des Auberges de Jeunesse	38 bd Raspail, 7e	45 48 69 84
18	F12	Maison des Gîtes de France	35 r. Godot-de-Mauroy, 9e	47 42 20 20
43	M13	Organisation pour le Tourisme Universitaire O.T.U.-Voyage	137 bd St-Michel, 5e	43 29 12 88
18	F12	Stations Françaises de Sports d'Hiver (Assoc. des Maires)	61 bd Haussmann, 8e	47 42 23 32
31	J14	Tourisme Régie Aut.Transports	53 bis quai Gds-Augustins, 6e	40 46 42 17
18	G11	— (RATP)	pl. de la Madeleine, 8e	40 06 71 45
41	L10	Union Nat. des Associations de Tourisme et de Plein Air	8 r. César-Franck, 15e	43 06 88 21
42	M12	Villages-Vacances-Familles (VVF)	38 bd Edgar-Quinet, 14e	43 20 12 88
19	G13	Wagons-Lits Tourisme (Agence)	32 r. du 4-Septembre, 2e	42 65 45 45

Maisons de Province
French Provincial centres, Vertretungen der Provinzen Frankreichs,
Casas de las Provincias de Francia

34	K20	Féd. Nat. des Groupes Folkloriques Originaires des Provinces Françaises	8 r. Voltaire, 11e	43 72 54 32
31	H13	Alpes-Dauphiné	2 pl. André-Malraux, 1er	42 96 08 43
17	G9	Alsace	39 av. des Champs-Élysées, 8e	43 59 44 24
30	H12	Auvergne	194 bis r. de Rivoli, 1er	42 61 82 38
31	H14	Aveyron	46 r. Berger, 1er	42 36 84 63
27	J5	Basque	10 r. Duban, 16e	42 24 98 87
42	L11	Bretagne	Centre commercial Maine Montparnasse, 15e	45 38 73 15
19	F13	Drôme	14 bd Haussmann, 9e	42 46 66 67
18	F12	Franche-Comté	2 bd de la Madeleine, 9e	42 66 26 28
19	F13	Gers et Armagnac	16 bd Haussmann, 9e	47 70 39 61
31	H13	Hautes-Alpes	4 av. de l'Opéra, 1er	42 96 05 08
31	K14	Hérault (Espace)	8 r. de la Harpe, 5e	
19	F13	Limousin	18 bd Haussmann, 9e	47 70 32 63
19	G13	Lot-et-Garonne	15-17 pass. Choiseul, 2e	42 97 51 43
31	K14	Lozère	4 r. Hautefeuille, 6e	43 54 26 64
34	H19	Morvan	25 r. St-Maur, 11e	47 00 53 15
19	F13	Nord-Pas-de-Calais	18 bd Haussmann, 9e	47 70 59 62
19	F13	Périgord	30 r. Louis-le-Grand, 2e	47 42 09 15
42	K11	Poitou-Charentes	68-70 r. du Cherche-Midi, 6e	42 22 83 74
19	G13	Pyrénées	15 r. St-Augustin, 2e	42 61 58 18
16	E8	Rouergue (Artisans du)	89 bd de Courcelles, 8e	43 80 84 48
19	F13	Savoie	16 bd Haussmann, 9e	45 23 05 50
17	D9	Tarn	34 av. de Villiers, 17e	47 63 06 26
18	F12	Antilles et Guyane	12 r. Auber, 9e	42 68 11 07
18	G12	La Réunion	1 r. Vignon, 8e	42 68 07 88
44	K15	Tahiti et ses Iles	28 bd St-Germain, 5e	

TRANSPORT
VERKEHRSMITTEL, COMUNICACIONES

Autobus Métro
Buses-Metro, Autobus-Metro

31	J14	**Régie Autonome des Transports Parisiens** (RATP) Renseign.	53 ter quai Gds-Augustins, 6e	40 46 41 41
			—	43 46 14 14

Consulter en outre le plan sur lequel figurent les itinéraires d'autobus p. 174 à 177, et le plan de métro p. 180 et 181.

Automobile
Motoring organizations, PKW, Automóvil

16	F8	**Chambre Syndicale des Constructeurs Automobiles**	2 r. de Presbourg, 8e	47 23 54 05
16	G7	**Féd. Nat. des Transports Routiers**	6 r. Paul-Valéry, 16e	45 53 92 88
17	E9	**Prévention Routière**	6 av. Hoche, 8e	42 67 97 17

Location de voitures
Car hire companies, Autovermietung, Coches de alquiler

29	K10	**Avis**	5 r. Bixio, 7e	45 50 32 31
37	N2	**Avis Train + Auto**	Boulogne - 72 av. P.-Grenier	46 09 92 12
6	C12	**Budget Milleville**	19 r. Ganneron, 18e	05 10 00 01
41	L9	**Cie Industr. Franç. Autom.** (CIFA-Peugeot)	80 bd Garibaldi, 15e	45 67 35 24
46	L19	**CITer**	11 r. Érard, 12e	05 05 10 11
18	E11	**C.L.V.-SOVAC**	17 r. de la Bienfaisance, 8e	40 08 28 28
42	M11	**EUROPCAR**	48-50 av. du Maine, 15e	43 21 28 37
29	H10	**Hertz**	Aérogare des Invalides, 7e	45 51 20 37
41	K9	**interRent**	42 av. de Saxe, 7e	45 67 69 07
55	N14	**Inter Touring Service**	117 bd A. Blanqui, 13e	45 88 52 37
17	F9	**LOCA-DIN**	79 av. Champs-Elysées, 8e	42 99 66 33
45	L18	**Mattei**	205 r. de Bercy, 12e	43 46 11 50

Compagnies de Taxis-radio

Taxis bleus 42 02 42 02
Alpha Taxis 47 30 23 23

Taxis G7 47 39 33 33 - 47 39 32 51
Taxis Radio-Étoile 42 70 41 41

Stations de taxis avec borne téléphonique
Taxi ranks with phone nos, Taxistationen mit Telefon, Paradas de taxis con teléfono.

Sur le plan, le signe ☎ signale les stations disposant d'une borne téléphonique (liste ci-dessous).

1er Arrondissement

31	H13	Pl. André-Malraux	42 60 61 40
32	J15	Pl. du Châtelet	42 33 20 99
30	G11	258 r. de Rivoli	42 61 67 60

2e Arrondissement

19	F13	7 pl. de l'Opéra	47 42 75 75
20	G16	19 bd St-Denis	42 36 93 55

3e Arrondissement

32	H16	64 r. de Bretagne	42 78 00 00
32	H15	20 r. Beaubourg	42 72 00 00

4e Arrondissement

32	J16	Métro St-Paul	48 87 49 39
32	K16	23 bd Morland	42 77 59 88

5e Arrondissement

44	M15	88 bd St-Marcel	43 31 00 00
44	L15	Pl. Monge	45 87 15 95
44	K16	Pont de la Tournelle	43 25 92 99
43	L14	26 r. Soufflot	46 33 00 00
31	J14	Pl. St-Michel	43 29 63 66
32	K15	Pl.Maubert	46 34 10 32

6e Arrondissement

31	K13	91 bd St-Germain	43 26 00 00
31	J13	Métro Mabillon	43 20 00 00
42	L11	Pl. du 18-Juin-1940	42 22 13 13
30	K12	Pl. A.-Deville	45 48 84 75
31	J13	149 bd St-Germain	42 22 00 00
43	M13	20 av. de l'Observatoire	43 54 74 37

7ᵉ Arrondissement

28	H8	2 av. Bosquet	47 05 66 86
28	J8	36 av. La Bourdonnais	47 05 06 89
29	J9	28 av. de Tourville	47 05 00 00
30	J12	Métro R. du Bac	42 22 49 64
41	L10	Métro Duroc	45 67 00 00
29	H10	Métro La Tour-Maubourg	45 55 78 42
30	H11	Métro Solférino	45 55 00 00
41	K10	7 pl. de Breteuil	45 66 70 17
30	H11	Pl. Prés.-E.Herriot	47 05 03 14
28	J7	Tour Eiffel	45 55 85 41
29	H10	27 bd de Latour-Maubourg	45 51 76 76

8ᵉ Arrondissement

17	F9	1 av. de Friedland	45 61 00 00
18	F11	8 bd Malesherbes	42 65 00 00
18	F11	44 bd Malesherbes	47 42 54 73
28	G8	Pl. de l'Alma	43 59 58 00
16	E8	Pl. des Ternes	47 63 00 00
17	G9	Rd-Pt Champs-Elysées	42 56 29 00
17	E10	Pl. Rio-de-Janeiro	45 62 00 00

9ᵉ Arrondissement

18	D12	Pl. de Clichy	42 85 00 00
18	E12	Église de la Trinité	48 74 00 00
19	E14	2 r. Pierre-Semard	48 78 00 00
19	F14	9 r. Drouot	42 46 00 00
19	E14	Square de Montholon	48 78 00 00

10ᵉ Arrondissement

| 21 | F18 | 137 av. Parmentier | 42 03 00 00 |

11ᵉ Arrondissement

34	K19	Métro Faidherbe-Chal.	43 72 00 00
34	G19	Métro Ménilmontant	43 55 64 00
34	H20	Métro Père-Lachaise	48 05 92 12
34	J19	Pl. Léon-Blum	43 79 00 00
47	K21	1 av. du Trône	43 73 29 58
33	G17	1 av. de la République	43 55 92 84

12ᵉ Arrondissement

33	K18	6 pl. de la Bastille	43 45 10 00
47	M21	9 pl. Félix-Éboué	43 43 00 00
48	N23	1 pl. E.-Renard	46 28 00 00
64	CT	Terminus RATP	48 08 00 00
		Château de Vincennes	

13ᵉ Arrondissement

55	N14	127 bd A.-Blanqui	45 80 00 00
57	P18	Carr. Patay-Tolbiac	45 83 00 00
56	P16	1 av. d'Italie	45 83 34 93
44	N16	Pl. Pinel	45 86 00 00
57	S17	36 av. de la Pte de Choisy	45 85 40 00
56	S16	Métro Pte d'Italie	45 86 00 44

14ᵉ arrondissement

53	N10	Métro Plaisance	45 41 66 00
53	P9	Métro Pte de Vanves	45 39 87 33
43	N13	Pl. Denfert-Rochereau	43 35 00 00
54	R12	1 pl. du 15-Août-1944	45 40 52 05
54	P12	228 av. du Maine	45 45 00 00
55	P14	1 av. Reille	45 89 05 71

15ᵉ arrondissement

40	M8	Mairie du 15e arr.	48 42 00 00
28	J7	Métro Bir-Hakeim	45 79 17 17
40	M7	Métro Boucicaut	45 58 15 00
40	M8	Métro Convention	42 50 00 00

40	K8	Métro La Motte-Picquet	45 66 00 00
41	L10	Métro Sèvres-Lecourbe	47 34 00 00
39	L6	Pl. Charles-Michels	45 78 20 00
52	N7	1 bd Lefebvre	48 28 00 00
41	N9	5 r. de Cronstadt	48 28 45 98
39	L5	Rd-Pt du Pont Mirabeau	45 77 48 00

16ᵉ Arrondissement

16	F7	1 av. Victor-Hugo	45 01 85 24
27	H6	10 bd Delessert	45 20 00 00
38	M4	23 bd Exelmans	45 25 93 91
27	G5	78 av. Henri-Martin	45 04 00 00
27	K5	Pl. du Docteur-Hayem	42 24 99 99
26	K4	Métro Jasmin	45 25 13 13
27	J5	Métro Muette	42 88 00 00
39	L5	Pl. de Barcelone	45 27 11 11
27	K5	Pl. Clément-Ader	45 24 56 17
38	K4	Pl. Jean-Lorrain	45 27 00 00
15	G6	12 pl. Victor-Hugo	45 53 00 11
27	H6	1 av. d'Eylau	47 27 00 00
38	L3	114 bd Exelmans	46 51 14 61
15	F5	Métro Pte-Dauphine	45 53 00 00
38	L3	27 bd Murat	46 51 19 19
38	M3	Pl. de la Pte-de-St-Cloud	46 51 60 40

17ᵉ Arrondissement

18	D11	Mairie du 17ᵉ arr.	43 87 00 00
6	C11	Métro Brochant	46 27 00 00
17	D10	Métro Villiers	46 22 00 00
16	D8	Pl. Aimé-Maillart	46 22 40 70
16	F8	1 av. de Wagram	43 80 01 99
16	D8	3 pl. Maréchal-Juin	42 27 00 00
5	D9	Pl. du Nicaragua	42 67 59 67
17	E9	Pl. Républ.-de-l'Équateur	47 66 80 50
5	C9	13 bis bd Berthier	43 80 00 00
4	D7	1 bd Gouvion-St-Cyr	47 66 22 77
5	B10	1 bd Berthier	46 27 90 06
6	B12	1 bd Bessières	42 63 00 00

18ᵉ Arrondissement

8	C15	Pl. du Château-Rouge	42 52 00 00
6	B12	Métro Guy-Môquet	42 28 00 00
7	B14	Pl. Jules-Joffrin	46 06 00 00
19	D13	Pl. Blanche	42 57 00 00
20	D16	Pl. de la Chapelle	42 08 00 00
7	D14	4 r. du Mont-Cenis	42 59 00 00
7	A14	1 av. de la Pte-de-Clignancourt	42 58 00 00
7	C13	2 r. Damrémont	42 54 00 00
8	C16	Métro Marx-Dormoy	46 07 88 00
7	C14	Métro Lamarck-Caulaincourt	42 55 00 00

19ᵉ Arrondissement

22	F20	5 r. Lassus	42 08 42 66
22	D19	Mairie du 19ᵉ arr.	42 06 00 00
22	E20	Métro Botzaris	42 05 00 00
21	E18	Pl. du Colonel-Fabien	42 08 00 00
23	E22	1 av. de la Pte-des-Lilas	42 02 71 40
11	C21	211 av. Jean-Jaurès	46 07 21 10
10	A20	Av. de la Pte-de-la-Villette	42 08 64 00
9	C18	185 r. de Crimée	42 39 28 27
21	D17	2 r. de Flandre	42 40 00 00

20ᵉ Arrondissement

35	H21	16 av. du Père-Lachaise	46 36 00 00
23	G22	2 pl. Paul-Signac	43 62 70 99
36	G23	Pl. de la Pte-de-Bagnolet	43 60 60 79
36	J23	Métro Pte-de-Montreuil	43 70 00 00
33	G18	Métro Pyrénées	43 49 10 00

French Railways, Franz. Eisenbahn, Ferrocarriles franceses

18	E12	**Soc. Nat. Chemins de Fer Français**	88 r. St-Lazare, 9ᵉ	42 85 60 00
		(SNCF) Direction Générale		
		— Renseignements téléphonés voyageurs		45 82 50 50
		— Réservations		45 65 60 60
45	L17	**Gare d'Austerlitz**	55 quai d'Austerlitz, 13ᵉ	
46	M19	**Gare de Bercy**	48 bis bd de Bercy, 12ᵉ	
20	E16	**Gare de l'Est**	pl. du 11-Novembre-1918, 10ᵉ	
42	M11	**Gare Montparnasse**	16-24 pl. Raoul-Dautry, 15ᵉ	
20	E16	**Gare du Nord**	18 r. de Dunkerque, 10ᵉ	
45	L18	**Gare de Paris-Lyon**	pl. Louis-Armand, 12ᵉ	
41	M10	**Gare de Paris-Vaugirard**	r. du Cotentin, 15ᵉ	
18	E11	**Gare St-Lazare**	r. St-Lazare, 8ᵉ	

French airlines, Franz. Fluggesellschaften, Compañías aéreas francesas

20	E8	**Aéroport du Bourget** (93)	Le Bourget	48 62 12 12
69-70		**Aéroport Charles-de-Gaulle** (95)	Roissy-Charles-de-Gaulle	48 62 22 80
67		**Aéroport d'Orly** (94)	Orly - Aérogare	48 84 32 10
16	F8	**Air France**	119 av. des Champs-Elysées, 8ᵉ	42 99 23 64
		Renseignements-réservations		45 35 61 61
		vols arrivée		43 20 12 55
		vols départ		43 20 13 55
29	H10	**Terminal Air France des Invalides**	Esplanade des Invalides, 7ᵉ	43 23 97 10
		arrêt d'autocars (vers Orly) :		
29	H10	— Invalides	2 r. R.-Esnault-Pelterie, 7ᵉ	43 23 97 10
42	M11	— Montparnasse	36 av. du Maine, 14ᵉ	43 23 97 10
		arrêt d'autocars (vers Roissy) :		
15	E6	— Palais des Congrès	rez-de-chaussée	42 99 20 18
16	F7	— pl. Charles-de-Gaulle	angle av. Carnot, 17ᵉ	42 99 20 18
30	G12	**Air Inter**	12 r. de Castiglione, 1ᵉʳ	45 39 25 25
39	N5	**Héliport de Paris**	4 av. de la Pte-de-Sèvres, 15ᵉ	
		Hélicap	—	45 57 75 51
		Hélifrance	—	45 57 53 67
		Héli-Location	—	45 57 66 33
18	F11	**Union Transports Aériens** (UTA)	3 bd Malesherbes, 8ᵉ	42 66 30 30

Compagnies aériennes étrangères, voir p. 57 à 68

French shipping companies, Franz. Schiffahrtsgesellschaften, Compañías marítimas francesas

65		**Cie Générale Maritime** (Siège)	**La Défense** - Tour Winterthur	49 03 94 00
18	F11	**Paquet**	5 bd Malesherbes, 8ᵉ	42 66 57 59
18	F12	**Sté Nat. Maritime Corse-Méditerranée**	12 r. Godot-de-Mauroy, 9ᵉ	42 66 67 98

Traffic information, Verkehrsinformationen, Información telefónica del estado de las carreteras

	F I P 514 (circulation à Paris)		45 25 50 50
	Voirie (fermeture du boulevard périphérique et des voies sur berge)		42 76 52 52
	Centre Régional d'Information et de Coordination Routière d'Ile-de-France		48 99 33 33

LÉGENDE

SIGNES CONVENTIONNELS

Voirie

Autoroute, boulevard périphérique . . . .

Rue en construction, interdite ou impraticable . . . .

Rue à sens unique, en escalier . . . .

Allée dans parc et cimetière - Rue piétonne . . . .

Chemin de fer, métro aérien . . . .

Passage sous voûte, tunnel . . . .

Bâtiments (avec entrée principale)

Repère important - Autre bâtiment repère . . . .

Culte catholique ou orthodoxe . . . .

Culte protestant - Synagogue . . . .

Caserne - Caserne de Sapeurs-Pompiers . . . .

Hôpital, hospice - Marché couvert . . . .

Bureau de poste - Commissariat de police . . . .

Sports et Loisirs

Piscine de plein air, couverte . . . .

Patinoire . . . .

Stade - Stade olympique - Terrain d'éducation physique . . . .

Centre hippique - Hippodrome . . . .

Aviron - Canoë-kayak - Ski nautique . . . .

Motonautisme - Club de voile . . . .

Signes divers

Monument - Fontaine - Usine . . . .

Station taxi - Station de métro . . . .

Parking avec entrée . . . .

Station-service ouverte nuit et jour . . . .

Numéro d'immeuble . . . .

Limite de Paris et de département . . . .

Limite d'arrondissement et de commune . . . .

Repère du carroyage . . . .

Repère commun à la carte Michelin n° 101 . . . .

Pa. At. 7

CONVENTIONAL SIGNS

Roads and railways
. . . . Motorway, ring road
. . . . Street under construction, No entry - unsuitable for traffic
. . . . One-way street - Stepped street - Pedestrian street
. . . . Arch, tunnel

Buildings (with main entrance)
. . . . Reference point : large building, other building
. . . . Catholic or orthodox church - Protestant church - Synagogue
. . . . Barracks - Police station - Fire station
. . . . Hospital, old people's home - Post office - Covered market

Sports - Leisure activities
. . . . Outdoor, indoor swimming pool - Skating rink
. . . . Olympic Stadium - Sports ground

Miscellaneous
. . . . Monument - Fountain - Factory - House no. in street
. . . . Main taxi ranks - Metro station
. . . . . Car park showing entrance - 24 hour petrol station
. . . . Paris limits ; adjoining departments
. . . . « Arrondissement » and « commune » boundaries
. . . . Map grid reference number
. . . . . . Reference no. common to Michelin map no. **101**
(Secteur en travaux) : Work in progress

ZEICHENERKLÄRUNG

Verkehrswege
. . . . Autobahn - Stadtautobahn
. . . . Straße im Bau - für Kfz gesperrt, nicht befahrbar
. . . . . . Einbahnstraße - Treppenstraße - Fußgängerstraße
. . . . Gewölbedurchgang - Tunnel

Gebäude (mit Haupteingang)
. . . . . . Wichtiger Orientierungspunkt - Sonstiger Orientierungspunkt
. . . . . Katholische oder orthodoxe Kirche - Evangelische Kirche - Synagoge
. . . . Kaserne - Polizeirevier - Feuerwehr
. . . . Krankenhaus, Altersheim - Postamt - Markthalle

Sport - Freizeit
. . . . Freibad - Hallenbad - Schlittschuhbahn
. . . . Olympianormen entsprechendes Stadion - Sportplatz

Verschiedene Zeichen
. . . . Denkmal - Brunnen - Fabrik - Hausnummer
. . . . Größere Taxistation - Metrostation
. . . . . Parkplatz und Einfahrt - Tag und Nacht geöffnete Tankstelle
. . . . Grenze : Pariser Stadtgebiet u. Departement
. . . . Arrondissement und Vorortgemeinde
. . . . Nr. des Planquadrates
. . . . . . Referenz-Zeichen für die Michelin-Karte Nr. **101**
(Secteur en travaux) : Das Viertel wird neugestaltet

SIGNOS CONVENCIONALES

Vías de circulación

Autopista, autovía de circunvalación . . . .
Calle en construcción, prohibida, impracticable . . . .
Calle de sentido único, con escalera - Calle peatonal . . . .
Paso abovedado, túnel . . . .

Edificios (y entrada principal)

Gran edificio, punto de referencia - Otro edificio, punto de referencia . . . . .

Iglesia católica u ortodoxa - Culto protestante - Sinagoga . . . .

Cuartel - Comisaría de Policía - Parque de Bomberos . . . .

Hospital, hospicio - Oficina de Correos - Mercado cubierto . . . .

Deportes y Distracciones

Piscina al aire libre, cubierta - Pista de patinaje . . . .
Estadio olímpico - Terreno de educación física . . . .

Signos diversos

Monumento - Fuente - Fábrica - Número del edificio . . . .
Estación principal de taxis - Boca de metro . . . .
Aparcamiento y entrada - Estación de servicio abierta día y noche . . . .
Límite de París departamento . . . .
Límite de distrito o de municipio . . . .

Referencia de la cuadrícula del plano . . . .
Referencia común al mapa Michelin No. 101 . . . .
(Secteur en travaux) : Sector en obras

Le pont Alexandre-III et les Invalides.

Utilisez le plan MICHELIN à 1/15 000 « Banlieue de Paris Nord-Ouest » n° 18

N 314 PONTOISE
N 13 ST GERMAIN-EN-LAYE

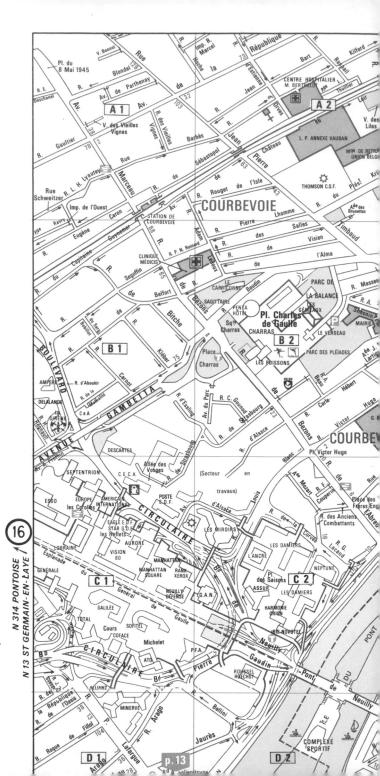

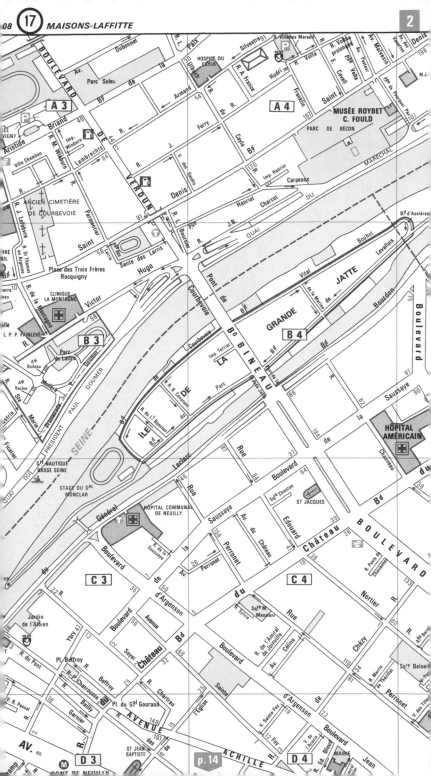

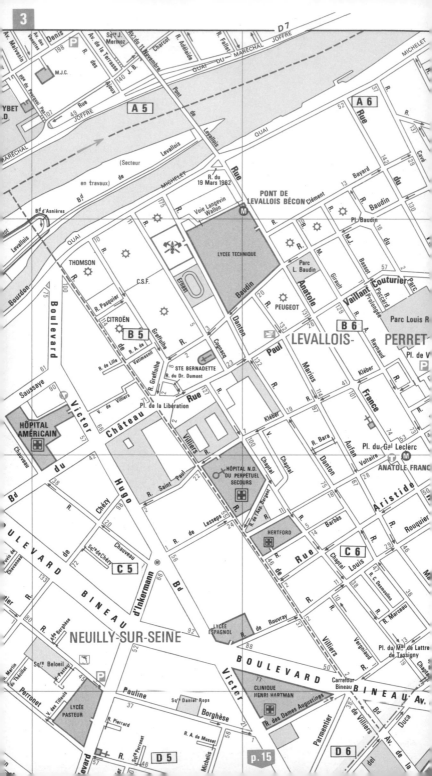

N 309

GAZ DE FRANCE

CIMETIÈRE DE
LEVALLOIS PERRET

A 7

Baudin

Café M. Ravel
Pl. du 11 Nov 1918

des Chasses

Jeanne
d'Asnières

A 8

Bac d'Asnières

STATION CLICHY LEVALLOIS

CIMETIÈRE S
DE CL

Belgrand

Collange

STE REINE

Raspail

Vaillant Couturier

Paul

Guesde

Camille

Vaillant

Marjolin

Pelletan

Brossolette

Victor Hugo

Briand

Gare
Gravel

Pl. du
8 Mai 1945

R. de Bretagne

Jaurès

B 7

ST JUSTIN

Av. du Gal
de Gaulle

Voltaire

MAIRIE
Pl. de la République

Aristide

Edouard

Rivay

Rue

Rue

Brossolette

Raspail

Jean Ferry

Rouquier

Youri

Gagarine

Dequingand

Lorraine

Alsace

d'

Rue

Victor

Hugo

R. Pablo

Neruda

B 8

Bo DU FORT DE VAU

Louis

Jules

Vaillant Jaurès

Imp. Genevoix

Allée

de

Alsace

P

STADE
LOUISON BOBET

PORTE
D'ASNIÈRES

BO DU FOR

Porte
d'A

du Prêt

Barbusse

Henri

Michel

Gabriel Péri

Jean

Wilson

R. G.
Eiffel

Parc G.
Eiffel

R. L.
Blanc

Guesde

Curnonsky

R. Ludwig

DE

REIMS

DE

REIMS

Olympiades

Brunetière

R. Marceaux

R. Redon

R. Suize

la

Porte

d'A

E

Barbusse

Louise

Carnot

France

Ibert

R. Perrier

Pge
d'Iéna

R. M. Ravel

Rue

T.E.P.

C 7

R. du Marquis
d'Arlandes

R. R. Pinet

R. R. Pinet

Av.

C 8

R. Pissarro

R. Gauguin

BERTHIER

Delorme

T

ESPACE
CHAMPERRET
Ostreicher

ORTE DE
HAMPERRET

MICHEL

Peugeot

SOMME

PORTE DE COURCELLES
Square
Ste Odile
STE ODILE

BOULEVARD

BOULEVARD

BOULEVARD

Av. E. et A. Massard

J. Gervex

Pte Paul
Leautaud

R. E. Flachat

GOURGAUD

AV.

COURCELLES

Roll

PEREIRE

R. Ch.
Gerhardt

R. Puvis de
Chavannes

R. de Neuilly

Café de l'Amérique
Latine

Pl. de la Porte
de Champerret

T

Capitaine Ménard

J. Moreau

STEPH. MALLARMÉ

Square
J. Bellat

Pl. Stuart
Merrill

M

PORTE DE
CHAMPERRET

LA

DE

BOULEVARD

AVE

Châtelain

R. A. Samain

PL. du Mal
Sqe A. Besnard

PÉREIRE-LEVALLOIS

D 8

L'YSER

R. Ch. Debussy

V. Berthier

D 7

p. 16

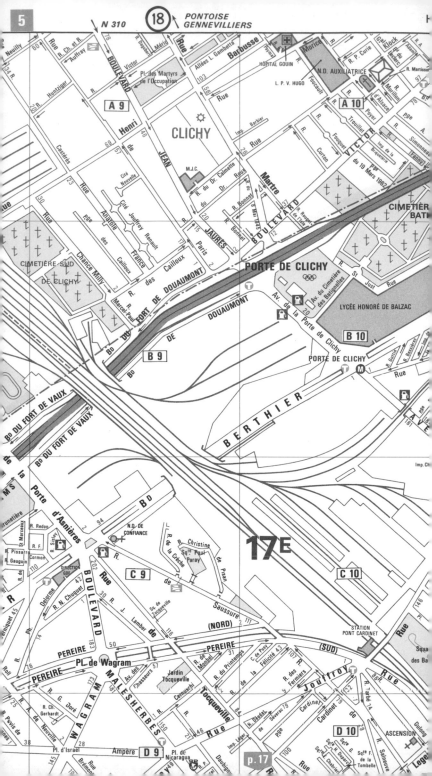

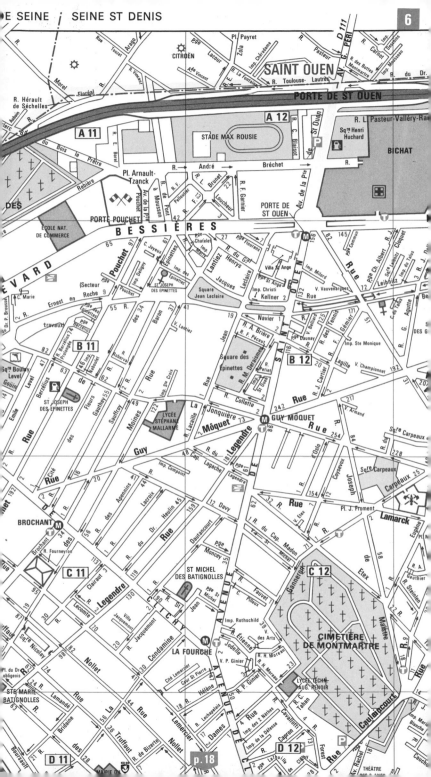

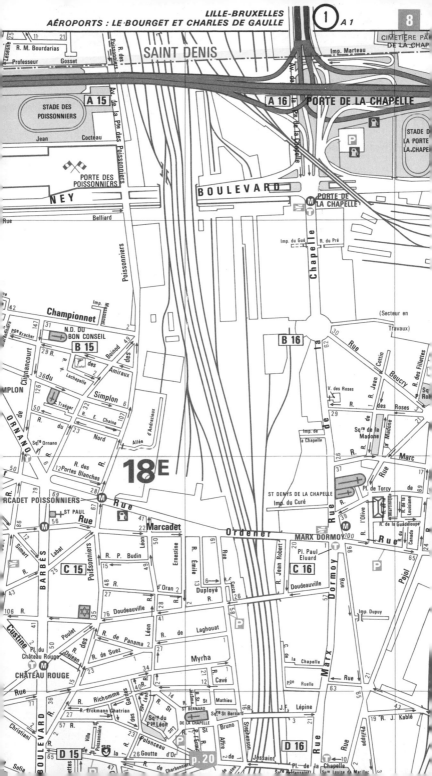

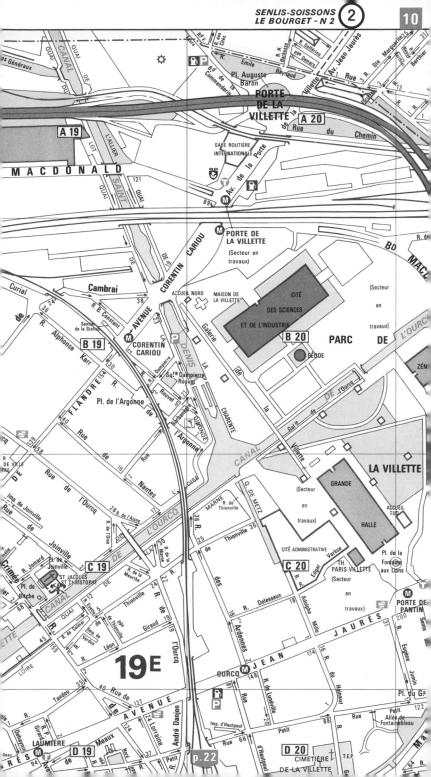

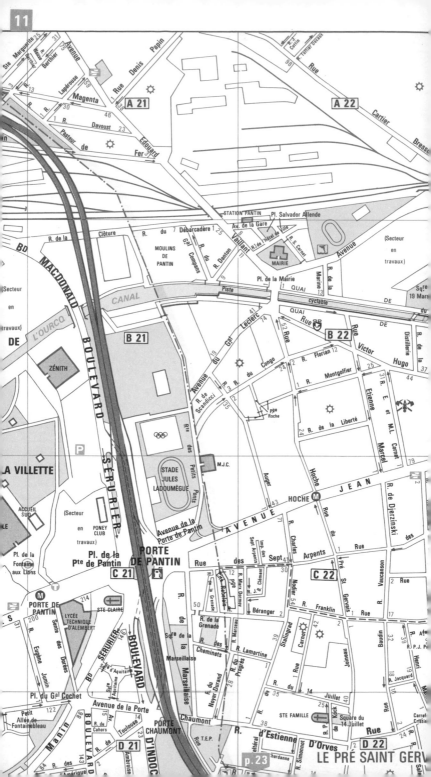

A 21

A 22

Cartier

Brasse

Magenta

Lagerouse

Berthier

Avenue

Ste Marguerite

Papin

Denis

Rue

Fer

Edouard

de

Pasteur

Davoust

Cetlin

R. Tratur Dreux

Rue

STATION PANTIN

Pl. Salvador Allende

Av. de la Gare

Débarcadère

Taillant

R. de l'Hôtel de Ville

S. Carnet

MAIRIE

Avenue

(Secteur

en

travaux)

R. de la

Clôture

R. du

Gal Compans

R. Denton

MOULINS
DE
PANTIN

Pl. de la Mairie

Marina

R. du

QUAI

Sofe
19 Mars

DE

CANAL

Piste

cyclable

DE

BD

MACDONALD

L'OURCQ

DE

BOULEVARD

B 21

QUAI

Leclerc

Gal

Rue

B 22

Rue

Victor

Hugo

Distillerie

ZÉNITH

Avenue

du

R. de
Scandicci

Congo

R. Florian

Montgolfier

Etienne

E. et M.L Carnet

Marcel

Pge
Roche

R. de la Liberté

Rte

des

Petits

Ponts

M.J.C.

Auger

Hoche

JEAN

R. de Dierzinski

des

P

STADE
JULES
LADOUMÈGUE

LA VILLETTE

ACCUEIL
SUD

(Secteur

en

travaux)

PONEY
CLUB

Avenue de la
Porte de Pantin

AVENUE

HOCHE M

Rue

Charles

R. Pte St Gervais

Rue

Rue

2

Pl. de la
Fontaine
aux Lions

M T

Pl. de la
Pte de Pantin

SÉRURIER

PORTE
DE PANTIN

C 21

PORTE
DE PANTIN

Rue

des

Sept

Arpents

C 22

Rue

2

Voivenauu

PORTE DE
PANTIN

LYCÉE
TECHNIQUE
D'ALEMBERT

STE CLAIRE

BOULEVARD

SÉRURIER

R.

de

la

R. Marx Dormy

Clément

Pge

J. B.

Nodier

R.
St
Gervais

R. Franklin

Rue

R.

Eugène

Jumin

Ste des
Dortes

Bd
d'Aquitaine

Sofe de la
Marseillaise

R. de la
Grenade

des

Béranger

Carnot

Henri

R. Jacquard

Rue

Pl. du Gal Cochet

Avenue de la Porte

PORTE
CHAUMONT

Chaumont

Petit
Allée de
Fontainebleau

R. de
Cahors

Toulouse

Ambroise

D 21

BOULEVARD

D'INDOC

Cheminets

R. Lamartine

Stalingrad

R.
du
Progrès

R. du
Noyer Durand

Rue

du

Juillet

Kick

Square du
14 Juillet

STE FAMILLE

R. P.

Rue

D'Orves

D 22

D'Estienne

T.E.P.

Rue

LE PRÉ SAINT GER

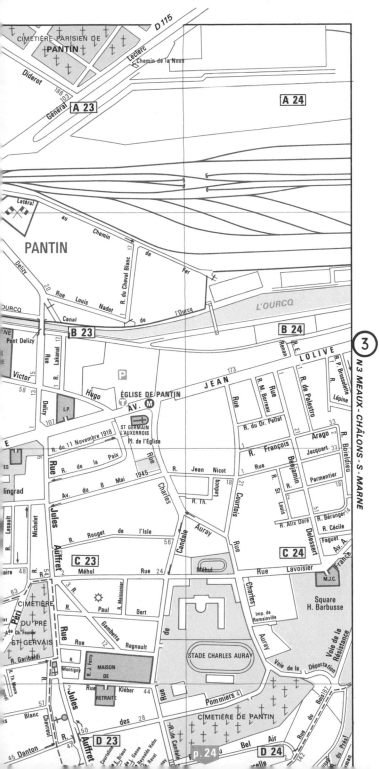

③ N 3 MEAUX - CHÂLONS - S - MARNE

CIMETIÈRE PARISIEN DE **PANTIN**

D 115

Leclerc

Chemin de la Noue

Diderot

Général

A 23

A 24

PANTIN

Latéral

au

Chemin

de

R. du Cheval Blanc

Fer

Delizy

Rue Louis Nadot

Canal de l'Ourcq

L'OURCQ

OURCQ

Pont Delizy

B 23

B 24

Rue Lakanal

Renan

R.E.

L O L I V E

R.P. Brossolette

Victor

Delizy

Hugo

ÉGLISE DE PANTIN

AV. Ⓜ

JEAN

Rue

R. M. Borreau

Rue

R. de Palestro

R.

Lépine

LP.

ST GERMAIN L'AUXERROIS Pl. de l'Eglise

R. du Dr. Pallat

Arago

R. Boïeldieu

R.-du 11 Novembre 1918

R. Jean Nicot

R. François

Jacquart

lingrad

Rue

R. de la Paix

Rue Charles

Rue

Langel

R. Courtois

Benjamin

Rue

R. St Louis

Parmentier

Av. du 8 Mai 1945

R. Th.

R. Alix Doré

R. Béranger

Michelet

Jules

Auffret

R. Rouget de l'Isle

Auray

Candale

R. Cécile

Faguet

Av. A.

R. Lesault

C 23

Méhul

Rue

Méhul

Rue

Lavoisier

C 24

France

M.J.C.

CIMETIÈRE DU PRÉ ST-GERVAIS

Aée Ch. Fourier

R.

Paul

Bert

R. Maissonat

Gambetta

Regnault

de

Charles

Imp. de Romainville

Square H. Barbusse

Voie de la Résistance

R. Garibaldi

R. Th. More

Rue

Montigny

R. J. Ferry

MAISON DE RETRAITE

Kléber

STADE CHARLES AURAY

Auray

Voie de la Déportation

Jules

Auffret

D 23

Rue

des

Rue

Pommiers

CIMETIÈRE DE PANTIN

Bel

Air

Rue du Bois

Danton

Chevreul

p. 24

D 24

Utilisez le plan MICHELIN à 1/15 000 « Banlieue de Paris Nord-Ouest » n° 18

HAUTS DE SEINE

R. Roque

R. Lafargue 36

Rue Arago

Jean 28

Bd A. Soljenitsyne

BOUTON

p. 1

PUTEAUX

SPORTIF

PARC
LEBAUDY

D 1

D 2

R. 60

R. des Pavillons

Sq a

Léon Blum

LE FRANCE

3

PUTEAUX

NEUILLY

Général

R. de Longchamp

R. V. Daix 2

R. F. Passy

R. du Bois

Boulevard

21

55

61

58

GODEFROY

BRAS

DE

DION

QUAI

GRAND

DE

BRAS

DE

NEUILLY

ÎLE

DE

STADE COMMUNAL
DE L'ÎLE DE
PUTEAUX

N 187

E 1

Général

Koenig

R.

103

R. Charles
Bernard Metman

Windsor

9

MUSÉE

R.

22

Longchamp

du

Delabordère

Saint James

Av.

6

12

91

Rd pt
St James

V. Léonard
de Vinci

E 2

Rue

Centre

Rue

la

R. 32

de

de

Rue

Pont

de Puteaux

Bd

du

Route

F 1

CHAMP

D'ENTRAÎNEMENT

26 R. Ernest Deloison 2

V. des Peupliers

17

Bd Julien Potin

141

5 Bd

Porte
de la Seine

LES ARCHERS
DE PARIS

Neuilly

D 1

Allée du Bord de l'Eau

de

Sèvres

Pl. de
Bagatelle

ST-LOUIS

Porte de Bagatelle

Richard

Rue

R. de Bagatelle

Av.

de

R. du Mal de
Lattre de Tassigny

Porte St James

Bretteville

15

23

Wallace

27

Bd

Carrefour de l
Porte de Madr

Champ

d'Entraînement

Queue

Longue

F 2

PARC

DE

la

Marguerite

Cavalière

des

BAGATELLE

de

Allée

Route

des

Reine

BOIS

DE

LONGC

Route

cyclable

Route
du Point du

Laca

à

G 1

p. 25

G 2

43

17

22

43

32

35

Bd

Piste

35

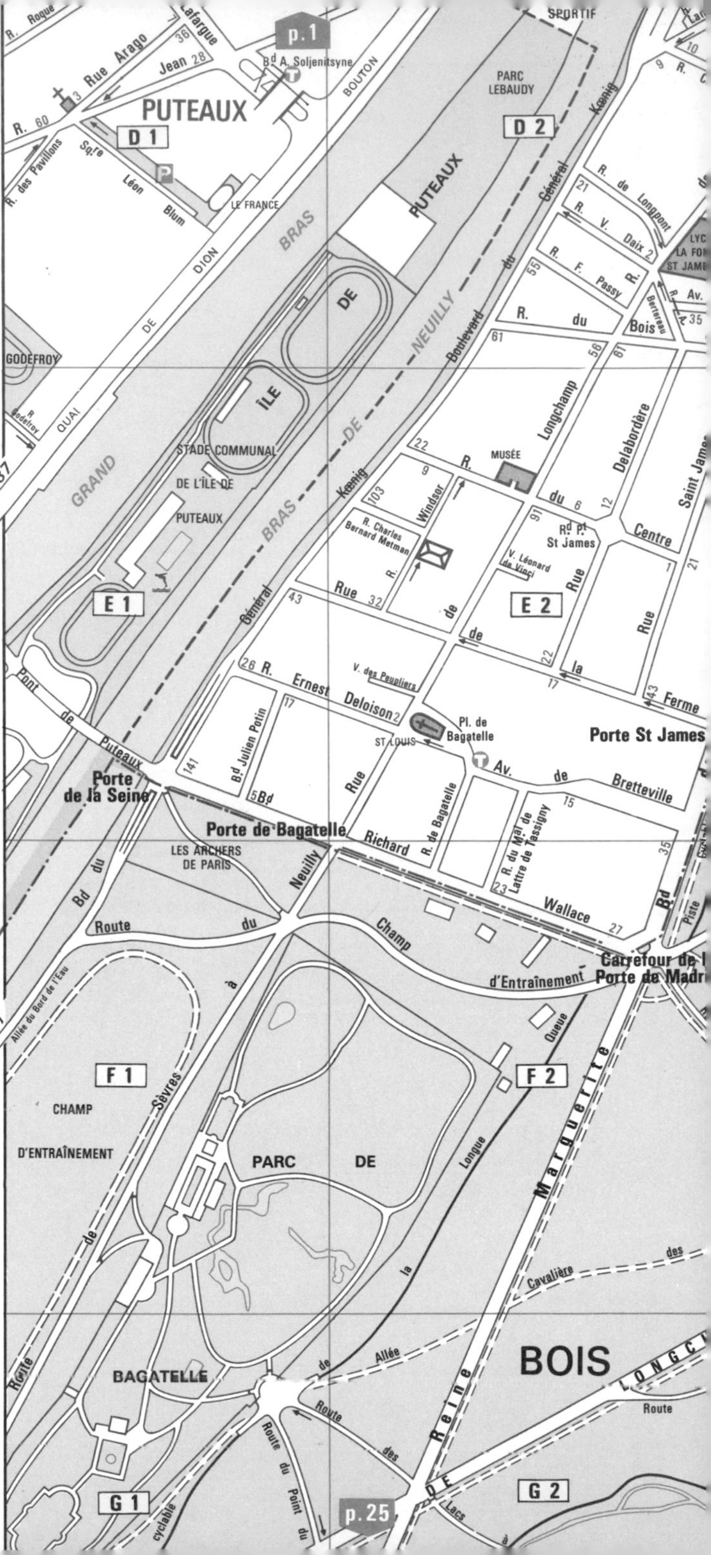

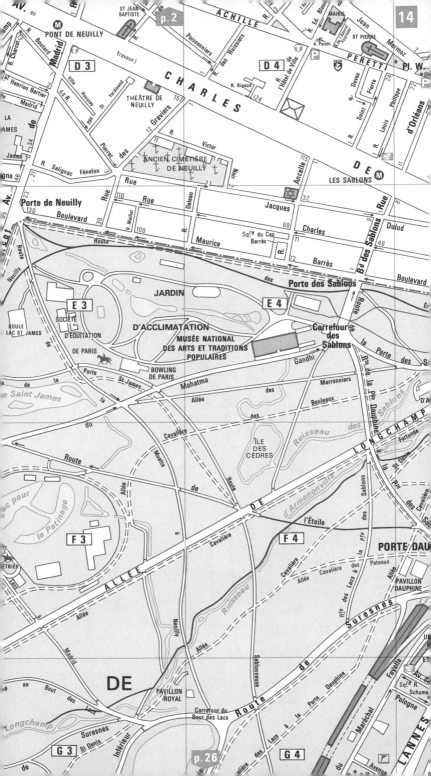

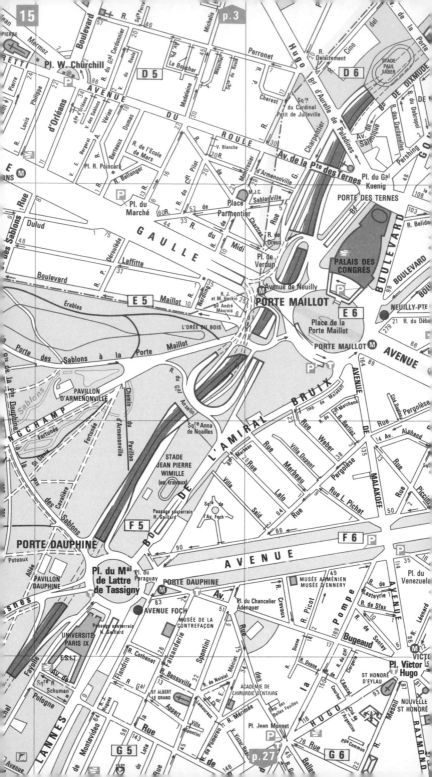

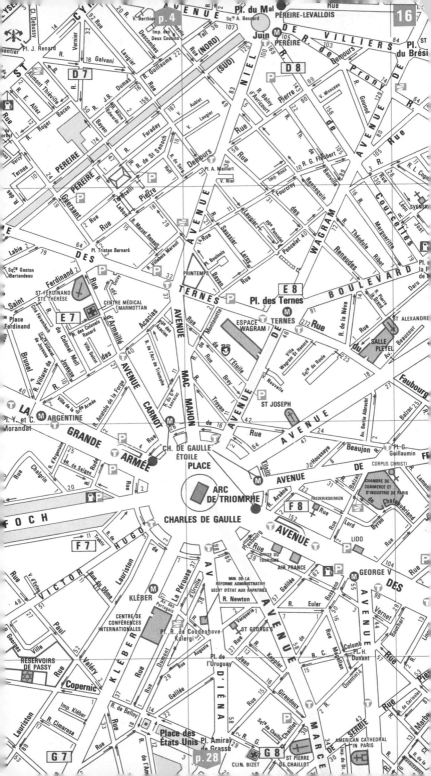

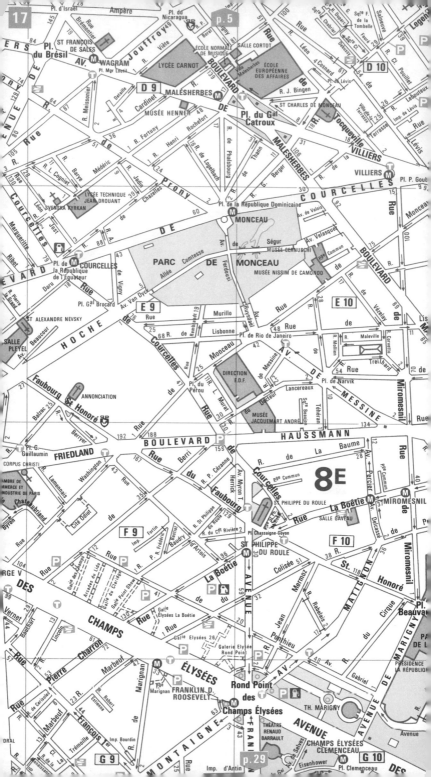

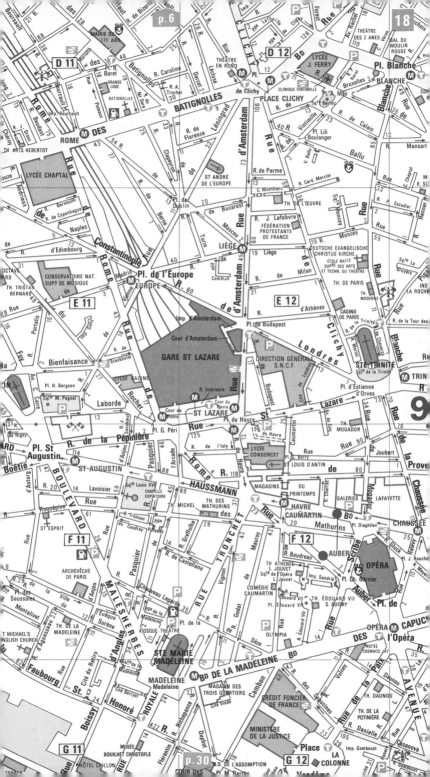

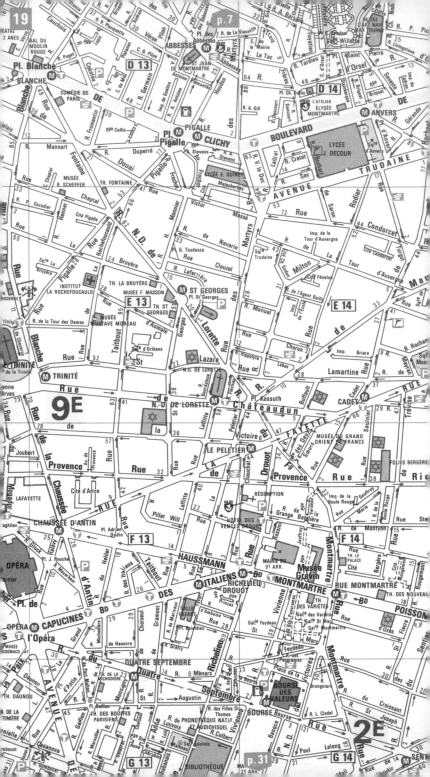

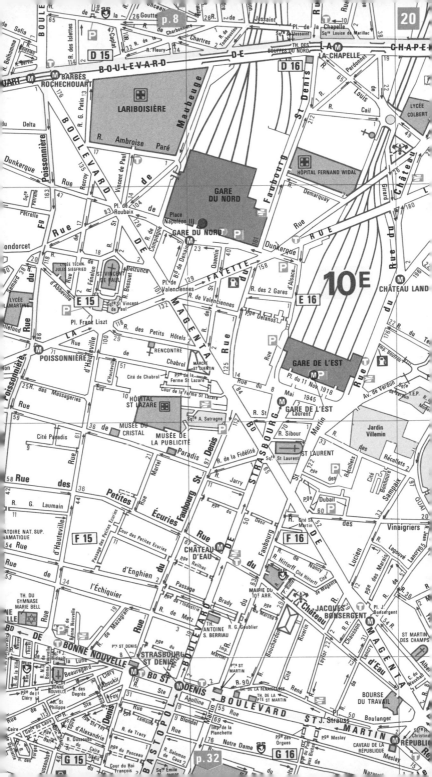

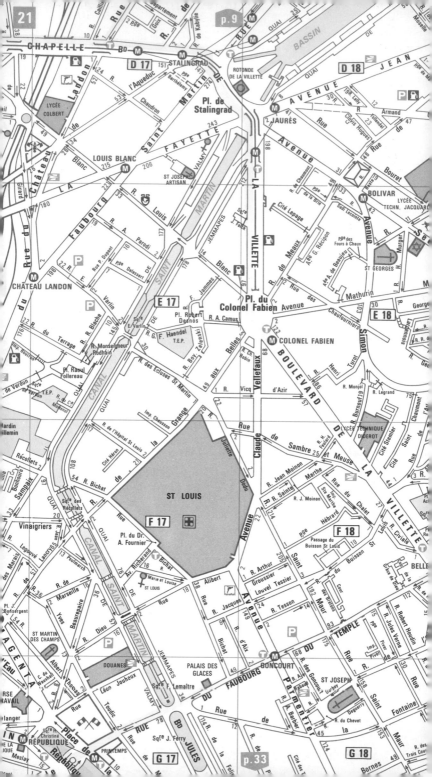

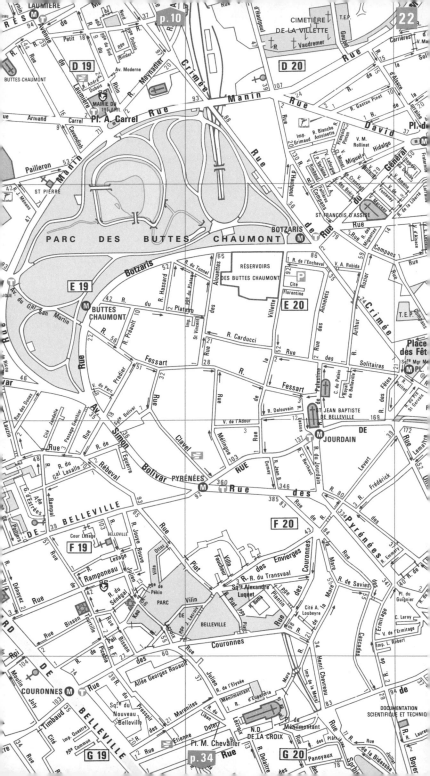

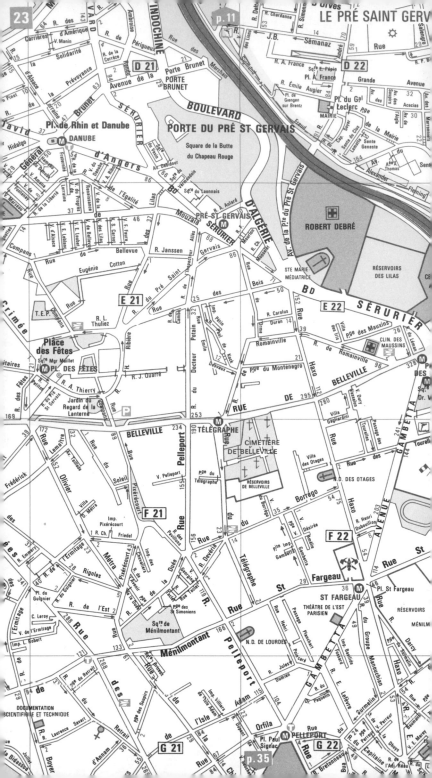

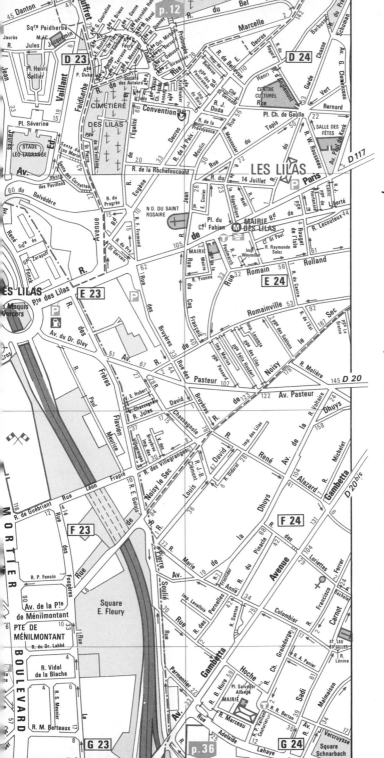

p. 12

Utilisez le plan MICHELIN à 1/15 000 « Banlieue de Paris Nord-Est » n° 20

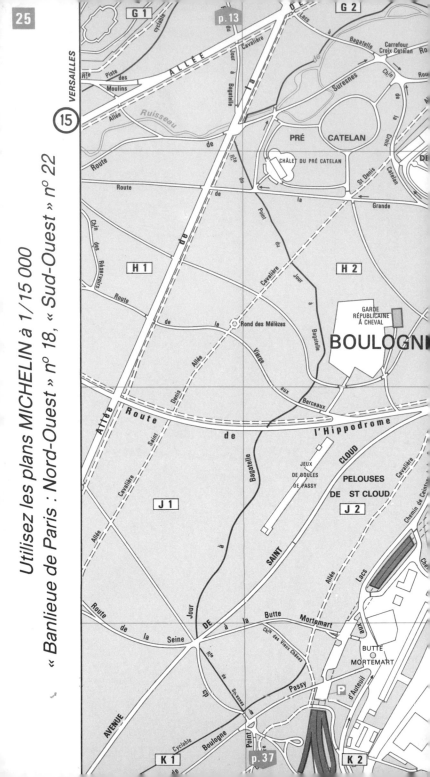

VERSAILLES

p. 13

15

Utilisez les plans MICHELIN à 1/15 000

« Banlieue de Paris : Nord-Ouest » n° 18, « Sud-Ouest » n° 22

G 1

G 2

Carrefour
Croix Catelan

cyclière
Allée

Piste
des
Moulins

Ruisseau

Route

Route

Chin des Réservoirs

Route

de

Allée

à

Jour
à
Bagatelle

Cavalière

la
de

Rte du

de

Point
du

Cavalière
Jour
à
Bagatelle

de

la
la

Suresnes

de
la
Croix

PRÉ   CATELAN

CHÂLET DU PRÉ CATELAN

St Denis
Grande

Catelan

DE

H 1

H 2

la   ◦ Rond des Mélèzes

Viaduc

aux

Berceaux

GARDE
RÉPUBLICAINE
À CHEVAL

BOULOGN

Allée   R o u t e

Saint

Denis

Allée

Cavalière

Allée

Route

de

de   la   Seine

à
Jour
DE

Bagatelle

à

Rte

de

Sevres

Passy

à

la   Butte

Chin des Vieux Chênes

l' Hippodrome

JEUX
DE BOULES
DE PASSY

CLOUD

PELOUSES
DE ST CLOUD

Cavalière

Chemin de Ceinture

Allée

Lacs

Châl

Cha

J 1

J 2

SAINT

Mortemart

BUTTE
MORTEMART

P
d'Auteuil

AVENUE

Cyclable   Boulogne

Point

à

K 1

K 2

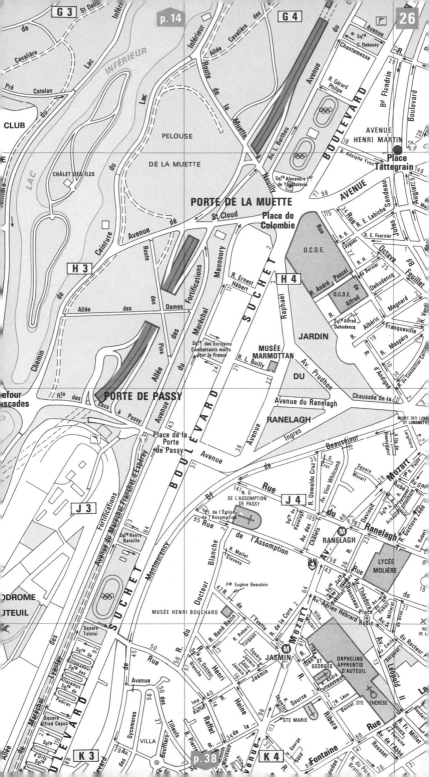

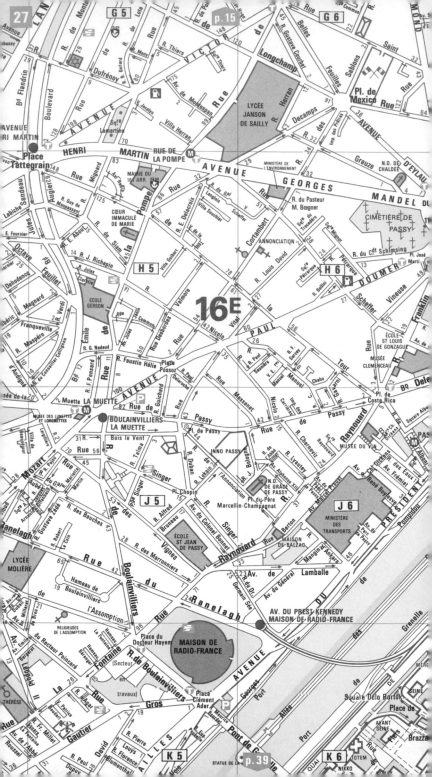

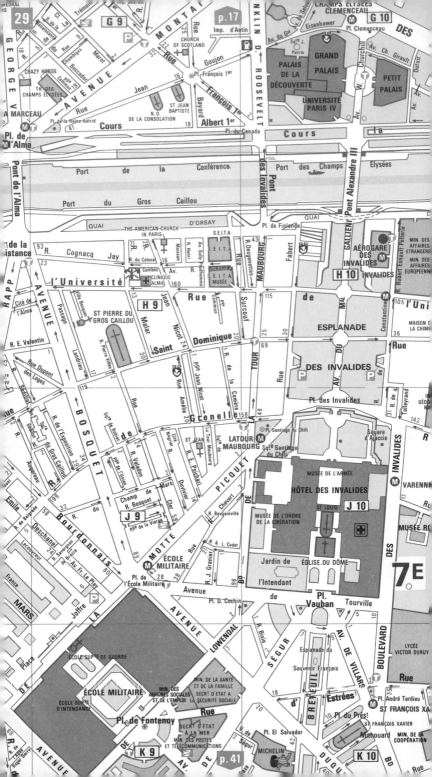

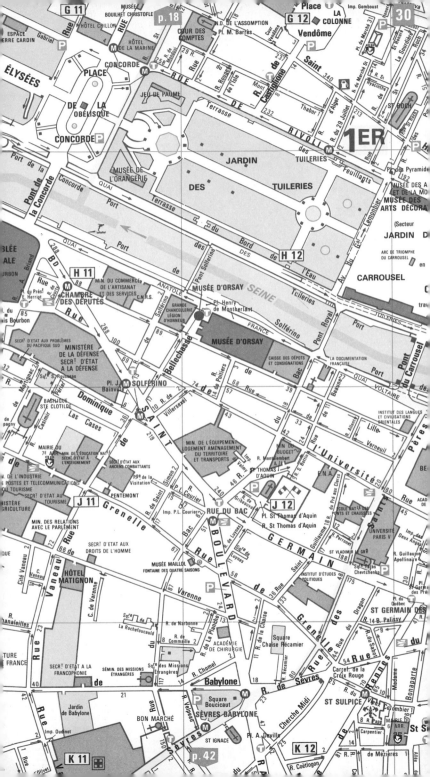

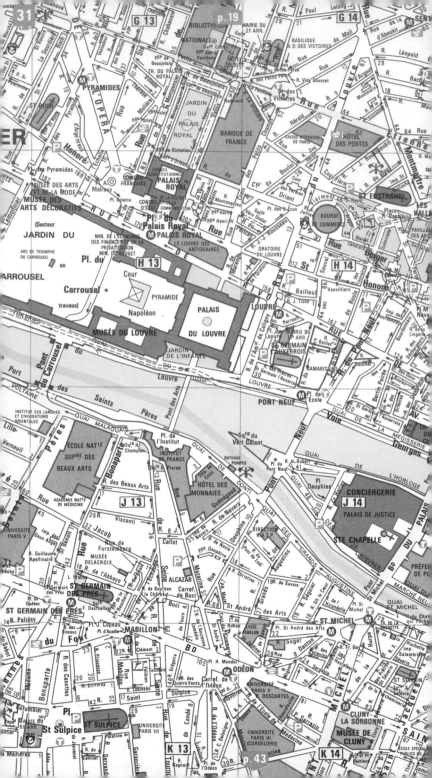

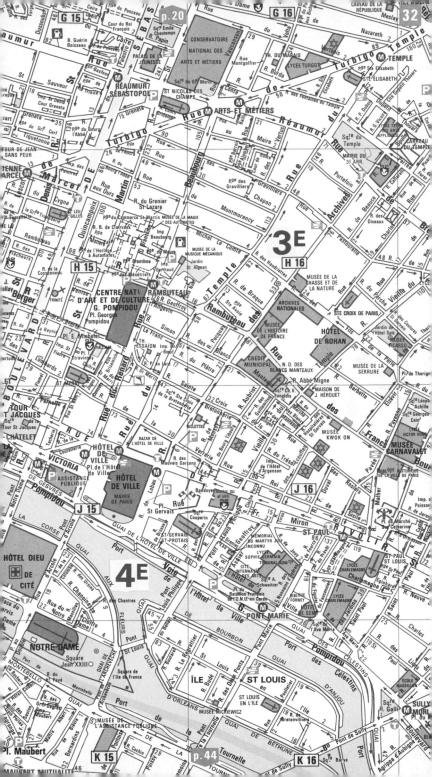

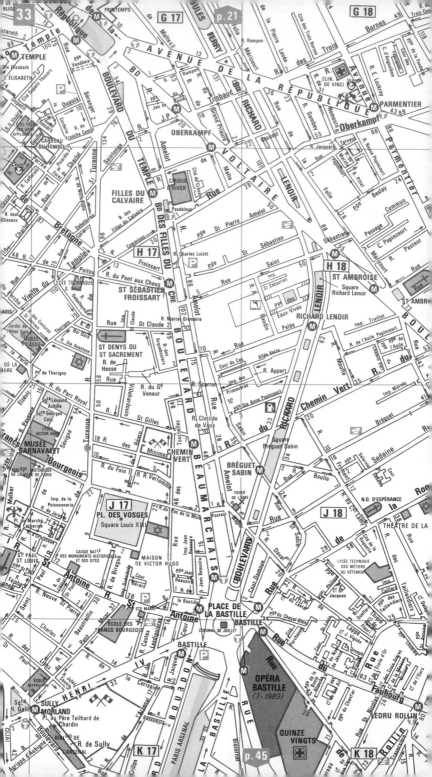

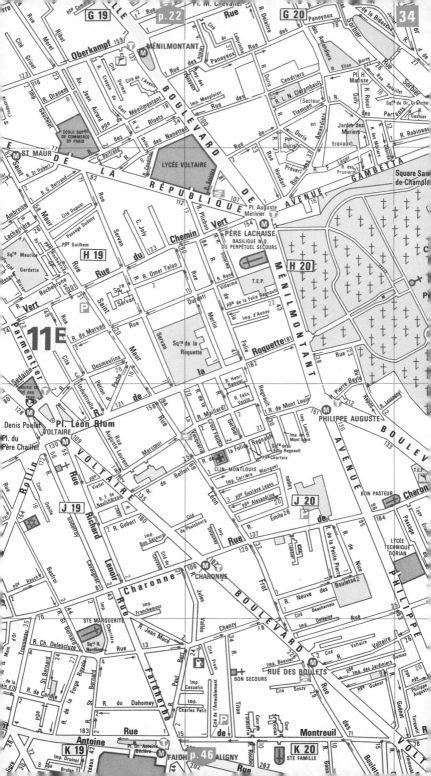

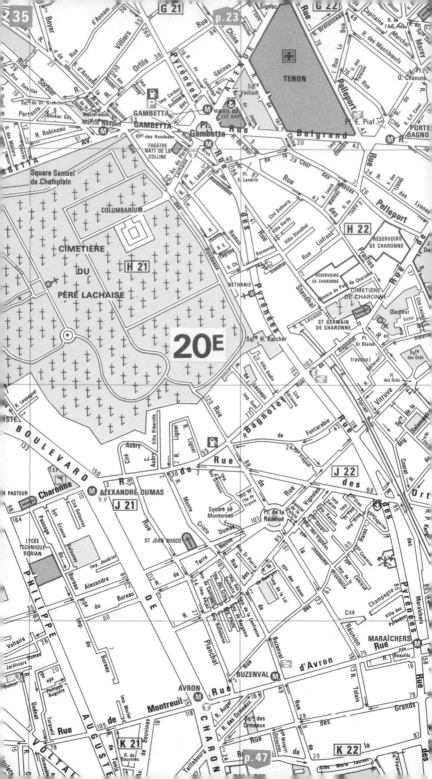

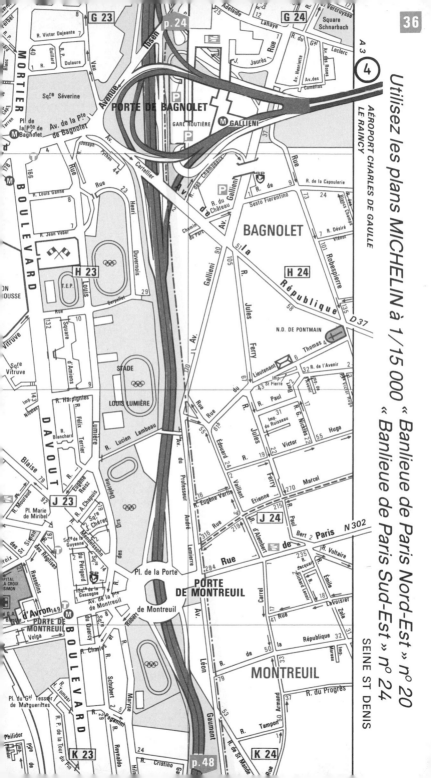

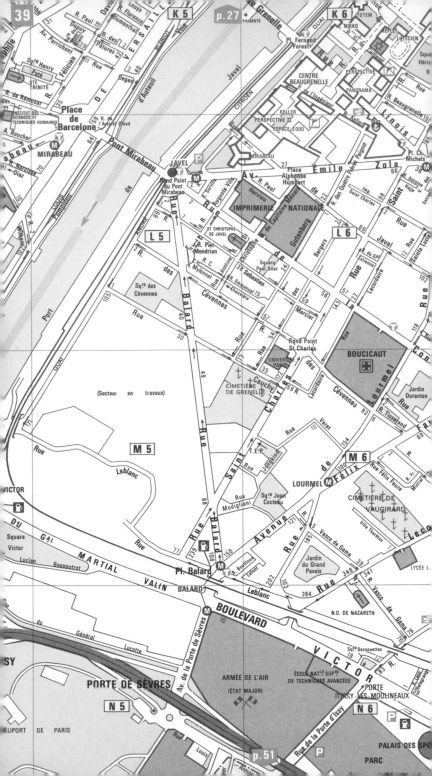

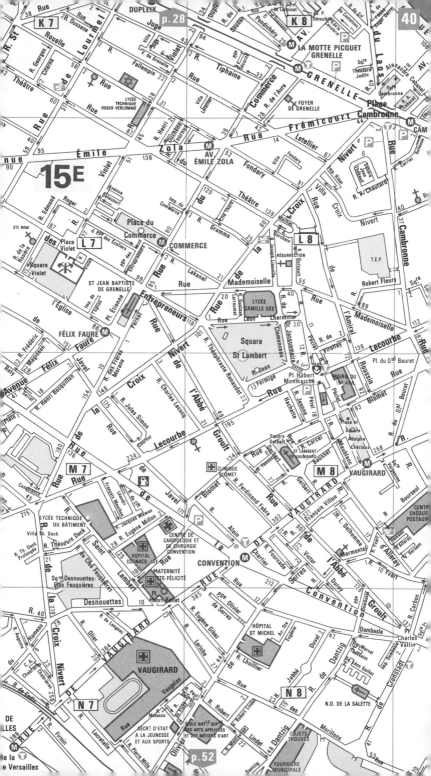

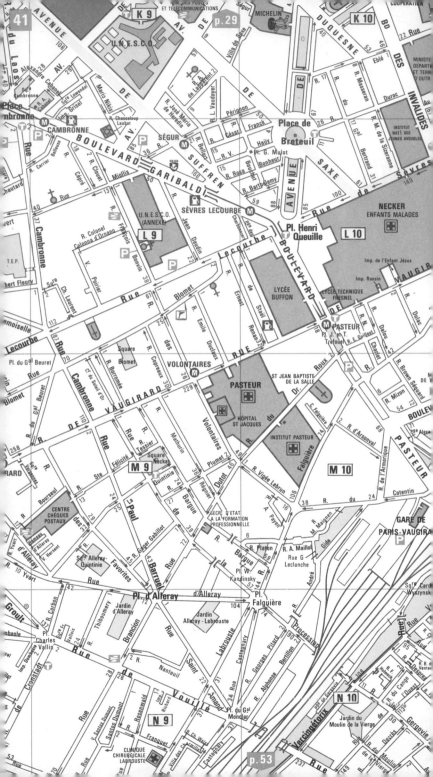

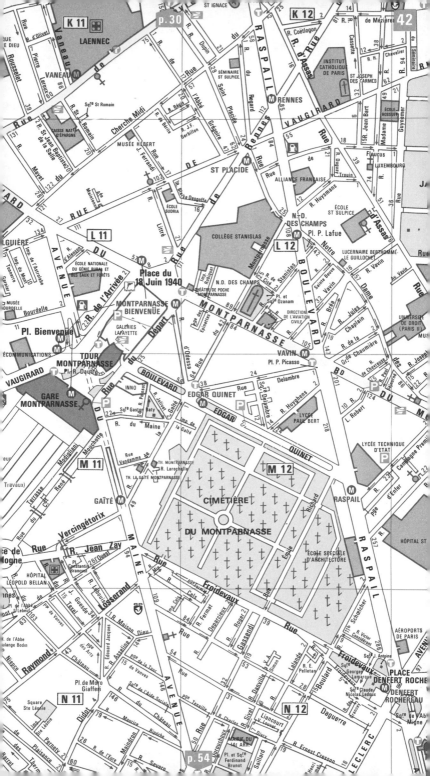

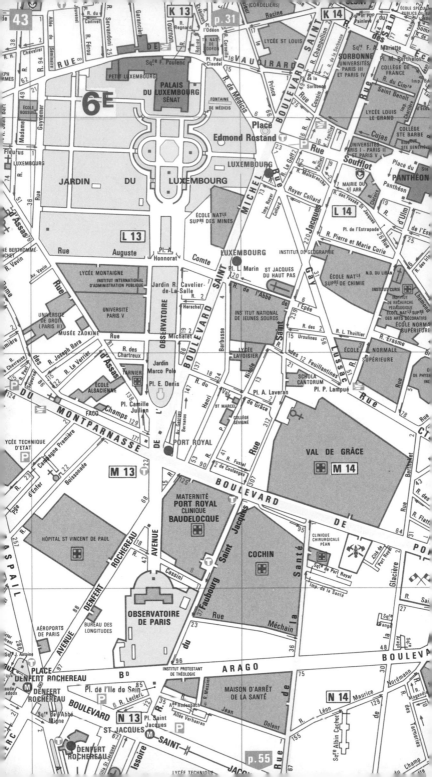

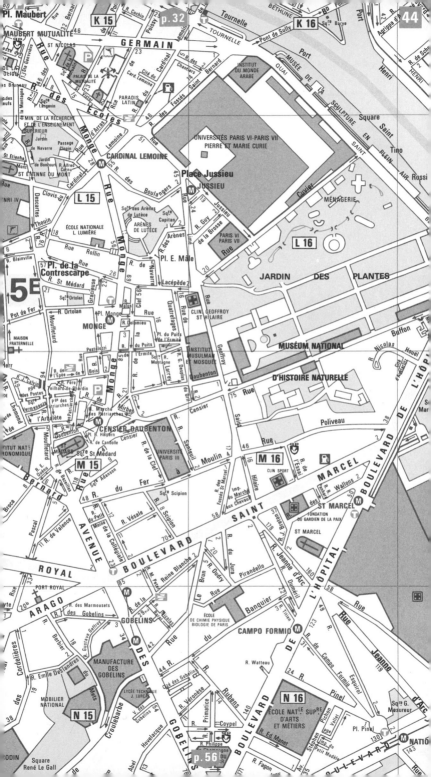

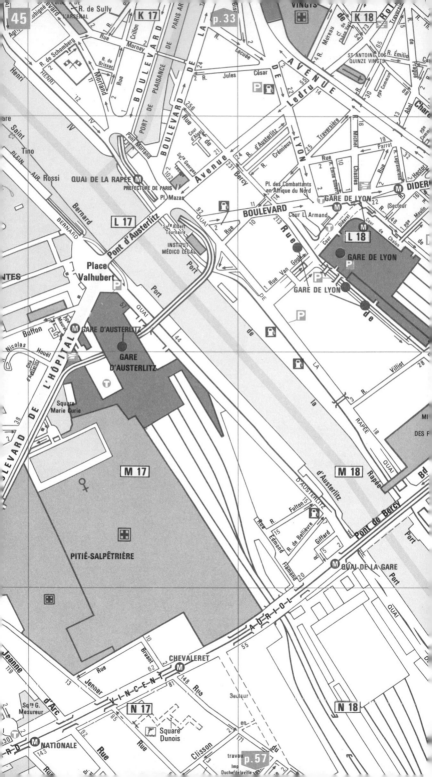

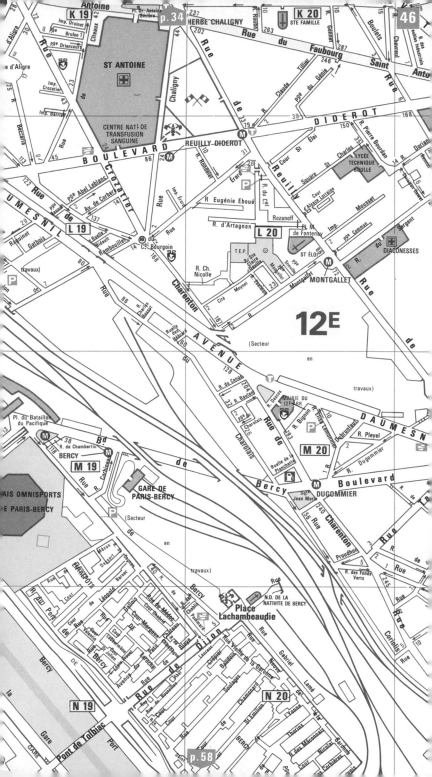

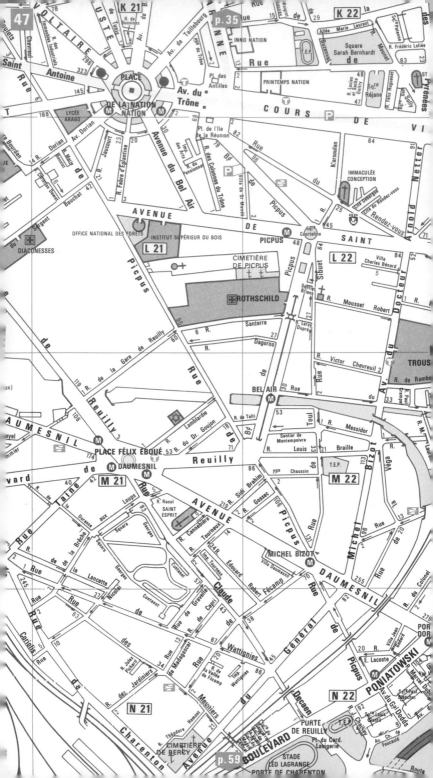

K 23   p. 36   K 24

Rue   de   Lagny

R. de St Mandé

R. de Lagny 102

LYCÉE
MAURICE
RAVEL

R. Lippmann

R. Louis Delaporte

CIMETIÈRE DE ST MANDÉ

Jeffre   Fays   Robert

Prévoyance

R. Noël Ballay

Albert Willemetz

R. l'Herminier

Plisson   ST LOUIS

R. Vitreu

R. Ch. Martinien

Céline

PORTE DE VINCENNES

PORTE DE VINCENNES

Av. de la Porte de Vincennes

des Vallées

Av. Galliéni

ST MANDÉ TOURELLE

Pl. du Gal Leclerc

Av. de Paris

R. du Talus du Cours

R. de l'Amiral Courbet

de   Gaulle

R. du Parc

Poirier

R. Cart

Gambetta

L 23   L 24

ST MICHEL

SAINT MANDÉ

Avenue

PORTE DE ST MANDÉ

Courteline   Av. Victor Hugo

Pl. Ch. Digeon

MAIRIE

R. Mongenot

INSTITUT DÉPAL DES AVEUGLES

Villa Kirti

T.E.P.

R. J. Lemaître

Square E. Cohl

Av. Maurice Ravel

Villa de l'Étang

Villa Suzanne

Square Georges Méliès

Émile   Laurent

R. de Bérulle

R. du Lac

PTE DE MONTEMPOIVRE

Renault

Sacrot

R. Benoît Lévy

LYCÉE PAUL VALÉRY

M 23

Paul   Bert   Allard

Sacrot   Rue Place Lucien

NOTRE DAME

L'Alouette

M 24

R. Grandville

R. du Gal Archinard

R. Baudin

R. de l'Abbé Pouchard

Pl. de la Libération

Jean   Mermoz

R. de l'Épinette

CIMETIÈRE SUD DE ST MANDÉ

Rue   Alphand

René

Mouchotte

R. Brière de Boismont

Faidherbe

R. de l'Aml La Roncière Le Noury

E.D.F.   G.D.F.

Marie

LYCÉE TECHN. ÉLISA LEMONNIER

MUSÉE DES TRANSPORTS

Sainte

Herbillon

Gaulle

MUSÉE DES ARTS AFRICAINS ET OCÉANIENS

Avenue   Avenue

Carrefour de la Demi Lune

CENTRE G. THILL

TE DORÉE E DE PICPUS)

N 23

A V E N U E   DAUMESNIL

N 24

Route   p. 60

BOULEVARD   SOULT

DAVOUT

Utilisez le plan MICHELIN à 1/15 000 « Banlieue de Paris Sud-Est » n° 24

COULOMMIERS LAGNY N 34

Av. de Paris (5)

VAL DE MARNE

Utilisez le plan MICHELIN à 1/15 000 « Banlieue de Paris Sud-Ouest » n° 22

N 1
p. 37
N 2

du Vie
Pont de Sèvres
124
139
R.
102
Boulevard
Rue
Jean
R. de Clamart
Salférino
45
R.
d'Issy
de
Rue
du
Heinrich
Rue
R.
Yves
R.
Kérmen
R.
R. Damiens
27
32 Traversière
Nationale
DE
QUAI
D1
P 1
111
45
R. Neuve St
Cours des Longs Prés
Pl. St Germain
des Longs Prés
Jules Ferry
DE STALINGRAD

IMMACULÉE CONCEPTION
Place Racine
Place Corneille
des
Longs
Prés
du
R. Molière
Point
106

Danjou
Jour
Avenue
Grenier
Pierre
Avenue
Seine
QUAI
DU
Sq⁺ᵉ des Moulineaux
Sq⁺ᵉ de l'Avre
P 2
65

Thiers
NOUVEAU CIMETIÈRE
DE BOULOGNE-BILLANCOURT
TÉLÉ-
Emile
Duclaux
POINT
BRAS
DE
BOULOGNE
SAINT

Pont de
Billancourt
ÎLE DE BILLANCOURT
Allée
du
Bas
Allée
Meudon
R 1
Pierre
Allée de
Av.
Billancourt
43
R.
Poli
Rue J. P. Timbaud
ÎLE
BRAS
D ISSY
QUAI
220
R 2
Jean
R. de la Gare

STATION LES MOULINEAUX-BILLANCOURT
Pl. de la Resistance
Rue
Rue
25
Pl. J. Gévelot
Sq⁺ᵉ Lombard
(Secteur
en travaux)
N 187 QUAI
DE
STALINGRAD
Miquel
Marcel
Rue
Av
de
Meudon
du
Viaduc
R. du Docteur
Lombard
STE LUCIE
MON DE RETRAITE
M. VIGNE
N 189
Avenue
152
de
Verdun
140
Av.
118
de
Rue
de
R. P.
Besnard
107
Rue
R. des
Montalets
S 1
Imp.
Gérard
R. des
Sorrières
R. des Mentelets
Voie de la Ferme
MEUDON
Paris
Voie Privée de St Cloud
Chin des
Montquartiers
Sentier des
Pucelles
S 2
Boulevard
CLAMART
Av. Henri
PERCY

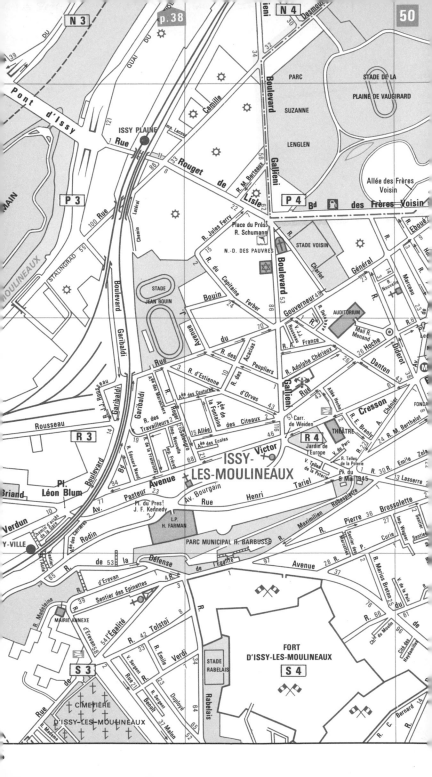

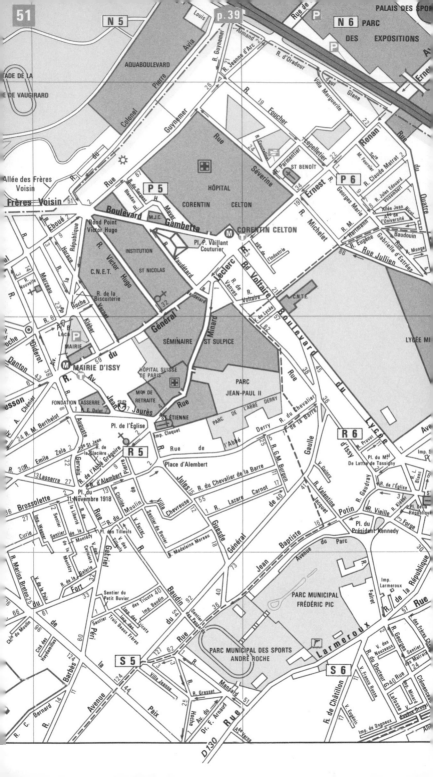

N 5

N 6 PARC
DES EXPOSITIONS

PALAIS DES SPOR

p. 39

Louis

Rue de

P

P

AQUABOULEVARD

STADE DE LA
E DE VAUGIRARD

R. Guynemer

R. Jeanne d'Arc

Armand

R. d'Oradour

Rue de

Pierre

Avia

Villa Marguerite

Glane

Renan

Ernest

Sorø

Colonel

du

Guynemer

Rue

R. du

Foucher

R. Séverine

St BENOÎT

R. Lepelletier

Parmentier

Rue

R. Claude Matrat

Allée des Frères
Voisin

HÔPITAL
CORENTIN CELTON

R. Georges Marie

R. Jules Édouard
Vaisonnat

Frères Voisin

Boulevard

Gambetta

Hartmann

R. Eugène

Gabrielle d'Estrée

Baudouin

Eboué

Rue

de la

République

M.J.C.

Rond Point
Victor Hugo

INSTITUTION
ST NICOLAS

CORENTIN CELTON

R. Michelet

R. M.

Rue Jullien

Marceau

R.

Victor

Hugo

C.N.E.T.

Vaudaxan

Pl. P. Vaillant
Couturier

Leclerc

Bd

Voltaire

rue de

l'Industrie

R. de la
Biscuiterie

Roche

Kléber

Vanard

Général

SÉMINAIRE

ST SULPICE

Minard

R. de
Vanves

C.N.T.E.

LYCÉE MI

MAIRIE

P

A. Locard

Danton

Biderot

M MAIRIE D'ISSY

Av.

Jean

HÔPITAL SUISSE
DE PARIS

Mon DE
RETRAITE

Rue

PARC
JEAN-PAUL II

Rue

du

Lycée

R.

Chénier

A.

FONDATION LASSERRE

R. E. Dolet

Auguste

Jaurès

ST ÉTIENNE

Imp. Cloquet

Rue

PARC DE L'ABBÉ DERRY

de

R. du Chevalier

R. du Chevalier de la Barre

Gaulle

R 6

d'Issy

R. Prevot

Pl. de l'Église

Rue

de

l'Abbé

Derry

Pl. du Mal
De Lattre de Tassigny

R 5

Emile Zola

R. 30

Place d'Alembert

Lasserre

R. de
la Glacière

R. de l'Abbé Grégoire

Gervais

Brossolette

Pl. St Jean de

R. de l'Alembert

L. Giudhe

Jules

R. du Chevalier de la Barre

R.G.M. Burgod

R. Valentine

R. Gaudray

R. de l'Église

Pl. du Mal

Curie

Brossolette

Sentier du Moulin

Ville Chevreuse

R. Lazare Carnot

de

Jacquet

R. Vieille

Pl. du
Président Kennedy

Forge

R. Mgr Bréton

R. des Tilleuls

R. Madeleine Moreau

Guesde

Général

Jean

Baptiste

du

Parc

Avenue

Imp.
Larmeroux

R. de la République

du

Fort

Sentier du
Petit Buvier

V. des Tricots

Imp. Baudin

Baudin

Rue

PARC MUNICIPAL
FRÉDÉRIC PIC

Rue

Barbès

de

Péri

Sentier

Trois Beaux Frères

Rue

Larmeroux

R. Franco Berra

S 5

PARC MUNICIPAL DES SPORTS
ANDRÉ ROCHE

Fg de Châtillon

S 6

Avenue

Paix

Hoche

Rue

Menier

R. Gressat

R. Arnaud

Rue

Imp. de Dagneau

D 130

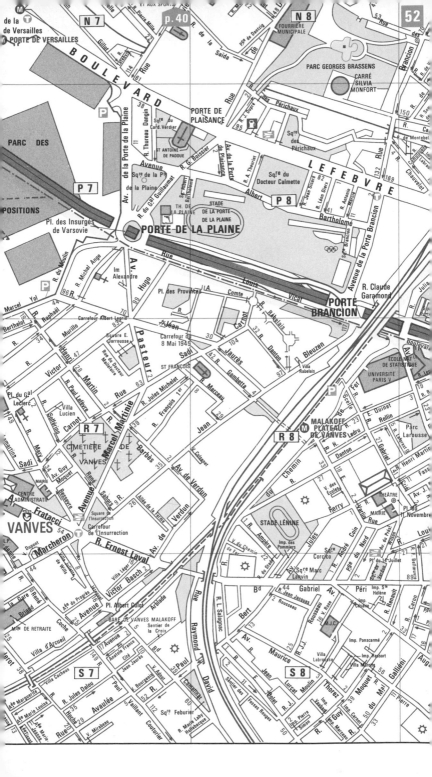

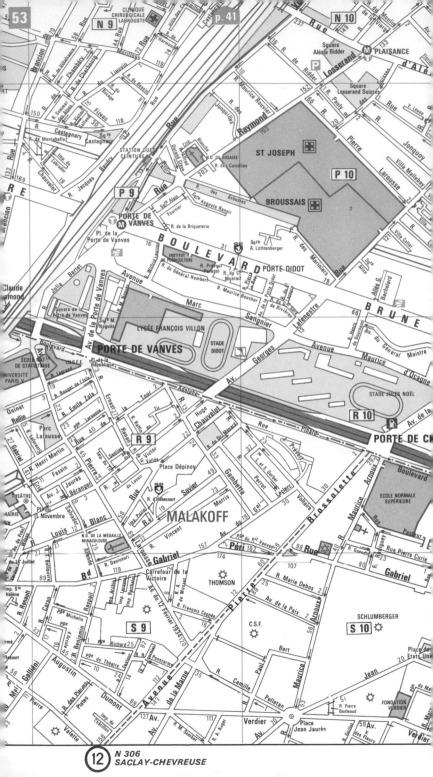

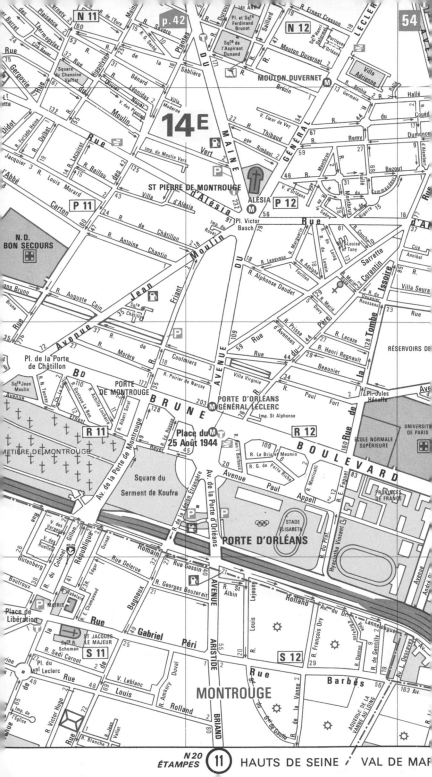

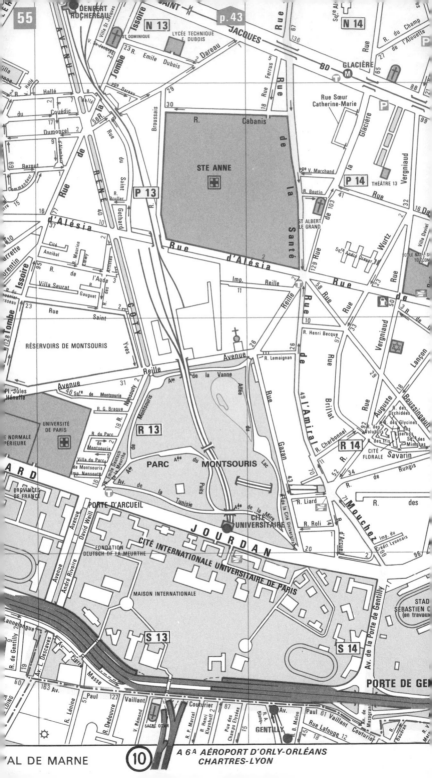

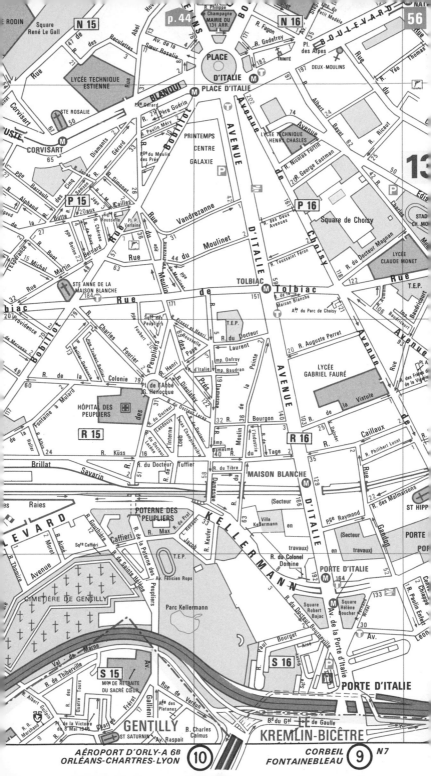

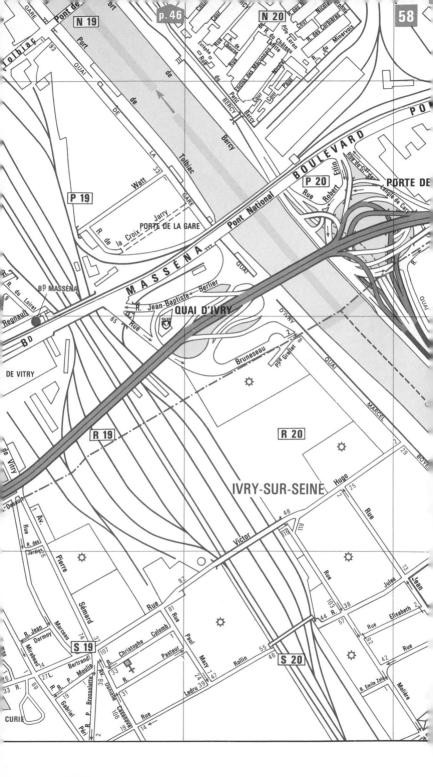

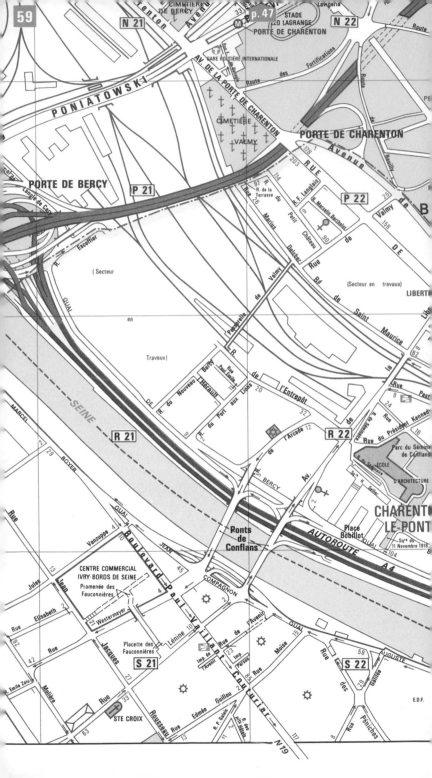

p. 48

N 23

N 24

PARC ZOOLOGIQUE

ÎLE DE BERCY

ÎLE DE REUILLY

Lac

Ceinture du

Daumesnil

TEMPLE BOUDDHIQUE

P 23

DE VINCENNES

P 24

Lac

Daumesnil

Carrefour de la Conservation

Route

Plaine

VÉLODROME JACQUES ANQUETIL

CIMETIÈRE DE CHARENTON

Dressée par la Manufacture Française des Pneumatiques MICHELIN
© MICHELIN et Cie, propriétaires-éditeurs, 1988
Sté en commandite par actions au capital de 875 000 000 de francs
R.C.S. Clermont-Ferrand B 855 200 507 Place des Carmes-Déchaux 63 Clermont-Ferrand (France)
Imprimée en France · 2 M IMPRESSIONS · Imp. MAILLET 75019 PARIS · Made in France · DL 1988 · 3e Trimestre

Avenue de Gravelle

6

VAL DE MARNE

Utilisez le plan MICHELIN à 1/15 000
« Banlieue de Paris Sud-Est » n° 24

R. d'Estienne d'Orves

Stinville

R. des Ormes

Leclerc

75

R.E. Détective

L.P. JEAN-JAURÈS

Av. Victor Basch

Général

Av. de Verdun

Guérin

THÉÂTRE MUNICIPAL

R 23

Rue du Col. Delmas

Rue

du

République

R 24

Parc

Conflans

Ville des Fleurs

Rue

de

Thiébault

R.E. Nocard

NANCY METZ-REIMS A 4

Pl. A. Briand

T

Rue

ST-PIERRE

Rue

Lattre

Pl. Ramon

MUSÉE DU PAIN

Pl. de l'Église

CHARENTON ÉCOLES

M

Rue Alfred

Savouré

Henri IV

Pte de la
Av. des Épinettes
des

ESP. TOFFOLI

P

R. Arthur

R. du Séjour

Rue

DE

Gabrielle

Marry

de

Sully

du

Mal.

R. de la Pompe

R.C.M.

R. du

Av. J.

R. Col.

R. du Mal Leclerc

MAIRIE

Pl. Arthur Dussault

M

TRIBUNAL

Rue

Gabriel

Périt

Square Jules Noël

R. du Séjour

PARIS

Sqre Jean Mermoz

M.J.C.

Rue de l'Abreuvoir

CARRIÈRES

6

ÎLE MARTINET

S 23

STADE HENRI GUÉRIN

S 24

Pont de Charenton

T

7

MARNE

QUAI DU DR. MASS

ALFORT ÉCOLE VÉTÉRINAIRE

M

QUAI

D'ALFORTVILLE

R. Vaillant Couturier

R. A. Maire

R. Bourgelat

T

8

MELUN N 6
FONTAINEBLEAU

N 19

TROYES
PROVINS

61

BOIS DE BOULOGNE

0 — 500 m

Voir légende pages suivantes
See key following pages
Zeichenerklärung s. folgende Seiten
Ver signos convencionales páginas siguientes

62

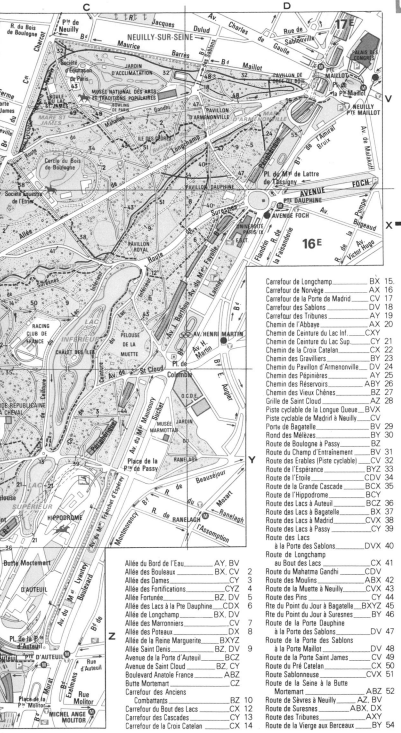

At. 15

63

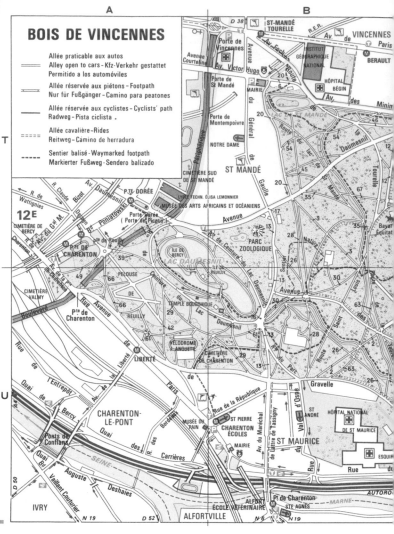

BOIS DE VINCENNES

═══	Allée praticable aux autos Alley open to cars – Kfz-Verkehr gestattet Permitido a los automóviles
┼┼┼	Allée réservée aux piétons – Footpath Nur für Fußgänger – Camino para peatones
────	Allée réservée aux cyclistes – Cyclists' path Radweg – Pista ciclista .
═════	Allée cavalière–Rides Reitweg–Camino de herradura
-----	Sentier balisé - Waymarked footpath Markierter Fußweg - Sendero balizado

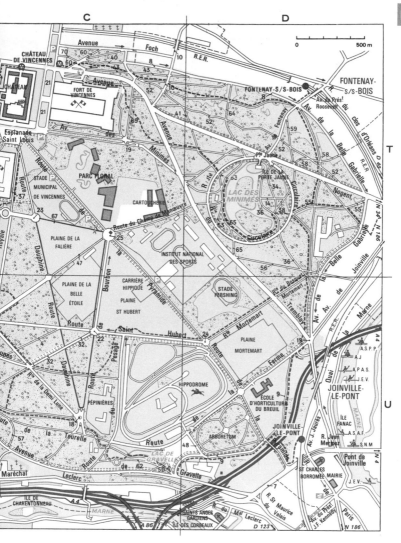

LA DÉFENSE

0 ————————— 200 m

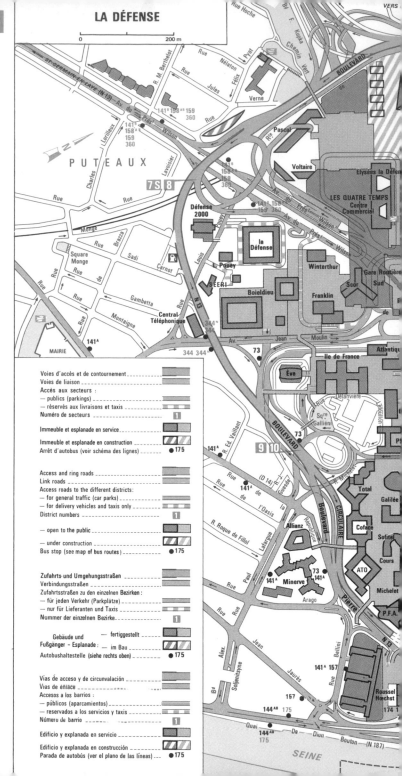

VERS

Rue Hoche

Bd F. Kupka

Chemin Vert

BOULEVARD

Rue Néaton

Rue Jules

R. M. Berthelot

Félix Pyat

Verne

ST-GERMAIN-EN-LAYE (N 13) — Av. du

Wilson

141ᴮ 158 ᴬᴮ 159 360

141ᴮ
158ᴬ
159
360

P U T E A U X

Charles — Lantieux

Rue

Lavoisier

Voltaire

Elysées la Défense

141ᴮ
158ᴬ
158
360

LES QUATRE TEMPS
Centre
Commercial

7S 8

Défense
2000

141 158
159 360

Av. du Prél

Av. du

Péri Wilson

Rue

Rue

Rue Monge

Brazza

Sadi

Square
Monge

Rue de

Carnot

Louis

Pouey

la
Défense

Winterthur

Gare Routière

Scor

Sud

SEERI

Boieldieu

Franklin

Rue

Gambetta

N 13

Montaigne

Central
Téléphonique

344ᴬ

de

141ᴬ

MAIRIE

344 344ᴮ

Av. Jean

Moulin

73

Ile de France

Atlantique

Éve

Rue

Delanvière

Sqre
Galliéni

BOULEVARD

73

141ᴬ

R. Ed. Vaillant

9 10

● 175

Rue

(D 14)

Guesde

R. Michelet

Total

Galilée

141ᴬ

de

de

R. Roque de Fillol

l'Oasis

Rawhangue

CIRCULAIRE

Boulevard

Allianz

Coface

Lafarque

Sofitel

Paul

141ᴬ

Minerve

73

141ᴬ

ATO

Cours

Rue

Arago

Michelet

Pierre

P.F.A.

Rue

Jean

Bellini

N 13

Alex

Soljenitsyne

141ᴬ 157

Jaurès

Bd

157

Roussel
Hœchst

174 ¹

Quai

De — Dion

Bouton — (N 187)

144ᴬᴮ
175

144ᴬᴮ 175

SEINE

Légende

Voies d'accès et de contournement ....
Voies de liaison ....
Accès aux secteurs :
— publics (parkings) ....
— réservés aux livraisons et taxis ....
Numéro de secteurs **1**

Immeuble et esplanade en service ....
Immeuble et esplanade en construction ....
Arrêt d'autobus (voir schéma des lignes) .... ● 175

Access and ring roads ....
Link roads ....
Access roads to the different districts:
— for general traffic (car parks) ....
— for delivery vehicles and taxis only ....
District numbers **1**

— open to the public ....
— under construction ....
Bus stop (see map of bus routes) .... ● 175

Zufahrts- und Umgehungsstraßen ....
Verbindungsstraßen ....
Zufahrtsstraßen zu den einzelnen Bezirken :
— für jeden Verkehr (Parkplätze) ....
— nur für Lieferanten und Taxis ....
Nummer der einzelnen Bezirke **1**

Gebäude und ——— fertiggestellt ....
Fußgänger – Esplanade : — im Bau
Autobushaltestelle (siehe rechts oben) .... ● 175

Vías de acceso y de circunvalación ....
Vías de enlace ....
Accesos a los barrios :
— públicos (aparcamientos) ....
— reservados a los servicios y taxis ....
Número de barrio **1**

Edificio y explanada en servicio ....
Edificio y explanada en construcción ....
Parada de autobús (ver el plano de las líneas) ... ● 175

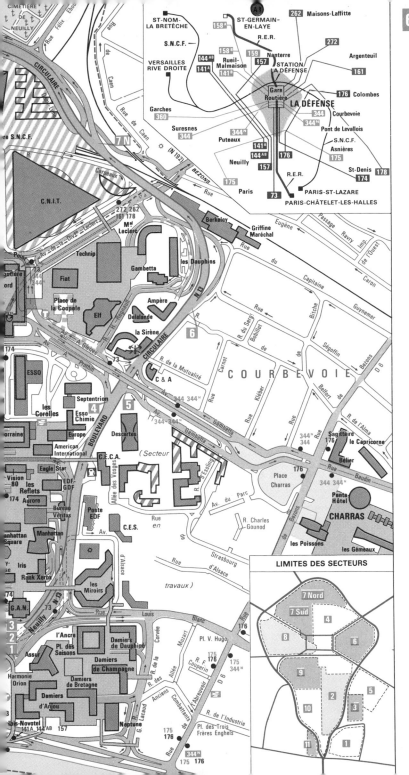

CIMETIÈRE
DE
NEUILLY

Rue Félix
Rue

ST-NOM-
LA BRETÈCHE
158ᴬ

ST-GERMAIN-
EN-LAYE
R.E.R.

262 Maisons-Laffitte

S.N.C.F.

158ᴮ

159 Nanterre

272 Argenteuil

VERSAILLES
RIVE DROITE
144 ᴬᴮ
141ᴬ
141ᴮ

157

STATION
LA DÉFENSE

161

Rueil-
Malmaison

176 Colombes

Garches
360

Gare
Routière

LA DÉFENSE

CIRCULAIRE

Suresnes
344

Rue de Caen

Puteaux

344ᴺ

Courbevoie
344

Pont de Levallois

S.N.C.F.
175

Asnières

Paris

Neuilly

141ᴬᴮ
144ᴬᴮ
157

176

St-Denis
174 178

7 N

(N 192)

175

R.E.R.

73

PARIS-ST-LAZARE

PARIS-CHÂTELET-LES-HALLES

C.N.I.T.

Carpeaux

272 262
161 178

Mᵉ
Leclerc

Berkeley

Griffine
Maréchal

Eugène

Passage
Ravry
Imp.

de l'Ouest

Technip

les Dauphins

Rue

du

73
344
344

Fiat

Gambetta

Caron

Place de
la Coupole

Elf

Ampère

Capitaine

Guynemer

Delalande

la Sirène

6

R.

R. du Sergt

Bablet

Rue

Bitche

Ségoffin

Bezons

174

Av. A. Gleizes

73

CIRCULAIRE

R. de la Mutualité

C & A

C O U R B E V O I E

D 6

ESSO

Prothin

Carnot

Rue

Kléber

Belfort

R de l'Alma

les
Corolles

Septentrion

4

5

Av.

344 344ᴺ

Rue

Sagittaire
176

le Capricorne

Lorraine

Esso
Chimie

Europe

American
International

BOULEVARD

Descartes

Av.
344ᴺ 344ᴺ

Gambetta

(Secteur

Rue

344ᴺ
344

Rue

Bélier

Rue

Baudin

Vision
80
174 Aurore

Eagle Star

EDF-
GDF

C.E.C.A.

Allée des Vosges

R. d'Essling

Place
Charras

176

344 344ᴺ

Penta
Hôtel

CHARRAS

Bureau
Véritas

Poste
EDF

C.E.S.

Rue
en

Av. du Parc

de

R. Charles
Gounod

Bezons

les Poissons

les Gémeaux

anhattan
Square

Manhattan

C.E.S.

Av.

Rue

Strasbourg
d'Alsace

travaux)

LIMITES DES SECTEURS

Iris
yse

Rank Xerox

les
Miroirs

d'Alsace

Rue

d'Alsace

7 Nord

74

G.A.N.

73

Neuilly

N 13

Rue

Louis

Blanc

Corvée

Pl. V. Hugo

Rue

176

7 Sud

4

3

l'Ancre

Damiers
de Dauphine

Mozart

R. F.
Couperin

175
176

175
344ᴺ

8

6

2
1

Assur

Pl. des
Saisons

Damiers
de Champagne

R. de la

Allée

d'Abreuvoir

D 6

9

5

Harmonie
Orion

Damiers
de Bretagne

Damiers
d'Anjou

R. des

Anciens
Combattants de

R. de l'Industrie

Pl. des Trois
Frères Enghels

10

3

Ibis-Novotel
141A 144ᴬᴮ 157

Neptune

Rue

175
176

344ᴺ
175 176

11

1

3

AÉROPORT D'ORLY

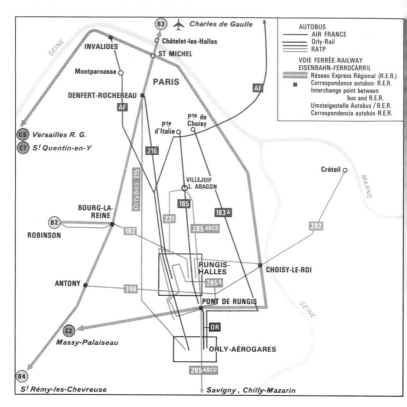

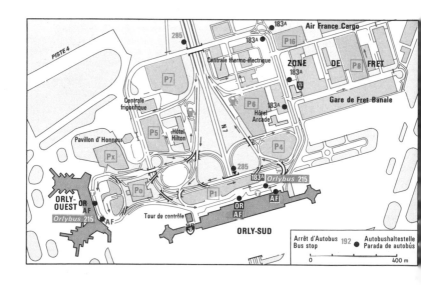

MARCHÉ DE RUNGIS (M.I.N.)

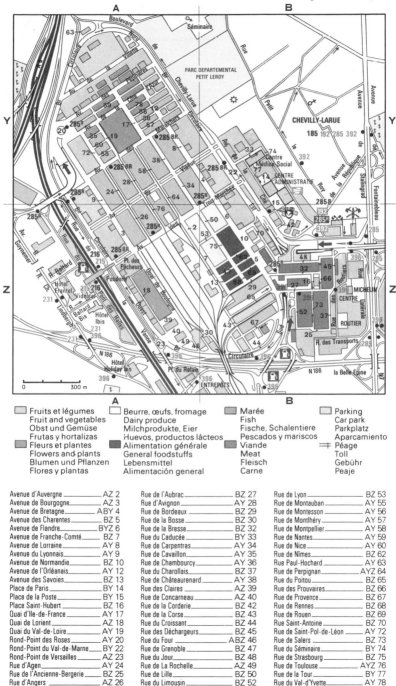

☐ Fruits et légumes Fruit and vegetables Obst und Gemüse Frutas y hortalizas	☐ Beurre, œufs, fromage Dairy produce Milchprodukte, Eier Huevos, productos lácteos	☐ Marée Fish Fische, Schalentiere Pescados y mariscos	☐ Parking Car park Parkplatz Aparcamiento
☐ Fleurs et plantes Flowers and plants Blumen und Pflanzen Flores y plantas	☐ Alimentation générale General foodstuffs Lebensmittel Alimentación general	☐ Viande Meat Fleisch Carne	⇌ Péage Toll Gebühr Peaje

AÉROPORT CHARLES DE GAULLE

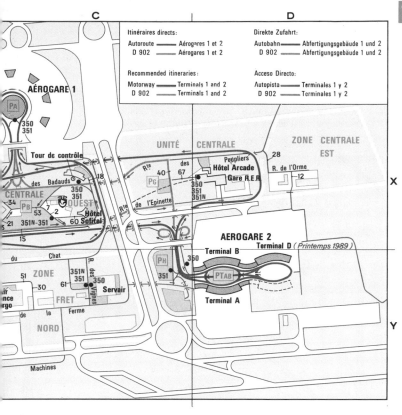

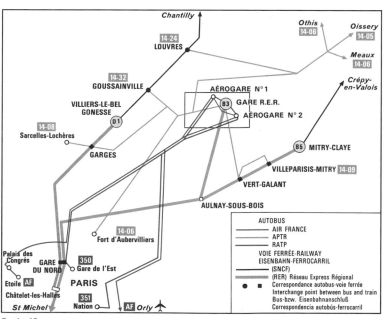

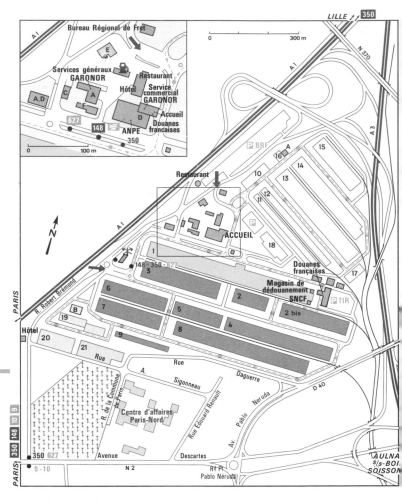

GARONOR

A — Dépannage tous véhicules — Vehicle repairs — Reparaturdienst für alle Fahrzeuge — Taller de reparación
B — Pièces détachées PL — Spare parts — LKW-Ersatzteile — Repuestos
C — Pneumatiques — Tyres — Reifen — Neumáticos
D — Location véhicule — Vehicle hire — Autovermietung — Coches de alquiler
E — Station lavage — Vehicle wash — Autowaschanlage — Lavado
F — Service médical — Infirmary — Ärztlicher Hilfsdienst — Servicio médico

● Arrêt d'Autobus

Bus stop — Autobushaltestelle — Parada de autobús

148	(RATP) — Église de Pantin — GARONOR
350	(RATP) — Gare de l'Est — GARONOR — Aéroport Charles-de-Gaulle
627	(TRA-RATP) — Aulnay-sous-Bois — Blanc-Mesnil — GARONOR
9	(APTR) — Fort d'Aubervilliers — GARONOR — Aulnay-sous-Bois (Rose des Vents)
10	(APTR) — Fort d'Aubervilliers — GARONOR — Aulnay-sous-Bois (Vélodrome)
●	Navette intérieure — Shuttle service — Interne Autobuslinie — Autobús de Servicio interior

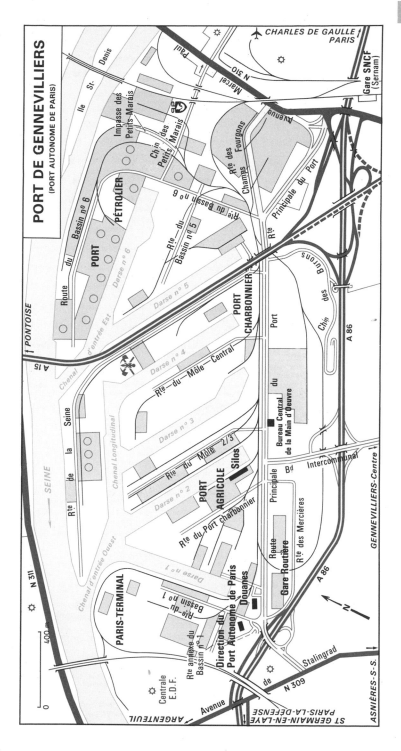

PORT DE GENNEVILLIERS
(PORT AUTONOME DE PARIS)

Service général de 7 h à 20 h 30 — Normal service from 7 am to 8.30 pm

service assuré jusqu'à minuit	■	buses running to midnight
service assuré les dimanches et fêtes	●	buses running on Sundays and holidays

20 ● Gare St-Lazare — Opéra — Sentier/Poissonnière-Bonne Nouvelle — République — Bastille — Gare de Lyon.

21 ■ ● Gare St-Lazare — Opéra — Palais Royal — Châtelet — Gare du Luxembourg — Berthollet-Vauquelin — Glacière-Auguste Blanqui — Pte de Gentilly.

22 Opéra — Pasquier-Anjou/Gare St-Lazare — Haussmann-Courcelles — Ch. de Gaulle-Etoile — Trocadéro — La Muette-Gare de Passy — Chardon Lagache-Molitor/Pt Mirabeau — Pte de St-Cloud.

24 Gare St-Lazare — Concorde — Pt du Carrousel/Pt Royal — Pt Neuf — Maubert-Mutualité/Pt de l'Archevêché — Gare d'Austerlitz — Bercy-Rapée — Pt National — Charenton-Pte de Conflans — Alfort-Ecole Vétérinaire.

26 ■ ● Gare St-Lazare — Carrefour de Châteaudun — La Fayette-St-Quentin-Gare du Nord/Magenta-Maubeuge-Gare du Nord — Jaurès-Stalingrad — Botzaris-Buttes Chaumont — Pyrénées-Ménilmontant — Pyrénées-Bagnolet — Cours de Vincennes.

27 ● Gare St-Lazare — Opéra — Palais Royal — Pt Neuf — Gare du Luxembourg — Berthollet-Vauquelin — Pl. d'Italie — Nationale — Pte de Vitry (■ : Pt Neuf — Pte de Vitry).

28 Gare St-Lazare — St-Philippe du Roule/Matignon-St-Honoré — Pt des Invalides — Ecole Militaire — Breteuil — Losserand — Pte d'Orléans.

29 Gare St-Lazare — Opéra — E. Marcel-Montmartre — Archives-Rambuteau/Archives-Haudriettes — Bastille — Gare de Lyon/Daumesnil-Diderot — Daumesnil-F. Eboué — Pte de Montempoivre.

30 Gare de l'Est — Barbès-Rochechouart — Pigalle — Pl. de Clichy — Malesherbes-Courcelles — Ch. de Gaulle-Etoile — Trocadéro.

31 ■ ● Gare de l'Est — Barbès-Rochechouart — Mairie du 18ᵉ — Vauvenargues — Brochant-Cardinet — Jouffroy-Malesherbes — Ch. de Gaulle-Etoile.

32 Gare de l'Est — Carrefour de Châteaudun — Gare St-Lazare — St-Philippe du Roule/Matignon-St-Honoré — Marceau-Pierre 1ᵉʳ de Serbie — Trocadéro — La Muette - Gare de Passy — Pte de Passy.

33 Gare de l'Est — Réaumur-Arts et Métiers/Réaumur-Sébastopol — Châtelet — Gare du Luxembourg — Denfert Rochereau — Pte d'Orléans (■ : Châtelet — Pte d'Orléans).

39 Gare de l'Est — Poissonnière-Bonne Nouvelle/Sentier — Richelieu-4 Septembre — Palais Royal — St-Germain des Prés — Hôp. des Enfants Malades — Mairie du 15ᵉ/Vaugirard-Favorites — Pte de Versailles.

42 Gare du Nord — Carrefour de Châteaudun/Le Peletier — Opéra — Concorde — Alma-Marceau — Champ de Mars — Charles Michels — Balard-Lecourbe.

43 Gare du Nord — Carrefour de Châteaudun — Gare St-Lazare — Haussmann-Courcelles — Ternes — Pte des Ternes — Neuilly-St-Pierre — Pt de Neuilly — Neuilly-Pl. de Bagatelle (● : Gare St-Lazare — Neuilly-Bagatelle).

46 ● Gare du Nord — Gare de l'Est — Goncourt — Voltaire-L. Blum — Faidherbe-Chaligny — Daumesnil-F. Eboué — Pte Dorée — St-Mandé-Demi Lune-Zoo (service partiel jusqu'au Parc floral d'avril à septembre).

47 Gare du Nord — Gare de l'Est — Réaumur-Arts et Métiers/Réaumur-Sébastopol — Châtelet — Maubert-Mutualité — Censier-Daubenton — Pl. d'Italie — Pte d'Italie — Le Kremlin Bicêtre-Fort.

48 Gare du Nord — Petites Ecuries/Cadet — Richelieu-4 Septembre/Réaumur-Montmartre — Palais Royal — St-Germain des Prés — Gare Montparnasse/pl. du 18 Juin 1940 — Institut Pasteur — Pte de Vanves.

49 Gare du Nord — Carrefour de Châteaudun — Gare St-Lazare — St-Philippe du Roule/Matignon-St-Honoré — Pt des Invalides — Ecole Militaire — Mairie du 15ᵉ/Vaugirard-Favorites — Pte de Versailles.

52 ● Opéra — Concorde/Boissy d'Anglas — St-Philippe du Roule — Ch. de Gaulle-Etoile — Belles Feuilles — La Muette — Pte d'Auteuil — Boulogne-Château — Pt de St-Cloud (■ : Ch. de Gaulle-Etoile — Pte d'Auteuil).

53 Opéra — Gare St-Lazare — Legendre — Pte d'Asnières — Levallois Perret-G. Eiffel.

54 République — Gare de l'Est — Barbès-Rochechouart — Pigalle — La Fourche — Pte de Clichy — Clichy-Landy-Martre/Clichy-Casanova — Asnières Gennevilliers-Gabriel Péri

56 Pte de Clignancourt — Barbès-Rochechouart — Gare de l'Est — République — Voltaire-L. Blum — Nation — Pte de St-Mandé — Vincennes-les Laitières — Chât. de Vincennes.

57 Gare de Lyon — Gare d'Austerlitz — Pl. d'Italie — Poterne des Peupliers — Mairie de Gentilly.

58 Hôtel de Ville — Pt Neuf — Palais du Luxembourg — Gare Montparnasse/pl. du 18 Juin 1940 — Château - Mairie du 14ᵉ — Pte de Vanves — Vanves-Lycée Michelet.

60 Gambetta — Borrégo — Botzaris — Ourcq-Jaurès — Crimée — Ordener-Marx Dormoy — Mairie du 18ᵉ — Pte de Montmartre.

61 Gare d'Austerlitz — Ledru Rollin-Fbg St-Antoine — Roquette-Père Lachaise — Gambetta — Pte des Lilas — Pré St-Gervais-Pl. Jean Jaurès.

62 ■ ● Cours de Vincennes — Daumesnil-F. Eboué — Pt de Tolbiac — Italie-Tolbiac — Glacière-Tolbiac — Alésia-Gal. Leclerc — Vercingétorix — Convention-Vaugirard — Convention-St-Charles — Chardon Lagache-Molitor/Michel Ange-Auteuil — Pte de St-Cloud.

63 ■ ● Gare de Lyon — Gare d'Austerlitz — Monge Mutualité/Maubert-Mutualité — St-Sulpice/St-Germain des Prés — Solférino-Bellechasse — Pt des Invalides-Quai d'Orsay — Alma-Marceau — Trocadéro — Pte de la Muette-Henri-Martin.

Normaler Busverkehr von 7 bis 20.30 Uhr — Circulación general de 7 h a 20 h 30

Busverkehr bis 24 Uhr ■ servicio hasta las 24 h

Busverkehr auch an Sonn- und Feiertagen ● servicio los domingos y festivos

65 Gare d'Austerlitz — Bastille — République — Gare de l'Est — Pl. Chapelle — Pte de la Chapelle — Aubervilliers-La Haie Coq — Mairie d'Aubervilliers (● : Pte de la Chapelle — Mairie d'Aubervilliers).

66 Opéra — Gare St-Lazare/Rome-Haussmann — Sq. des Batignolles — Pte Pouchet — Clichy-Bd V. Hugo.

67 Pigalle — Carrefour Châteaudun — Richelieu-4 Septembre/Réaumur-Montmartre — Palais Royal/Louvre-Rivoli — Hôtel de Ville — St-Germain-Cardinal Lemoine — Buffon-Mosquée — Pl. d'Italie — Pte de Gentilly.

68 Pl. de Clichy — Trinité — Opéra — Pt Royal — Sèvres-Babylone — Vavin — Denfert Rochereau — Pte d'Orléans — Montrouge-Etats Unis/Montrouge-Verdier-République — Montrouge-Cim. Bagneux (● : Pte d'Orléans — Montrouge-Cim. Bagneux).

69 Gambetta — Roquette-Père Lachaise — Bastille — Hôtel de Ville — Palais Royal/Pt Carrousel — Grenelle-Bellechasse/Solférino-Bellechasse — Invalides-La Tour Maubourg/La Tour Maubourg-St-Dominique — Champ de Mars.

70 Hôtel de Ville — Pt Neuf — St-Sulpice/St-Germain des Prés — Hôp. des Enfants Malades — Peclet — Charles Michels — Pl. du Dr Hayem-Radio-France.

72 Hôtel de Ville — Palais Royal/Pt Carrousel — Concorde — Alma-Marceau — Pt Bir Hakeim — Pt Mirabeau — Pte St-Cloud — Boulogne Billancourt-J. Jaurès — Pt 'St-Cloud (● : Concorde — ■ : Pte St-Cloud — Pt St-Cloud).

73 Musée d'Orsay — Concorde — Rond Point des Champs Elysées — Ch. de Gaulle-Etoile — Pte Maillot — Neuilly-Hôtel de Ville — Pt de Neuilly — La Défense.

74 Hôtel de Ville — Louvre-Rivoli — Réaumur-Montmartre/Richelieu-4 Septembre — Carrefour de Châteaudun — La Fourche — Pte de Clichy — Clichy-V. Hugo — Clichy-Hôp. Beaujon (■ ● : Pte Clichy — Hôp. Beaujon).

75 Pt Neuf — Archives-Haudriettes/Grenier St-Lazare — République — Grange aux Belles — Armand Carrel-Mairie du 19e — Pte de Pantin.

76 Louvre — Hôtel de Ville — Bastille — Charonne-Ph. Auguste — Pte de Bagnolet — Mairie de Bagnolet — Bagnolet-Malassis.

80 ● Mairie du 15e — Ecole Militaire — Alma-Marceau — Matignon-St-Honoré/St-Philippe du Roule — Gare St-Lazare — Damrémont-Caulaincourt — Mairie du 18e (*les dimanches et fêtes seulement, prolongation de ligne Mairie du 18e* — Mairie du 15e *jusqu'à la* Pte de Versailles).

81 Châtelet — Palais Royal — Opéra — Trinité/Gare St-Lazare — La Fourche — Pte de St-Ouen.

82 ●Gare du Luxembourg — Pl. du 18 juin 1940 — Oudinot — Ecole Militaire — Champ de Mars — Kléber-Boissière — Pte Maillot — Neuilly-St-Pierre — Neuilly-Hôpital Américain.

83 Friedland-Haussmann — St-Philippe du Roule — Rd-Pt des Champs-Élysées — Gare des Invalides — Sèvres-Babylone — Observatoire — Les Gobelins — Pl. d'Italie — Pt d'Ivry.

84 Pl. du Panthéon — Gare du Luxembourg — Sèvres-Babylone — Solférino-Bellechasse — Concorde — St-Augustin — Courcelles — Pte de Champerret.

85 Gare du Luxembourg — Châtelet — Louvre-Rivoli — Réaumur-Montmartre/Richelieu-4 Septembre — Cadet/Carrefour de Châteaudun — Muller — Pte Clignancourt — Mairie St-Ouen (■ ● : Pte Clignancourt — Mairie St-Ouen).

86 St-Germain des Prés — Mutualité — Bastille — Faidherbe-Chaligny — Pyrénées/Pte de Vincennes — St-Mandé-Tourelle — St-Mandé-Demi Lune-Zoo.

87 Champ de Mars — Ecole Militaire — Duroc-Oudinot/Vaneau-Babylone — St-Germain des Prés/St-Sulpice — Mutualité — Bastille — Gare de Lyon — Charenton-Wattignies — Porte de Reuilly.

89 Gare d'Austerlitz — Cardinal Lemoine-Monge — Gare Luxembourg — Pl. du 18 Juin 1940 — Cambronne-Vaugirard/Vaugirard-Favorites — Pte de Plaisance — Vanves-Lycée Michelet.

91 ■ ● Gare Montparnasse — Observatoire-Port Royal — Gobelins — Gare d'Austerlitz — Bastille.

92 ■ ● Gare Montparnasse — Oudinot — Ecole Militaire — Alma-Marceau — Ch. de Gaulle-Etoile — Pte de Champerret.

93 Rd-Pt des Champs-Elysées — St-Philippe du Roule — Friedland-Haussmann — Ternes — Pte de Champerret — Levallois-Pl. de la Libération.

94 Gare Montparnasse — Sèvres-Babylone — Solférino-Bellechasse — Concorde — St-Augustin — Malesherbes-Courcelles — Pte d'Asnières — Mairie de Levallois.

95 ■ ● Gare Montparnasse — St-Germain des Prés — Palais Royal — Opéra — Gare St-Lazare — Damrémont-Caulaincourt — Pte de Montmartre.

96 ● Gare Montparnasse — St-Germain des Prés — St-Michel — Hôtel de Ville — Turenne-Francs Bourgeois — Parmentier-République — Pyrénées-Ménilmontant — Pte des Lilas (■ : Châtelet — Pte des Lilas).

PC ■ ● Pte Auteuil — Pte Passy — Longchamp — Pte Maillot — Pte Champerret — Pte Clichy — Pte St-Ouen — Pte Clignancourt — Pte Chapelle — Pte Villette — Pte Chaumont — Pte Lilas — Pte Bagnolet — Pte Vincennes — Pte Charenton — Pte Vitry — Pte Italie — Cité Universitaire — Pte Orléans — Pte Vanves — Pte Versailles — Bd Victor — Pte Auteuil.

Montmartrobus ● Pigalle — Sacré-Cœur — Mairie du 18e.

PARIS AUTOBUS

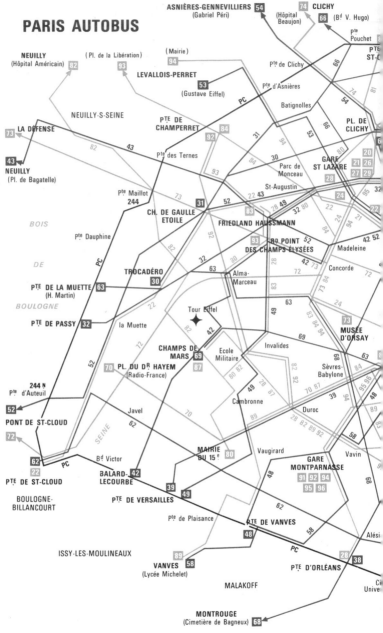

A   Châtelet — Louvre — Concorde — Champs Élysées — Pl. Charles de Gaulle-Étoile — Pt de Neuilly.

B   Châtelet — Palais Royal — Opéra — Gare St-Lazare — Pte Champerret - Levallois-Mairie.

C   Châtelet — Louvre — Carrefour-de-Châteaudun — Pigalle — Pl. Clichy — Pte Clichy — Clichy-Mairie.

D   Châtelet — Palais Royal — Gare du Nord — Pte de Clignancourt — Pte Montmartre — St-Ouen-Mairie.

E   Châtelet — Arts-et-Métiers — Gare de l'Est — Stalingrad — Pte Pantin — Pantin-Église.

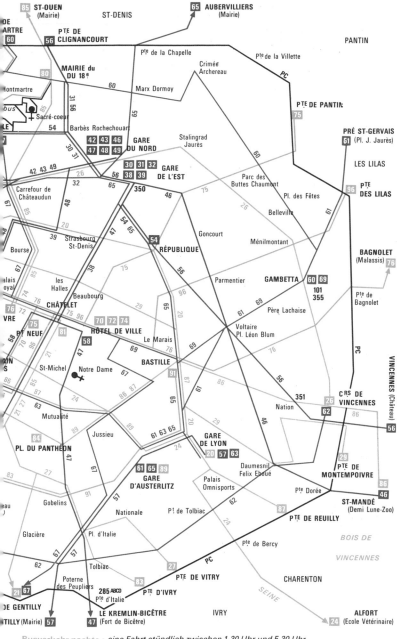

Busverkehr nachts : *eine Fahrt stündlich zwischen 1.30 Uhr und 5.30 Uhr.*

Líneas nocturnas : *todas las horas de 1 h 30 a 5 h 30 de la mañana.*

F	Châtelet — Arts-et-Métiers — République — Belleville — Pte des Lilas — Les Lilas-Mairie.
G	Châtelet — République — Voltaire — Gambetta — Pte de Bagnolet — Montreuil-Mairie.
H	Châtelet — Bastille — Nation — Pte de Vincennes — Vincennes-Château.
J	Châtelet — St-Michel — Luxembourg — Denfert Rochereau — Pte d'Orléans.
R	Châtelet — Maubert Mutualité — Gobelins — Pl. d'Italie — Pte d'Italie — Kremlin Bicêtre — Villejuif — Thiais — Chevilly Larue — Rungis-M.I.N. Marée.

RÉSEAU EXPRESS RÉGIONAL (RER)

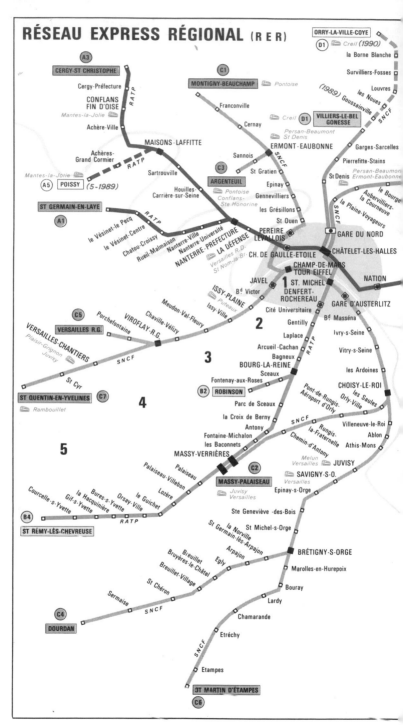

NOTES

MANUFACTURE FRANÇAISE DES PNEUMATIQUES MICHEL

Société en commandite par actions au capital de 875 000 000 de francs
Place des Carmes-Déchaux - 63 Clermont-Ferrand (France)
R.C.S. Clermont-Fd B 855 200 507
© **Michelin et Cie, Propriétaires-Éditeurs 1988**
Dépôt légal - 3e trim. 1988 - ISBN 2.06.000.148-X

Printed in France - 7-88-41
Photocomposition : IOTA-MIS, Nanterre - Impression : MAME Imprimeurs, Tours n° 13782

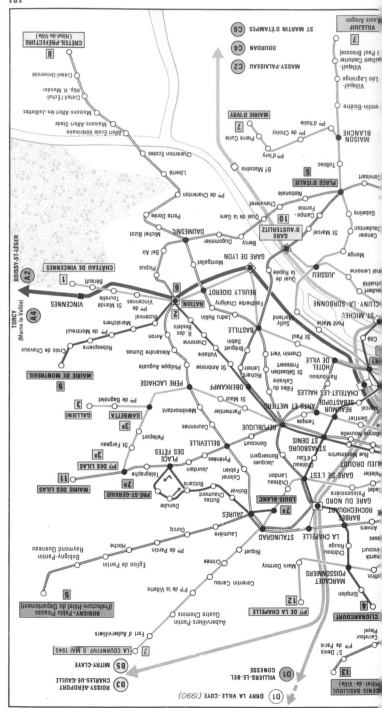

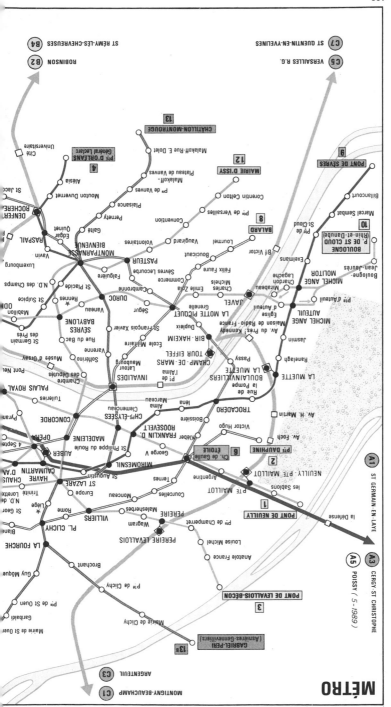

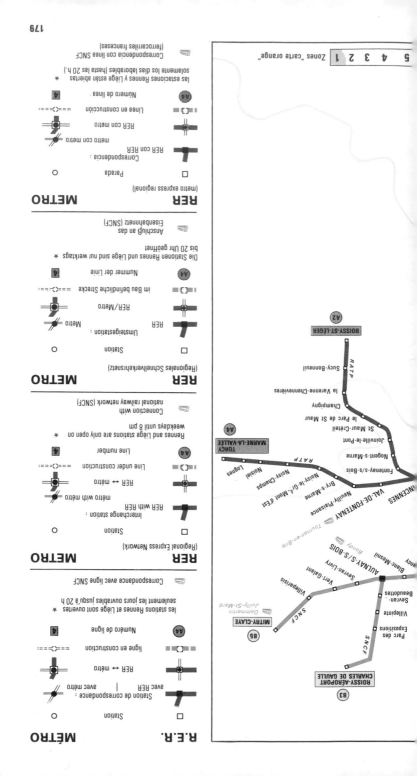

R.E.R. / MÉTRO

MÉTRO

R.E.R.

Station □ O

Station de correspondance :
avec RER | avec métro
RER ↔ métro

ligne en construction ===()===

Numéro de ligne (A4) [4]

* les stations Rennes et Liège sont ouvertes seulement les jours ouvrables jusqu'à 20 h

Correspondance avec ligne SNCF

MÉTRO

RER (Regional Express Network)

Station □ O

Interchange station :
RER with métro
métro with métro
RER ↔ métro

Line under construction ===()===

Line number (A4) [4]

* Rennes and Liège stations are only open on weekdays until 8 pm

Connection with national railway network (SNCF)

MÉTRO

RER (Regionales Schnellverkehrsnetz)

Station □ O

Umsteigestation :
RER
Metro
RER/Metro

im Bau befindliche Strecke ===()===

Nummer der Linie (A4) [4]

* Die Stationen Rennes und Liège sind nur werktags bis 20 Uhr geöffnet

Anschluß an das Eisenbahnnetz (SNCF)

MÉTRO

RER (metro express regional)

Parada □ O

Correspondencia :
RER con RER
metro con metro
RER con metro

Línea en construcción ===()===

Número de línea (A4) [4]

* las estaciones Rennes y Liège están abiertas solamente los días laborables (hasta las 20 h.)

Correspondencia con línea SNCF (ferrocarriles franceses)